COMPREHENSIVE SECURITY IN SOUTH ASIA

Comprehensive Security in South Asia

Edited by

DEV RAJ DAHAL
NISHCHAL NATH PANDEY

FRIEDRICH EBERT STIFTUNG, KATHMANDU

INSTITUTE OF FOREIGN AFFAIRS, KATHMANDU

MANOHAR
2006

First published 2006

ISBN 81-7304-663-8

Published by
Ajay Kumar Jain *for*
Manohar Publishers & Distributors
4753/23 Ansari Road, Daryaganj
New Delhi 110002
in association with
Friedrich Ebert Stiftung and
Institute of Foreign Affairs, Kathmandu

Printed at
Lordson Publishers Pvt. Ltd.
Delhi 110007

Distributed in South Asia by
FOUNDATION BOOKS
4381/4, Ansari Road
Daryaganj, New Delhi 110 002
and its branches at Mumbai, Hyderabad,
Bangalore, Chennai, Kolkata

Contents

Introduction

Lying between the Himalayas and the Indian Ocean, South Asia forms an organic security zone—a zone that had historically shaped regional security by spreading the messages of civilization, cooperation and peace. Aware of historical reasoning about the political and psychological causes of war, ancient statesmen had jettisoned the policy of balance of power, self-help and state-centric order in favour of freedom of the movements of people, trade and commerce. The varied and deep economic and social links among the South Asian countries—Bangladesh, Bhutan, India, Maldives, Nepal, Pakistan and Sri Lanka helped to generate a strong political will to build cooperation that disposed the governments to define security on welfare–maximizing terms. The consideration of the well-being of over one billion people of the region still constitutes the central objective of comprehensive security at inter-state and inter-societal level.

Europe is increasingly getting united towards a shared economic, defence and foreign policies. A common threat perception shapes the Association of South East Asian Nations (ASEAN), its security and autonomy encapsulated in the ideas of Zone of Peace, Freedom and Neutrality. South Asia, however, is struggling to form a collective identity through shared values and interests in cooperation and engagement in restraint, non-confrontation and consultation. Does it mean that the region is making a paradigm shift from the hitherto 'internationalization of security policy' to regionalization? Beneath a vision of greater interdependence of the regional peoples and the states and shared interests in the promotion of peace and progress underlies the leitmotif of comprehensive security. By definition, comprehensive security encompasses the full range of survival, well-being and identity-related issues and the complex links between the domestic order and international relations. Besides, it subsumes vital strategic concerns of the states, markets and civil societies, all acting together to achieve a higher source of public order based on social justice and equal access to achieve regional commonality. Institutional development of regional policy objectives is essential to achieve coordinated action in issue areas. A secure region is that whose statesmen and citizens have the reason to believe that internal and external environment are peaceful and all the levels of security assessment—individual, sub-national, state, regional and global—are co-dependent, mutually beneficial and cohesive.

South Asia can neither be separated from the global geopolitical contest nor from the main international security, political, economic and technological developments. Growing cooperation between the region and other global powers, including India and Pakistan, harmonization of positions of regional states on a number of international issues, including agreement on free trade areas (SAFTA), the World Trade Organization (WTO) and ratification of the Additional Protocol to the Convention on Suppression of Terrorism spell out the evolution of a realpolitik entente. Substantive dialogue on Kashmir, exchange of information on missile tests, opposition to open-ended arms race and promise to create a violence-free environment indicate a growing recognition towards mutual responsibility. Greater economic integration of South Asia based on the foundation of the SAARC Social Charter, binds all countries to work together to increase efficiencies in poverty alleviation, education, trade, investment and environment management and reinforce the commitment to common responsibility for a stable peace.

Comprehensive security requires the creation of a viable regime with healthy bilateral relations between India and its South Asian neighbours and effective multilateralism seeking the cooperation of the international community for an inclusive transformation of regional societies for effective governance.

The principle of comprehensive security is a protective manifestation of the solidarity of peaceful states as opposed to that which sets exclusive national interests above those of the community interests of states and peoples. The structural character of the South Asian ties defines distinct perception about each nation's self image, the other's character, intentions and capabilities. This structural context describes the rational choices available to each state, rules of the game for cooperation and the conceptual conclusion of policy decisions. In this context, how can comprehensive security offer reasonable benefits for individual states that correspond with regional interests also? Lord Buddha invented the idea of Panchasheel to regulate the conduct of human beings. On 29 April 1954 India and China reiterated its historical relevance for durable inter-state relations in Asia and tried to reduce the states' sovereign potential for conflict.

Panchasheel, based on Asian language, culture, feeling and textuality, received further fillip during the Bangdung Conference of Afro-Asian states and subsequently served an ideological bedrock of the non-aligned movement's pursuit for independence, equality and freedom for Asian, African and Latin American countries. Strengthening of the state's efficiency was the order of the day. Weak states can neither ensure security to their citizens nor their neighbours without depleting resources which can be put to other uses. The five principles of coexistence underlined in Panchasheel ideally constitutes the cardinal principles of comprehensive security and at the same time forms the reason, art and method of multilateralism, the regional countries are pursuing in the SAARC, the UN and non-aligned movements in the name of collective security. Regional civil societies and market institutions are already creating a 'multiple space' for post-national activities and have been emphasizing conflict prevention and conflict resolution by the use of civilian means. Soft-regionalism is also developing on other fronts and drawing important powers into a loose network of economic, political and social relations for civil coexistence.

CIVIL COEXISTENCE

Civil coexistence is not just a methodology. It is a virtue that can keep all the regional states cohesive enough to address the growing gap between traditional politics and social revolutions, seek evolutionary stability in state-society relations and support regional policies compatible with national aspirations. A propensity for evolutionary change is essential to create a critical leverage abroad in reaping the positive opportunities offered by the diffusion of international regimes, including the processes of globalization. Multi-lateral institutions established by SAARC have begun to deal with certain aspects of global governance. Adoption of a foreign policy of lower risk and greater accommodation has also begun to foster regional harmony and rectify the compulsion of adopting 'tilted' non-alignment as well as distorted communication.

South Asia's harmonious development is possible if India-Pakistan ties improve and growing cooperation in 'soft politics' binds shared interests in 'hard politics'—security, economy and international relations. Intensified political dialogues, Confidence Building Measures (CBM) and social, economic, ecological and technological cooperation can create necessary conditions for reducing the threat of tension and rebellion and promote the foundation for economic and social justice, peace and progress in South Asia. The challenge to peace springs from the fundamental inability to see security as anything other than a defence concern. When globalization is breaking the discipline and boundaries of the Westphalian system and reconnecting the regions and people, it is important to strengthen comprehensive security to enable South Asia to adjust in the existing multi-polar, hierarchical and competitive international system.

SENSE OF COMMUNITY

The utility of SAARC lies in deepening and enlarging the areas of soft-politics with an aim of beefing up efforts to meet the need for comprehensive security in the region. Its political future rests on effectiveness in utilizing its principles, objectives and means and coherence on institutional routines designed to regulate exchange of relationship in functional areas of cooperation. Regime growth begins if performance remains firm and common interests and consensus among them continue to grow. It requires the coherence of three approaches—bilateral coordination of action, regional coalition and global solidarity for collective action. Both the spirit and letter of the SAARC charter encourage the member states to strengthen the general structure of regional peace. South Asia can overcome its backwardness if its leadership can articulate the possibilities for an understanding between its public and the world.

The genesis of the concept of comprehensive security came from the realization that threats to national and human security originate from many directions and it is these that need to be addressed, analysed and properly assessed in the context of the dynamics at work in the region. While relations between nations is one aspect, internal political and economic situations are other features bearing an impact on the overall security of a region. The idea of comprehensive security does not necessarily exclude military capabilities and does not envisage a weak state but rather places emphasis on the non-military threats to security and ways and means to fuse these into a larger state security apparatus.

In the case of South Asia, structural causes of any kind of on-going conflicts are largely embedded in economic depravity, political instability, racial or religious discord, search for a separate identity, corruption, state mishandling, environmental devastation or scarcity of renewable resources. Disparities in addressing the challenges of globalization, territorial disputes, arms race, refugee crises, civil war in states and political tension among states prevents stability and thwarts peace and cooperation. Besides the weakening of traditional states, demographic pressures, pressures of globalization, low level of inter-state trade, fragile governments, weak political institutions, poverty, marginalization of *dalits*, gender discrimination, drug trafficking and proliferation of armed militia are other factors that have hindered progress in South Asia tossing the region into the bottom of human development indicators. A deliberation on comprehensive security in the region cannot divorce itself from all these factors mentioned above.

While it was not possible to deliberate upon all the causes and impact of non-traditional threats to security in the region, the assembly of erudite and well known personalities throughout South Asia for a regional conference on 'Comprehensive Security in South Asia' organized jointly by the Institute of Foreign Affairs and the Friedrich Ebert Stiftung (Nepal) on 19–20 November 2004 in Kathmandu deliberated upon many of the issues at hand.

Both the Institute of Foreign Affairs and the Friedrich Ebert Stiftung are grateful to all the participants of the conference who have authored insightful papers collected in this volume. The then Prime Minister of Nepal Sher Bahadur Deuba is also thanked for kindly inaugurating the regional meet. We would also like to thank Mr Ramesh Jain of Manohar Publishers, New Delhi for bringing out this book.

DEV RAJ DAHAL
NISHCHAL NATH PANDEY

CHAPTER 1

Trade Liberalization and Human Security in South Asia

INDRA NATH MUKHERJI

Over the past decade all South Asian countries have undertaken substantial trade liberalization as an essential component of structural adjustment programmes at the behest of the Britton Woods Institutions in the early 1980s. For some countries the pace of liberalization was slow and halting in the early 1980s, but gathered momentum in the 1990s. Currently the peak tariffs in most South Asian countries have been brought to around 20 per cent (excluding agriculture) from the very high levels exceeding 100 per cent in the 1970s and 1980s.

The reduction in tariff barriers was accompanied by the removal of quantitative restrictions through prohibitions. In Bangladesh, quantitative restrictions were greatly reduced from 315 products in 1989–90 to 124 in 1997. In India, all quantitative restrictions on exports were removed for all South Asian countries in August 1998 and for all other countries from April 2001.

There is no evidence to show that trade liberalization has adversely affected the rate of growth of South Asian countries. In fact, the rate of growth improved along with trade liberalization in India and Bangladesh. In Pakistan and Sri Lanka, due to political reasons, this link is tenuous.

Trade liberalization when targeted at essential raw materials, intermediate products, and capital goods can make some industries competitive by making available to them cheaper inputs which could facilitate industrialization. Again, when trade liberalization is directed to essential consumer goods or articles of daily consumption, they help to keep the cost of living down, benefiting the consumer. Further, by fostering competition with domestic industries, they induce improvement in resource use and bring down prices.

However the pace and pattern of trade liberalization have to be so calibrated that the governments' revenues are not adversely affected or the livelihood concerns of a large number of domestic producers put at stake. Governments would need to widen their tax base in the domestic economy to obtain alternative sources of revenue lost due to import liberalization. The increased requirement for foreign exchange would have to be earned through enhanced exports. Besides, in any democratically elected government, the interests of various stakeholders affected by reforms would need to be factored in.

The objective of this paper is to highlight the point that import liberalization, while being desirable, must be so calibrated as not to adversely affect the livelihood concerns of a large section of the population (particularly in agriculture). Further, trade liberalization can work best on a level playing field. In this context we will highlight the various legitimate instruments available with South Asian countries to safeguard the livelihood concerns of a vast majority of their population, which could be adversely affected by global pressure to hasten the indiscriminate opening up of their economics, with particular reference to agriculture.

Although the World Trade Organization (WTO) Agreement on Agriculture (AoA) emphasizes the importance of trade in improving the agricultural sector in WTO member countries, it also highlights the need to give due recognition to the various non-trade concerns in this sector.

The countries participating in discussions on AoA have emphasized two sets of issues. The first is what may broadly be termed as the multifunctional character of agriculture, where the European countries have enunciated the range of functions that agriculture performs, apart from providing food and fibres. These relate primarily to the environment in general and the conservation of biodiversity in particular. The second, emphasized by developing countries, is the more critical aspect of food security, which needs to have a non-trade perspective. It has been argued that if trade is made the singular basis of policy making in the agricultural sector in particular, domestic production of food grain could be seriously undermined which, in turn, threatens the realization of food security, an essential component of human security.

In the following sections some of the instruments available to South Asian countries to protect human security in general and food security in particular while at the same time participating in the process of globalization. In particular, we shall highlight the 'July Package', the WTO General Councils' post-Cancun decision declared on 31 July 2004.

AGRICULTURAL TARIFFS

For the reasons stated earlier, agricultural products have been subject to high tariff, both in the industrial and in the developing countries.

The AoA contains provisions in three broad areas of trade and agriculture policies: market access, export subsidies, and domestic support. Under market access, the agreement states that there can be no restrictions on farm trade except through tariffs. This means that the quantitative restricions (quotas, import restrictions through bans, permits, import licensing) that were in existence before the agreement came into being, were to be replaced by tariffs on imports to provide the same level of protection, and were then to be followed by a progressive reduction of tariffs levels. Tariffs resulting from the 'tariffication process' as well as other tariffs are to be reduced by a simple average of 36 per cent over six years in the case of the developed countries, and 24 per cent over ten years in the case of developing countries.[1]

In order to ensure the security of its agricultural population threatened by cheap subsidized imports from industrial countries, India had bound its tariffs at a high level, viz., 100 per cent for primary products, 150 per cent for processed products and 300 per cent for edible oils (except for some items that were historically bound at a lower level in the earlier negotiation.[2]

It is now well documented that developed countires extend subsides in three forms to their agriculture: (a) 'Amber' subsidies are intended to encourage more production; (b) 'Blue Box' subsidies provide incentives to limit production; and (c) 'Green Box' subsidies are provided primarily in the name of research and development. The total subsidy extended by the developed countries to their farmers has been increasing year by year, in spite of the agreement, and currently its value stands at US$ 320 billion or nearly a billion dollars per day. Such heavy subsidization keeps the prices of primary agricultural products down. As a consequence, in spite of having a comparative edge in agriculture, the South Asian countries not only fail to export their available surplus grains to the industrial world, but in fact, are vulnerable to becoming the dumping ground for the industrial countries.

While in the industrial countries the agricultural population accounts for no more than around 5 per cent of their total population, in developing South Asian countries, the rural population accounts for around 70–80 per cent of the total population. Whereas in the industrial countries agriculture is looked upon as a commercial enterprise, in the developing South Asian countries agriculture provides food security and livelihood concerns for millions of farmers and their families.

In view of these factors, and given that tariffs become the sole instrument for protecting the farmers, India chose to bind its tariffs at a very high level, even though its actual tariffs on most agricultural products were much lower. Nevertheless the binding of tariffs at a high level gave India some leverage against sudden possible surges in subsidized exports from industrial countries disrupting the domestic agricultural market and depriving farmers of their employment. This also provided India some bargaining strength when negotiating the limitation or removal of farm subsidies by the industrial countries.

In contrast to India, Sri Lanka chose to bind its agricultural tariff under the Uruguay Round AoA at a modest level of 50 per cent, while allowing the applied rate to be at 35 per cent. In 1998, all non-tariff barriers (NTB) were removed. While this was acclaimed by the global community as a demonstration of 'free-trade', the social consequences of such a decision were far from honourable, particularly given that Sri Lanka is a relatively high-cost producer of agricultural products. With the disbanding of NTBs and fixing tariff at 35 per cent on agricultural commodities, Sri Lanka faced a surge of imports of 'sensitive' agricultural crops into the country. This impacted negatively on production and the incomes of farmers, as well as on rural employment in areas where these crops are cultivated. Consequently, commodity specific taxes had to be introduced in the short term to prevent permanent damage to the agricultural community. However, Sri Lanka's options in this regard were limited, since it had agreed to maintain its bound tariff rates at no more than 50 per cent.[3]

INDUSTRIAL TARIFFS

The Doha Ministerial declaration in November 2001 sought to reduce or eliminate, tariffs on industrial products, including reduction in tariff peaks, high tariffs, and tariff escalation, as well as non-tariff barriers, in particular on products of export interest to developing countries. The declaration noted the special needs of the developing and least developed countries and recognized the need for less than full reciprocity in their reduction requirements. To this end, the Negotiating Group on Market Access was created at the first meeting of the Trade Negotiations Committee in early 2002.[4]

NON-TARIFF MEASURES

Article VI of the GATT provides for the right of contracting parties to apply anti-dumping measures, that is, measures against imports of a product at an export price below its 'normal' value,[5] if such dumped imports cause injury to a domestic industry in the territory of the importing country. If the domestic price cannot be used to make a comparison because of the peculiar market situation, then the cost of production could be used to draw a comparison.

Rules on anti-dumping were concluded at the end of the Tokyo Round. The revised agreement provides for greater clarity and more detailed rules in relation to the method of determining if a product has been dumped. Among other provisions, a new provision requires the immediate termination of an anti-dumping investigation in cases where the authorities determine that the margin of dumping is *de minimus*: defined as less than 2 per cent, expressed as a percentage of the export price of the product, or that the volume of the dumped imports is negligible.[6]

According to a study by the USA-based Institute for Agriculture and Trade Policy (IATP) in 2003, the US has been dumping major agricultural commodities like wheat, soya bean, maize, rice, and cotton since 1990 in world agricultural markets. According to this study, from 1990 to 2001, the levels of US dumping floated around 14 per cent for wheat, 57 per cent for cotton and between 25 and 30 per cent for maize.[7]

A recent study of Oxfam, released on 14 April 2004, threw new light on EU taxpayers paying 819 million every year to six sugar companies to dump sugar in world agricultural markets.[8]

Can South Asian countries protect their agriculture under existing dumping disciplines in GATT/WTO? A comparison of export prices with the cost of production can establish the extent of dumping. Nevertheless dumping becomes actionable only when it can be proved to have resulted in material injury to the domestic industry.

In the field of agriculture, notwithstanding clear evidence of dumping leading to material injury, no anti-dumping duties are being imposed on imports of agricultural commodities. The reason for this is that farmers in developing countries, apart from being ignorant of the discipline on dumping, are far too scattered and unorganized. In this context, a valuable suggestion has been made to have a separate discipline on agricultural dumping. Under this discipline, a separate *de minimus* dumping margin for different agricultural commodities, depending on the sensitivity of each commodity, should be determined. Once this margin is violated, material injury should be presumed and the importing country would have the right to impose anti-dumping duties on agricultural commodities. This would enable many marginal and subsistence farmers to protect themselves from sudden, unanticipated surges in imports of sensitive agricultural products adversely affecting on their food and livelihood security.[9]

AGREEMENT ON SANITARY AND PHYTOSANITARY MEASURES (SPS)

The WTO Agreement on SPS measures relates to the application of sanitary and phytosanitary measures concerning food safety and animal and plant health regulations. The agreement recognizes that governments have the right to take SPS measures, but they should be not be applied only to unjustifiably discriminate between member countries where identical or similar conditions prevail.[10]

In order to harmonize SPS measures on as wide a basis as possible, members are encouraged to base their measures on international standard guidelines and recommendations where they exist. However, members may maintain or introduce measures that result in higher standards if there is scientific justification or as a consequence of consistent risk decisions based on an appropriate risk assessment. The agreement includes provisions on control, inspection and approval procedure.[11]

The basic purpose of health and safety standards is to protect human, animal, and plant life as well as preserve the environment. The foods and drugs that people consume need to be safe for their health. A country's right to protect its consumers and environment against substandard products, both local and foreign, is undeniable. This implies that these standards have to be applied with both MFN and national treatment principles so that there is no discrimination between imported products by origin or between imported products on the one hand and those produced domestically in terms of regulations.

SPS measures are applied on trade in both developed as well as developing countries. However, along with the gradual removal or reduction in tariff barriers, SPS measures are being strengthened, particularly in the industrial countries. For example, the rules imposed by the US on imports to pre-empt terrorism, requiring prior notice to the US Food and Drug Administration, have proved enormously complex as well as costly in terms of compliance by the developing countries. This places the developing countries, whose major markets lie in the industrial countries, at a disadvantage.[12]

AGREEMENT IN SAFEGUARDS

Article XIX of the WTO Agreement allows a member to take 'safeguard' measures to protect a specific domestic industry from an unforeseen increase of imports of any product which is causing, or which is likely to cause, serious injury to the industry.

The agreement sets out the items for 'serious injury and the factors which must be considered in determining the impact on imports'. Generally, the duration of a measure should not exceed four years though this could be extended up to a maximum of eight years, subject to confirmation of continued necessity by the competent national authorities and if there is evidence that the industry is adjusting. Safeguard measures would not be applicable to a product from a developing member country, if the share of the developing member country with less than 3 per cent import share collectively accounts for no more than 9 per cent of total imports of the product, concerned.[13] The South Asian countries have not been using this measure to safeguard their domestic industries. However, many international institutions such as the World Bank have been suggesting that safeguard measures should be used in lieu of anti-dumping measures.

RULES OF ORIGIN (ROO)

The ROO is particularly relevant under Regional Trading Arrangements (RTA). Under RTAs, member states reduce mutual trade restrictions without doing the same from non-members to encourage intra-regional trade. However, the member states under such arrangements are free to set their tariff levels with non-members at a level they deem appropriate. Under such a situation, member states having relatively lower tariffs with non-members could deflect trade to member states maintaining relatively higher tariffs on similar products. Under such a situation, the markets of the latter members state could be flooded with low-tariff imports from the former member state. In order to prevent this happening, most RTAs set ROO that specify the minimum local raw material component on products required for eligibility for preferential treatment.

In this context, we may recall the progressive liberalization of the Indo–Nepalese Trade and Transit Treaties over the years, culminating in the Treaty of 1996, which totally waived the ROO requirement for Nepalese imports to India. Only a certification by a competent authority in Nepal was all that was required. This led to a surge in imports of a number of sensitive products into the Indian market. Nepalese imports of a number of products such as copper wire rods, scrap and sheet, polyethylene granules, vegetable oil, and acrylic yarns had increased rapidly, far above the domestic needs of the country. These were deflected in large quantities to the Indian market, taking advantage of the loophole in the Treaty. This caused a large number of vegetable oil processors and acrylic fibre manufacturing units in northern Indian states to shut down their operations, threatening the livelihood security of a large number of operators and those employed in their units. Consequently, a revised protocol to Article V and the new protocol to Article IX of the treaty had to be incorporated in the Indo–Nepal Treaty of Trade from March 2002, setting a minimum ROO criteria of 25 per cent.[14]

IMPLICATIONS OF THE 'JULY PACKAGE'

This section examines the General Council's post-Cancun decision on the Doha Agenda works programme agreed on 31 July 2004, setting the framework for future negotiations that could impact on the livelihood security of vast rural populations in South Asia.

It might be recalled that the Cancun round ended in a fiasco because of the stubborn refusal of the US and EU countries to discuss the reduction of agricultural subsidies, but instead to push Singapore issues, namely investment, competition, government procurement and trade facilitation. Since India, Brazil, China, Indonesia, Egypt, Malaysia, the Philippines, Bangladesh, and other developing countries voiced their strong opposition to the Cancun (2003) draft, the negotiations ended in total failure.

The Indian Commerce and Industry Minister, Kamal Nath, has claimed that the Geneva framework has been able to extract substantial gains from the export of industrial goods and services while at the same time safeguarding the interests of farmers.

The developed countries have agreed to do away with the direct and indirect subsidies provided to their exports. They have also agreed to bring about a substantial reduction in the domestic support provided to their farmers. In particular, the Geneva Framework required that there would be a minimum reduction in such support to 80 per cent of the pre-existing levels in the very first years 'and throughout the period of implementation'.

The Blue Box support has been capped at 5 per cent of a

member's average total value of agricultural production during a historical period, to be established in the negotiation.

The framework recognizes the need for special and differential treatment for developing countries in terms of the quantum of tariff reduction, tariff rate quota expansion, number and treatment of sensitive products, and the length of the implementation period.

Further, the developing countries have the right to identify the number of special products, based on the criteria of food security, livelihood security and rural development needs, which could be eligible for flexible treatment.

Finally, a Special Safeguard Mechanism has been provided in the framework against disruptive imports, the details of which are to be worked out. The developed countries have also accepted the adoption of the less-than-full reciprocity principles for the developing countries. While on paper the Geneva Framework appears to be a step forward in addressing the needs of developing countries, some analysts have recommended caution about the real outcome.

While the developed countries have agreed to eliminate export subsidies, it is not clear as to the time frame that is involved. Only ongoing negotiations will reveal this.

One major weakness of the Framework is that Blue Box subsidies have been legitimized. The declaration states: 'Members recognized the role of the Blue Box for promoting agricultural reforms'. Besides, the Framework states: 'in cases where a member has placed an exceptionally large percentage of its trade distributing support in the Blue Box some flexibility will be provided on a basis to be agreed to ensure that such a Member is not called upon to make a wholly disproportionate cut'.[15] Similarly, the declaration accepts that the Green Box subsidies will not be subject to reduction commitments in future. Given this, it is quite probable that for the developing countries will shift some of their subsidies from Amber and Green Box to Blue Box, a practice they have been following for the past several years. A statement made by Senator Charles Grassely, Chairman of the Senate Finance Committee that oversees trade agreement legislation, confirms this. He reassured American farmers in a radio broadcast on 3 August 2004, that the WTO framework agreement would not bring about changes in the US farm programmes until after the current Farm Bill expires (2007), and said that US subsidies would likely be shifted from one category to another, but not necessarily reduced. He stated: 'I see in the final analysis, maybe the total support for American agriculture not being decreased but being changed from production-related subsidies to . . . (support for) environmental practices'.[16] Grassely further stated that the Framework provides new flexibility for US counter-cyclical payments. Under the Framework such payments can be shifted from the Amber Box of trade distorting supports to the Blue Box of subsidies that are decoupled from production and are considered less trade distorting. Counter cyclical payments, included in the 2002 Farm Bill, are used to compensate US farmers when global prices for commodities fall below government fixed targets.[17]

On agricultural subsides, the Framework says: 'As the first installment of the overall cut, in the first year and throughout the implementation period, the sum of all trade-distorting support will not exceed 80 per cent of the sum of final bound total AMS[18] plus permitted *de minimus* plus the Blue Box at the level to be determined in Paragraph 15.' However, since the actual AMS in the EU is less than the bound commitment level, the level of actual as opposed to bound AMS based total support plus *de minimus* support, plus Blue Box support, stood at ECU 78.0 billion in 2000–1, which is lower than the post-minimal reduction level of ECU 81.2 billion. This would enable EU members not only to retain their existing level of subsidies, but in fact, to even raise them.[19]

Regarding non-agricultural market access, the July Package recognized that a formula approach was the key to reducing tariffs peaks and escalation through a non-linear formula applied on a line-by-line basis, which would take into account the special needs and interests of developing and LDCs, including less than full reciprocity in reduction commitments. The package specifies the flexibilities that could be so applied.

1. Applying less than formula cuts upto 10 per cent of the tariff lines provided that the cuts are no less than half the formula cuts and that these tariff lines do not exceed 10 per cent of the total value of member participants' imports.

2. Keeping as an exception, tariff lines unbound, or not applying the formula cuts for upto 5 per cent of tariff lines provided they do not exceed 5 per cent of the total value of member participants' imports.
3. LDCs from applying the formula or participating in sectoral approach, but are required to substantially increase their binding commitments.

Another notable feature of the package is that developed countries (and other participants who agree), should offer duty-free and quota-free market access for non-agricultural products originating from LDCs by the year to be decided.

CONCLUSION

Global trade liberalization is expected to improve the efficiency of resource use and thereby enhance human welfare. However, this assumes a level playing field for all participants, both developed and developing. For the latter group of countries, special and differential treatment is endorsed in the WTO rules. However, these countries must work out how they could protect their vulnerable population, both in agriculture and in non-agriculture, while making the best use of the flexibilities that are available to them. This would involve, among other measures, identification of the products they could include in their sensitive lists. Since LDCs have been provided considerable protection, it is up to the non-LDCs in the developing world, particularly in South Asia to make the best use of flexibilities offered to them. However even with the best use of flexibilities the protection may not be adequate so long as the industrial countries find ways and means to avoid capping their agricultural subsidies and eliminating them or reducing them substantially.

NOTES

1. E:\human Security \Focus on India and WT agric.htm.
2. Ibid.
3. N.F.C. Ranawerea, 'Agreement Trade Polices and Further Subsides—its Impact in Sri Lanka', paper presented at the Regional Workshop on Trade Polices in South Asia, Colombo, 2–3 October 2003.

4. www.wto.org.
5. Usually the price of the product in the domestic market of the exporting country.
6. http//www.wto.org/English/dogs_e/legal-eursum-e.html//to Agreement.
7. Ranjan Prabhash, 'Anti dumping—Anti-dote to Farm Subsidy Venon', in *World Trade Review*, vol. 4, no. 16, 16–31 August 2004.
8. Ibid.
9. Ibid.
10. Ibid.
11. Ibid.
12. For details see H.H. Zaidi, 'Non-traditional Trade Barriers', *World Trade Review*, 16–31 August 2004.
13. Zaidi, 'Non-traditional Trade Barriers'.
14. Indo–Nepal Treaty of Trade, letters exchanged between Government of India and His Majesty's Government of Nepal, 2 March 2002.
15. Ibid., para 15.
16. A.Q. Suberi, 'A False Unfolding', in *World Trade Review*, 10–15 September 2004.
17. Ibid.
18. Aggregate Measurement of Support.
19. Ibid.

CHAPTER 2

Environmental Security in South Asia: Dimensions, Issues and Problems

B.C. UPRETI

The fast depletion of natural resources resulting in the scarcity of resources and the degradation of the environment and the growing conflict over resources within and between the states has given rise to a growing concern for environmental security all over the world. It is being widely accepted that environmental scarcity and environmental degradation pose a threat to national security. Hence there is a close linkage between environmental degradation and national security.[1] There are scholars to whom these propositions are not convincing.[2] Yet in recent years it has been widely accepted that environmental security is a significant dimension of the national and regional security frameworks of the nation-states.

In fact, it is true to say that in recent years there has been a growing concern for the environment. It may be pointed out here that since the beginning, man has been imposing his needs and demands on the environment. Therefore, the concern of human beings for the environment has been always and obvious. But it is only now that the concern for environmental security is being advocated. Why has such a need for environmental security arisen now? What has necessitated it? Is the depletion or scarcity of natural resources a threat to the environment? To what extent does overpopulation have a bearing on the environment? Is human dislocation creating environmental hazards? Are natural disasters a cause and effect of the environmental degeneration? Then how can we secure the environment? These are some of the issues and problems

*Paper presented at a regional workshop on 'Security in South Asia', Institute of Foreign Affairs, Kathmandu, Nepal, 5–6 September, 2004.

that need deeper probe in order to understand the phenomenon of environmental security and its relevance.

In this paper an attempt has been made to analyse these issues in the context of the South Asian region. As a preliminary note, it can be said that in a highly populated (rather overpopulated) and resource-scarce region with ill-coordinated development activities, threats to the environment become more prominent. Therefore there is a greater need for securing the environment in such areas. It may also be added here that in such a situation, any stress on the environment can cause conflicts involving violence of a low to a very high magnitude within the state boundaries as well as between the states.[3]

ENVIRONMENTAL SECURITY: A CONCEPTUAL FRAMEWORK

After the end of the Cold War, there has been an urge to redefine national security and build up a comprehensive view of it several studies have advocated a rethinking on the concept of national approaches and provided alternative approaches.[4] The thrust of the comprehensive view of security has been to secure social, economic and environmental dimensions, along with securing the boundaries of the state.[5] The traditional concept of security was cenetred on defending the territory and political integrity of a country. The state was responsible for defending its sovereignty and integrity and the armed forces were assigned to this duty.[6] The state alone had to perform this responsibility as there were no such other institutions that could share it.[7] With the end of Cold War and the decreasing importance of geo-strategic considerations, national security is being viewed from a comprehensive perspective. While there is no denying the fact that the military dimensions of security are relevant, there is an added emphasis on the non-military dimensions of security. It is not sufficient to secure the territory and the sovereignty of the state. It is equally important to secure the people and their surroundings. It is in this perspective that a comprehensive view of national security has emerged. It may be noted here that the comprehensive national security approach is a deviation from the state-centric view of security.

Japan was the first country to talk about a comprehensive approach to national security.[8]

The comprehensive view of national security is based on the notion that it is not the state alone that needs security. The people, the resources, and the socio-economic structures within the state also need to be secured. In fact, it is now strongly believed that the security of the state is meaningless unless the people are secure. Therefore, some scholars have tried to define national security in terms of human security. The concept of human security gives the impression that the securing of the human beings should not remain confined to state boundaries. The comprehensive view of national security obviously includes social, economic, and environmental security, along with the security of the state. Thus, both the military and non-military dimensions are important in the changed framework of national security.

Environmental security has become an important dimension of comprehensive national security. Environmental security as a concept was officially mentioned for the first time in the General Assembly of the UNO in 1987.[9] Since then, it has become a significant aspect of security studies in both theoretical and empirical contexts. It has been widely accepted that the indiscriminate attitudes of the people and the governments towards the environment, self-interest, over-exploitation of resources, etc., have caused a scarcity of resources and their fast depletion as well as the degradation of the environment. This has caused conflicts and violence among and between the states.[10] The scarcity of resources may give rise to a conflict for the remaining resources. Therefore there is a need to secure the environment. The security of the environment needs a positive attitude towards it. Thus environmental security may be defined as the avoidance of the negative linkages between human activities and the environment.

The notion of environmental security underlines the need to explore and propagate the interlinkages between resource use and environmental degradation; because the environment can be properly protected and managed only when we understand urgency behind it. In this context, environmental security can be viewed as an effective measure towards sustainable development.[11]

Since the environment can be a cause of conflicts, violence, and a threat to peace and stability, securing the environment would mean, in a broader perspective, removing the causes of environmental conflicts, as well as the causes of environmental scarcity.[12] This would require sustainability of the biotic resources of the earth and this is possible through environmental security.[13]

Thus environmental security means ordering and managing the resources and biosphere activities. It is related to the establishment of a proper human–nature relationship.

APPROACHES TO ENVIRONMENTAL SECURITY

It is clear that the central thrust of the environmental security is to secure the environment. But the point is how to determine the phenomenon of the environment. In this regard, there can be two approaches to define the environmental concerns.

The first approach confines the environment to the nature and the problems and constraints related to it. It can be termed as the ecological approach. This approach is too narrow in its scope, as nature alone is not responsible for many types of hazards. How it is being exploited and protected are equally important.

The other approach has been termed as the maximize approach, and it includes both the ecology and its human domains. This approach takes into consideration the interaction between the two. It believes that the excessive dependence of human beings affects the environment, and the depletion and degradation of the environment affect the human beings. Environmental security has to include both the domains and understand their interlinkages. In fact, the uses of the environment and its proper maintenance are related to the human domains.

It may also be added here that the question of environmental security has to be addressed in a broader perspective. Both the living non-human domains and the human domains have to be included within the purview of environmental security. It is also important that a futuristic attitude has to be adopted in securing the environment. Today's environmental hazards can be environmental challenges tomorrow. Therefore, it is not sufficient that today's needs and demands are kept in view. It is equally important that the possible human–environment interlinkages are taken into consideration in securing the environment.

SOUTH ASIA: SOME ECOLOGICAL FEATURES

The South Asian region is a compact geo-ecological zone with several geographical variations ranging from the high Himalayan region to the maritime zones. A region of nearly 4,082 sq. km., South Asia is characterized by Indo-centricity. India forms borders with almost all the countries of South Asia but no other country forms borders with another. India is the largest of the countries of the region. Its size, population, resources, economic development, scientific and technological advancement, and military strength are heavily disproportionate in comparison to the other countries of the region. India alone holds 76 per cent of the land area. Its population is three times higher than the combined populations of the rest of the countries of the region. It contains 78 per cent of the total GNP of the region. This kind of asymmetry in terms of size and resources is a source of numerous problems in the region including sharing and managing the resources of the region. Such a situation also accelerates conflicts over resources.[14]

The South Asian states are not synchronized with the eco-geographical region due to the artificial divisioning of the state into different regions. India, Pakistan, and Bangladesh emerged as independent countries out of one geographic unit. As a result, these independent states share a common geography. Therefore mutual sharing and conflict over resources are obvious. This also necessitates the development of a common approach to environmental security.

The three major river systems of South Asia—the Indus, the Ganga and the Brahmaputra—are shared by most of the countries of the region. It is therefore obvious that they also share the hazards emanating from these river systems.

Nepal and Bhutan are landlocked countries and Sri Lanka and the Maldives are island countries. This asymmetrical incongruity between the states of the region accounts for many of the disputes and conflicts.

It can be said on the basis of this brief overview that the very nature of the South Asian region makes it prone to various kinds of environmental issues and problems.

MAJOR ENVIRONMENTAL ISSUES IN SOUTH ASIA

South Asia faces a number of major evironmental issues, some of which will be discussed in this section.

Population Explosion

Population has a direct bearing upon resources and the environment at large. There has to be a balance between the population and the resources. An imbalance is bound to create environmental hazards. South Asia is one of the most densely populated regions of the world. The total population of South Asia is 1,366 million (2001). The region holds more than 23 per cent of the world's total population, while it has only 3.5 per cent of the total land area of the world. This shows that the region has much greater population in relation to its land area. India holds the largest share of the population of the region, with 1,033 million people, Pakistan has a population of 146 million, Bangladesh 141 million, Nepal 24 million, Sri Lanka 19 million, Bhutan 2.13 million, and the Maldives 0.30 million. India is the second-most populated country in the world. Similarly, Bangladesh is overpopulated in terms of its land area. The average annual population growth of South Asia is 1.8 per cent, which is more than the average annual population growth of the developing countries (1.6 per cent). The Maldives has the highest population growth with 3.1 per cent, followed by Bhutan 2.8 per cent, Nepal 2.3 per cent, Pakistan 2.7 per cent, India 1.7 per cent and Sri Lanka 0.9 per cent.[15]

It is clear that all these countries are overpopulated. The excessive pressure of the population on the resources causes numerous environmental problems and constraints. The problems of environmental depletion and environmental scarcity are closely associated with the problem of uncontrolled population growth.

Poverty

There is a direct correlation between population, poverty, and environmental degradation.[16] The poor countries are more vulnerable to environmental changes. Hence they are more prone to environmentally induced conflicts.[17] Poverty and underdevelopment affect the environment by causing environmental depletion and scarcity thereby contributing to environment-related conflicts.[18] The poverty conditions in South Asia can be understood from the fact that the region generates only 1.2 per cent of the world's total income.[19] The Human Development Report for South Asia states that 32.3 per cent of the total population is below the poverty line in the region. Nepal has the highest number of poor with 37.7 per cent, followed by Bangladesh 36.0 per cent, and India 34.7 per cent.

The per capita GNP ($45, 2001) is 448 in South Asia. The GDP growth rate has been 5 per cent during 2000–1. South Asia's human development index has been 0.560 (2000). Nearly 22 per cent of the total population is without access to health services, 63 per cent population without access to sanitation facilities, and 11 per cent without access to safe drinking water. This data clearly shows that the South Asian countries are faced with the challenges of poverty and underdevelopment.

Threat to Biodiversity

The South Asian region is rich in biodiversity. The different ecological regions, like the mountains, hills, plains, deserts, and sea coasts have specific varieties of flora and fauna. The hilly countries of Nepal and Bhutan have numerous varieties of plants, many of which have medicinal value. The Maldives has the world's best coral reef formations. Road development, dam construction, fast depletion of forests, pollution of rivers, and excessive exploitation of plant species and floral varieties for individual and commercial uses threaten the biodiversity. The issues involved here are biodiversity conservation and growth, protection of intellectual property rights, patents, security from bio-imperialism, etc.[20]

Natural and Other Hazards

The region is prone to numerous kinds of natural hazards which have a direct effect on the environment.

In South Asia, forests play an important role in the developmental process, as well as catering to the needs of the people. People have depended on forests for food, firewood, fodder, manure, medicinal herbs, timber, etc. Forests play a significant role in soil and water conservation, the reduction of air pollution and improvement of the environment, wildlife preservation and conservation, storage of water, and controlling the greenhouse effect. Countries like India, Nepal, and Bhutan were once quite rich in forest resources. However, excessive exploitation of forest resources and the lack of reforestation policies, over dependence on forest resources, urbanization, increasing demand for cultivable land, etc., has caused fast depletion of the forests. South Asia has only 15 per cent of land area under forests. India has a forest area of 19.5 per cent. Bangladesh has 9 per cent. The annual rate of deforestation is the highest in Nepal, at 1.8 per cent.[21] The depletion of forests has serious ecological effects such as soil erosion, siltation, shrinking of water resources, etc.

Floods are a common problem for countries like India, Bangladesh, Nepal, and Pakistan. The annual floods cause losses to people and property, sedimentation, etc. Bangladesh has been viewed as one of the most disaster prone countries of the world, and has experienced some of the most devastating floods.[22] In Bangladesh, 18 to 19 million people are affected by floods every year.[23] There is a direct co-relationship between environmental change and floods.

In the case of Bangladesh, it is said that one-third of the country may be submerged by 2050 due to the rise in the sea level. It has been estimated that a one-metre rise in the sea level would cover 14 per cent of the land area of the country, thereby displacing 10 per cent of its total population.[24] In the case of the Maldives as well, it is said that the country is in danger of disappearing under the sea in a few years.

The Himalayan region is highly sensitive to seismic activity and has witnessed some of the world's most devastating earthquakes. India, Bangladesh, Sri Lanka, the Maldives, and Pakistan are affected by cyclones, tidal waves, sea storms, coastal area pollution, etc. Bangladesh is also faced with the problem of water salinity and arsenic poisoning.[25]

India, Pakistan, Bangladesh, and Sri Lanka are subject to acute draughts. These draughts result in a fall in agriculture production causing food scarcity, scarcity of fodder, scarcity of drinking water, hunger, and unemployment.[26] Air pollution is also becoming a problem in some areas of India, Pakistan, and Bangladesh, due to urbanization and industrialization and other types of infrastructural growth. There are also problems of water logging, water pollution, etc.

South Asian countries are predominantly agriculture societies. With the rise in populations, there is increased demand for agriculture productivity. In some countries the cultivable land is already exhausted. There is heavy pressure on agriculture land, giving rise to conflicts. The demand for higher productivity has necessitated the use of fertilizers and chemicals, which has generated many problems such as deterioration in the quality of soil productivity.

Most of the countries of South Asia are also faced with the problems of water pollution, decline in the quality of water, decline of the groundwater level, etc. India's annual renewable resources are 1,878 cu.m., Bangladesh 9,238 cu.m., Nepal 9,122 cu.m., and Sri Lanka 2,708 cu.m.[27] But the depletion of renewable resources is believed to occur faster than their natural replenishment.[28]

ENVIRONMENTAL INTERLINKAGES AND CONFLICTS IN SOUTH ASIA

South Asia is a compact geographic unit and it is one ecological zone. Therefore, most of the environmental problems extend beyond national boundaries and are shared by more than one country. There are some environmental issues that are beyond the jurisdiction of any one country of the region.[29] These are regional issues indeed. The regional interlinkages of environmental issues and problems have given rise to bilateral and multilateral conflicts. Thus, it can be said that the environmental problems are a threat to regional peace and stability in South Asia.

The population explosion, underdevelopment, and poverty have resulted in large-scale cross-country movements of population as illegal migrants, economic migrants and refugees.[30] This has caused disputes between the local inhabitants and the outsiders, given rise to ethnic conflicts and violent movements, and caused bilateral disputes between the countries involved. For example, migration has become a serious issue between India and Bangladesh, and India and Nepal. Similarly, the question of migrants and refugees has caused tensions in Nepal–Bhutan relations.

The pollution caused by infrastructural developments in one country does not remain confined to that country alone. It also affects the ecology of the other countries of the region. The issues related to unilateral uses and withdrawal of river waters by one country are a cause of concern for the other country, whether it is India, Pakistan, Bangladesh, or Nepal. Similarly, the sharing of river water has caused disputes and misunderstandings between India and Bangladesh, India and Nepal, and India and Pakistan.

Floods in India have a more devastating effect in Bangladesh. The same is true between Nepal and India and India and Pakistan. Environmental hazards like soil erosion, desertification, sedimentation, earthquakes, coastal-area pollution, deforestation threats to biodiversity, and their multiplied effects, are issues that are not confined to one single country.

NEED FOR A REGIONAL APPROACH ON ENVIRONMENTAL ISSUES

Environment-related problems and their implications are regional issues as the countries of the region, in most of cases, share them. It is true that there has been a growing awareness on environmental issues in almost all the countries of South Asia in the last few years.[31] Individual countries have adopted environment-friendly policies in certain sectors. Attempts have been made towards reforestation, flood control, controlling desertification, etc. However, there are two issues that need to be looked at more closely:

1. Some of the measures taken for environmental management and protection have not been effective as the sources of environmental degradation lie in some other country.
2. All the countries of the region are not conscious about environmental protection on the same scale. Their excessive dependence on natural resources, lack of alternative sources, scarcity of capital resources and technical know-how have proved to be a serious bottleneck in making adequate efforts towards environmental protection.

A common approach to securing the environment at the regional level may involve the following aspects:

- sharing of knowledge and expertise regarding population control measures, policies, and programmes,
- cooperation for development and poverty eradication,
- regularization of inter-state migrations, evolving a regional framework for controlling, repatriation, and rehabilitation of refugees,
- establishment of a system of disaster management and disaster preparedness at the regional level,
- exchange of knowledge and researches on seismic tremors, earthquakes, landslides, their causes and possibilities,
- evolving common flood-control measures and a regional flood warning system, and
- common measures for increased agriculture productivity, treatment of salinity, development of cyclone warning systems, reforestation, development of water resources, air pollution control systems, etc.

All these measures can be covered within the framework of a Regional Environmental Security Treaty. Such a treaty will provide an institutional basis for the growth of a common approach to environmental protection and management in South Asia. The South Asian Association for Regional Cooperation (SAARC) can take a lead in this regard and prepare the necessary background for a Regional Environmental Security Treaty. The SAARC can further consolidate its environmental protection measures; because it is through regional cooperation alone that many of the environment related issues can be settled.[32]

CONCLUSION

After the end of Cold War, there has been much debate on the comprehensive approach to national security. It is widely accepted that national security has to be viewed in a wider perspective. Environmental security constitutes a significant dimension of the comprehensive national security.

The environment too has to be viewed in a wider perspective where human and non-human living beings are also important, along with the nature. The environment and living organs are closely interlinked. Hence environmental security must take into consideration a balanced and sustained inter-relationship between the two.

In South Asia, environmental issues have become significant in the overall framework of security due to high population growth, excessive dependence on nature, uneven infrastructural development, poverty, underdevelopment, and the fragile ecology.

While there is urgent need to take measures for environmental protection, a regional approach alone can bear fruit because of eco-geographical interlinkages and interdependence in the region. Therefore, along with the strengthening of SAARC, a Regional Environment Security Treaty can be suggestive. Given the socio-political realities of the South Asian region, the conflictual relations between the states of South Asia, the complexities, identity crises, over-consciousness about resources, big-power, small-power angularities, and the slow progress of SAARC and its ineffectiveness in many cases, the realization of the goal of a Regional Environment Security Treaty is not an easy task. There are several constraints. But it is not a difficult task either if there is mutual confidence, trust, and understanding between the countries of the region. It has to be realized that environmental security in South Asia is possible only through a regional approach only. Therefore, the efforts made by the individual countries need to be coordinated in a regional framework.

NOTES

1. J. Riftin, *Biospheric Politics: A New Consciousness for a New Century*, New York: Crown Books, 1991; Norman Myers, 'Environment and Security', *Foreign Policy*, no. 74, Spring 1989; Arthur H. Westing (ed.), *Global Resources and International Conflict: Environmental Factors in Strategic Policy and Action*, New York: Oxford University Press, 1986.
2. Daniel Deudney, 'The Case Against Linking Environmental Degradation and National Security', *Millennium*, vol. 19, no. 3, Winter, 1990; L. Brock 'Security Through Defending the Environment: An Illusion', in E. Boulding (ed.), *New Agenda for Peace Research: Conflict and Security Re-examined*, Boulder, 1992; Richard H. Moss, 'Environmental Security? The Illogic of Centralised State Responses

to Environmental Threats', in Paul Painchand (ed.), *Geopolitical Perspectives on Environmental Security*, Quebec, 1992.

3. Homar Dixon, 'On the Threshold: Environmental Changes as Causes of Acute Conflict', *International Security*, vol. 16, no. 2, Fall 1991.
4. Barry Buzan, 'Rethinking Security after the Cold War', *Nordic Journal of International Studies*, vol. 32, no. 1, March 1997; B. Weston (ed.), *Alternative Security: Luring Without Nuclear Deterrence*, Boulder: Westview Press, 1990; A.L. Powers and M. Sommers (eds.), *The Conquest of War: Alternative Strategies for Global Security*, Boulder, 1990.
5. Berry Buzan, *The Logic of Anarchy*, New York: Columbia University Press, 1992, p. 34.
6. M.P. Leffer, 'The American Conception of National Security and the Beginning of the Cold War 1945–48', *American Historical Review*, vol. 89, 1984, pp. 246–81.
7. Narottam Gann, 'Environmental Security: An Appendage to Geo-political World Order of the United States', *BIISS Journal* (Dhaka), vol. 24, no. 3, July 2003, p. 428.
8. Robert W. Barnett, *Beyond War: Japan's Concept of Comprehensive National Security*, Washington, 1984.
9. *Our Common Future*, UCED, Oxford: Oxford University Press, 1987.
10. F. Thomas and Homer Dixon, *Environment, Security and Violence*, Princeton, 1999, p. 48. Paul F. Diehl and Nils Potter Gleditsch (eds.) *Environmental Conflict*, Boulder: Westview Press, 2001; Michael Dobkowski and Isidor Wallimann (eds.), *On the Edge of Scarcity: Environment, Resources, Population, Sustainability and Conflicts*, Syracuse: Syracuse University Press, 2002.
11. Abul Kalam, 'Environment and Development: Widening Security Frontier and the Quest for a New Security Framework in South Asia', *BIISS Journal*, vol. 19, no. 2, 1989, pp. 122–3.
12. Gann, 'Environmental Security', *BIISS Journal*, p. 452.
13. Shaukat Hassan, 'Emerging Environmental Concerns in South Asia', in Dipankar Banerji (ed.), *Security Studies in South Asia: Change and Challenges*, New Delhi: Manohar, 2000, p. 28.
14. Lawrence S. Prabhakar, 'Security Studies in India: Continuity and Change in the Post-Cold War Era', in Banerji (ed.), *Security Studies in South Asia*, p. 72.
15. *Human Development in South Asia 2003*, Karachi: Oxford University Press, 2004, p. 193.
16. Kalam, 'Environment and Development', *BIISS Journal*, p. 122.
17. Homer Dixon, 'Environmental Changes as Causes of Acute Conflict', in Richard K. Belts (ed.), *Conflict After the Cold War: Agreements on Causes of Conflict and Peace*, New York: Macmillan, 1994, p. 426.

18. Michael Renner, *National Security : The Economic and Environmental Dimensions*, Washington, 1989.
19. B.C. Upreti, *Contemporary South Asia*, Delhi: Kalinga Publications, 2004, p. 5.
20. Surender Singh Chauhan, *Biodiversity, Biopiracy and Biopolitics: The Global Perspectives*, Delhi: Kalinga Publications, 2001.
21. *Human Development in South Asia*, p. 196.
22. Abdur Rob Khan, 'Bangladesh', in *Comprehensive Security for South Asia*, New Delhi: Delhi Policy Group, 2001, p. 16.
23. Dilara Chaudhary, 'Security Studies in Bangladesh: Continuity and Change', in Banerji (ed.), *Security Studies in South Asia*, p. 153.
24. Khan, 'Bangladesh', p. 22.
25. Mohammad Humayun Kabir (ed.), *National Security of Bangladesh in Twenty First Century*, Dhaka, 2000.
26. B.C. Upreti, 'Comprehensive National Security in India: A View from Western India', in *Comprehensive National Security for India*, New Delhi: Delhi Policy Group, 2002.
27. *Human Development in South Asia.*
28. Gann, 'Comprehensive Security for South Asia: An Environmental Approach', *BIISS Journal*, vol. 20, no. 2, 1999, p. 103.
29. R.B. Jain, 'Regional Cooperation in Environmental Management, Problems and Prospects on South Asian Countries', in Lok Raj Baral (ed.), *South Asia, Democracy and the Road Ahead*, Kathmandu: POLSAN, 1992, p. 223.
30. Upreti, 'Population Movement in South Asia: Causes and Consequences', SAJOSPAS, December 2004 (to be published).
31. Khan, *Comprehensive Security for South Asia.*
32. Ashok Swain, 'Environmental Cooperation in South Asia', in Ken Conca and Geoff Daberke (eds.), *Environmental Peacemaking*, Washington: Woodrow Wilson Centre Press, 2002.

CHAPTER 3

Major Powers and South Asia

C.V. RANGANATHAN

Winston Churchill is quoted as having said, 'America will do the right thing, once it had exhausted all the alternatives'. There is a remarkable contemporary ring to this remark if one chooses to be an optimist. One might also transpose it to apply to India, given the international and regional developments over the last few years.

It is self-evident that the policies of the major powers towards countries of South Asia are related to the dynamics of their relationship inter se. However since 2002, counting from roughly a year and a half ago, prospects have been opening up for active dialogue to solve all outstanding issues between India and Pakistan. The summit meeting of South Asian Association for Regional Cooperation (SAARC) in Islamabad in 2004 resulted in firm commitments to press forward in many needed directions. The Indian economy and polity is moving steadily to make it more capable of driving regional cooperation in South Asia in old and new areas. Indian entrepreneurs are reviving Indian industry while adapting to the promises and pitfalls of globalization. The skill sets and business acumen required to lay the base for knowledge industries are growing. The present and future impact of the policies of major powers vis-à-vis South Asia would therefore need to be looked at in the context of the current global issues—rather than purely in the context of the extant bilateral disputes in South Asia. For the defining feature of our contemporary world is the global and transnational character of the challenges confronted, whether they are in the realm of international security or in development.

OVERVIEW OF INDIA–CHINA RELATIONS

It would be appropriate to begin with China as it is the largest and immediate neighbour of four South Asian countries. While it is a fact that the poor state of relations between India and Pakistan has held progress in the SAARC hostage till the beginning of 2004, no one can deny that the state of India–China relations from the 1950s to at least the late 1970s cast a malign shadow on South Asia. As an Indian, one needs to acknowledge that strategic experts and opinion makers in India were in the habit, in those years, of looking at China, and relations between individual South Asian countries and China, through the psychological prism of poor Sino–Indian relations. It would be equally true to assert that various Chinese policies and actions in the same period had the definite objective of hurting Indian interests or displaying insensitivity to some Indian interests. Such policies and actions were in evidence when China's own world view was fundamentally different from the external policies adopted from the late 1970s.

Certain chronological landmarks in Chinese actions vis-à-vis South Asia are relevant as they explain the then prevailing negative balance sheet: 1950 (Tibet), 1962 (Sino–Indian war), 1965 (Indo–Pak war), 1971 (liberation of Bangladesh). Domestic circumstances during the Cultural Revolution in China, the prevalence of the Cold War, when India relied so much on the Soviet Union (from 1962 onwards), the bitterness of the Sino–Soviet dispute which USA exploited from the early 1970s and which reached an apogee in 1979 when Soviet troops invaded Afghanistan, cumulatively contributed to an unfortunate hiatus in Sino–Indian relations for more than two decades. Feelings of hurt and humiliation in India caused by events surrounding Sino–Indian relations from the 1950s to the late 1970s impacted negatively on the Indian mindset years after Jawaharlal Nehru's death in 1964.

Then came the beginning of the reform era in China, in 1978, initiated by the great Chinese leader Deng Xiaoping. Intrinsic to this great era of domestic socio-economic reform was his policy of consciously working for a peaceful neighbourhood. A sea change in China's external relations with her erstwhile enemies, the USA and the former Soviet Union, and with most countries of South-

East Asia came about through the 1980s. India too benefited from this change by restoring friendship with China. The major chronological landmarks in this restored relationship were 1988 (Rajiv Gandhi's visit to China), 1993 (Narasimha Rao's visit to China, when an agreement on Peace and Tranquility along the lines of actual control in the India–China border was signed), 1996 (the visit of President Jiang Zemin to India and its neighbours and a follow-up agreement on confidence building measures), 1999 (the Kargil conflict), and 2003 (A.B. Vajpayee's visit to China). Cummulatively, from 1988 a very positive balance sheet has thus been established in the India–China relationship in marked contrast to the situation prevailing till the late 1970s.

A direct result of this positive balance sheet is its beneficial impact on the South Asian region. From the very inception of SAARC, China has been enthusiastic about its potential, albeit unrealized. In a statement made at the Senate in Pakistan on 2 December 1996, the former Chinese President gave authoritative expression to Chinese goodwill towards the success of SAARC. He also advised South Asian countries to put aside their differences if they could not be resolved in the larger interest of deriving benefits from economic cooperation. With regard to conflict situations, such as was witnessed at Kargil in 1999, China called for mutual respect of established de facto lines of control. It has been supportive of solutions to all outstanding disputes through peaceful dialogues and consultations within countries and between countries in the region. Needless to add, China is against forcible regime changes. With stability at home being the overall rubric under which socio-economic development can take place, China is very averse to instability in its neighbourhood caused by extremist or fundamentalist movements. Such movements have spillover effects on China itself.

Many Chinese academicians and some at official levels, have pronounced consistently from the 1990s that improvements in Sino–Indian understanding and better relations between the countries would have a good effect on India's neighbours. Vice versa, good relations between India and her neighbours, especially between India and Pakistan, would reinforce the growing India–China friendship. In the present times numerous Western financial institutions and multinationals and prominent Asia-based ones speak of India and China as the drivers of Asia's economic growth and the shift of global political and economic centres of gravity to Asia. Arising from its democratic political stability, its economic growth which is showing signs of sustainability, and its defence capabilities, India is showing the needed self-confidence to deal with all the major powers including China. The tried and tested Panchsheel (or Five Principles) and growing mutual sensitivity to each other's regional and global concerns will continue to propel forward India–China relations. These have acquired maturity, a good measure of substance, and are backed up by a web of institutional arrangements aimed at solving existing differences as well as investigating areas of possible cooperation over diverse areas of bilateral and international importance.

Some welcome features of the relationship are the increasing exchanges of visits at the high political levels and at the levels of personnel from the security and defence establishments, growing trade and mutual investments, denser interactions between academicians from diverse disciplines, and greater flow of tourists from both directions following the establishment of direct air connections.

USA AND IRAQ: IMPACT ON SOUTH ASIA

Turning next to the other superpower that has an impact on South Asian security, namely the USA, it is inevitable that we look at global issues. The impact of the global policies of the Bush administration would naturally be of great concern even as we are uncertain about their contours. Given the geographical positioning of South Asia, it is understandable that the interests of this region stretch in a wide arc from the Gulf, West Asia to Central and South-East Asia and it is in these areas that the USA is heavily engaged.

When Osama bin Laden rejoiced at the disintegration of the World Trade Center in New York he may have demonstrated his belief that the only relationship acceptable between the West and Islam was one of violent confrontation. The chain of events starting from 11 September 2001 (9/11), involved Afghanistan and its neighbourhood in Pakistan. This was followed by the US led military actions in Iraq, which have currently intensified. In Iraq there is as yet no sign of the USA or its few partners making much headway in creating a self-sustaining state. The emergence of an independent sovereign state in Palestine with secure borders for Iraq and itself, is yet to become a reality.

The challenge after 9/11 is how to deal with problems of extremism and fundamentalism without wounding the self-respect of the Islamic world. The juxtaposition of terrorism and Islam has hurt the Muslim psyche across the continents from Africa to South-East Asia. South Asia with perhaps the largest concentration of populations of believers in Islam has had a long history of co-existence of people of different faiths and subcultures and can perhaps play an exemplary role in selling the example of vibrant democracies respecting the plurality, diversity and tolerance inherent in its peoples. This in turn would immunize South Asian countries from the possible spillover from the unilateralist military actions undertaken in Iraq. As for the USA and the Bush administration and its allies, it would be a vital contribution to peace and security if the four pillars on which a viable international order are based are restored as soon as possible. Two American scholars who wrote on Iraq in the journal *Foreign Affairs* (November/December issue), have identified these as its commitment to international law; its acceptance of consensual decision making, a reputation for moderation and identification with the preservation of peace.

NON-PROLIFERATION OF WEAPONS OF MASS DESTRUCTION

The conduct of nuclear tests in 1998 by India and Pakistan and their self-proclaimed nuclear-weapons status has ensured that all the major powers, the countries of South Asia, and the international community will view tensions and possible armed conflicts between them with fears of escalation. Fortunately, statesmanlike leadership in both countries has set in motion a whole series of dialogues on Confidence Building Measures (CBM), including in the nuclear field and in those relating to all outstanding issues of concern to each. This all-inclusive approach demonstrates the political will in both countries to reverse the tide of adverse relations and to work for a better future. However, the question of preventing the proliferation of weapons of mass destruction remains to be addressed. The North Korean example of pursuing a weapons programme and the commercial gains that individuals seek through sharing knowledge of dangerous technologies, as was the case with A.K. Khan, have underlined the importance of finding peaceful solutions to the problem of their non-proliferation.

Additional measures need to be devised by the international community involving the states that have nuclear capabilities, who are outside the NPT framework but who have a proven track record for responsible behaviour where non-proliferation is concerned. The flaws in the original treaty are evident but it exists as a reality and cannot be wished away. India and Pakistan have accepted voluntary restraints on further testing, and their bilateral dialogues could result in assuring security to each other as nuclear weapons states. This would have a spillover effect on the security in South Asia. The problem is one of perfecting export controls which are internationally acceptable, the prevention of weapons of mass destruction from falling into the hands of non-state actors, and finally, of removing discriminatory measures which prevent the development of nuclear energy for peaceful purposes. In all this, the USA and other developed countries have a crucial role to play.

TERRORISM AND SOUTH ASIA

In South Asia, unfortunately, transborder terrorism continues to pose a threat to domestic security, but the resolute counter-terrorism fight cannot be seen in the context of any prevailing anti-Islamic sentiment. Terrorism is resorted to in the pursuit of extremist ideologies that do not believe in available democratic instruments for the redressal of socio-economic and political grievances. It is being resorted to for territorial expansion. Bases from which terrorists can operate against neighbours are provided in countries that wish to destabilize them for the achievement of political objectives. Experience has shown that those who provide such bases are themselves overwhelmed by threats to their domestic security and harmony. Trans-border targets thus could shift to domestic ones.

In view of this, South Asian countries need to consciously create an environment for the total rejection of terrorism as unacceptable in any form regardless of the apparent causes that terrorists espouse. Loss of innocent civilian lives cannot be condoned under any circumstances. The SAARC Regional Convention on the Suppression of Terrorism and the signing of the Additional Protocol to it need to be assiduously implemented by the South Asian countries.

NEED FOR SOUTH ASIA TO LOOK IN ALL DIRECTION

Threats to the security of South Asia on account of armed confrontations have abated thanks to the leadership of the governments and civil societies of India and Pakistan. But the monumental social and economic deficits surrounding poverty, ill health, illiteracy and a myriad other ills in the majority of South Asian countries are fertile breeding grounds for non-conventional threats to security. In the medium and long terms the task of removing these appear to be more Herculean than the removal of conventional military threats. The primary responsibility for correcting these deficits lies with individual countries. However, with the fresh and welcome winds capturing the sails of SAARC after the Islamabad Summit, the time has come to lay the foundations for a more ambitious vision of regional integration which includes and transcends the geographical and sovereign limits of South Asian countries. Regional integration through cooperation in regional and subregional organizations is not antithetical to globalization. Rather it is a necessary complement to the exploitation of the physical and human resources of parts of countries or whole countries. The geography of South Asia demands an omni-directional external outlook if its countries are to attain the physical and human security to which its huge population is entitled. In other words, cooperation within regions and between regions is today the urgent requirement for ensuring comprehensive security for the vast populations in South Asia.

India had, in earlier decades, missed the opening to the more rapidly developing parts of Asia, which the 'Look East' policy initiated in the early 1990s has substantially redressed. In a continuum from 1992 to 2002, India is today a summit-level partner of the Association of South East Asian Nations (ASEAN). Its relations with this regional organization has thus assumed a strategic direction in foreign policy. It is sustained by a structure of annual summits, supplemented by meetings of foreign ministers, the ministers of trade and industry and senior officials. The responsibility for several programmes of socio-economic significance has been assumed by India. India is also making the necessary investments through the engagement of its navy and security establishments in the maintenance of the safety of sea lanes, in combating international terrorism, and other security concerns. India and ASEAN have signed a framework Agreement on Comprehensive Economic Cooperation including a Free Trade Area in goods, services, and investment. One important feature which is the key to closer multifaceted ties between India and ASEAN, and which should be of interest to countries of South Asia, is connectivity—whether by rail, air, road, sea or inland waterways. In many of these areas, projects are under serious discussion, involving India, Myanmar and Thailand. A more liberal air services policy would allow for different urban centres in India to be linked with ASEAN countries.

BIMSTEC

Another key prong of India's 'Look East' policy is the subregional organization known as 'Bay of Bengal Initiative for Multi-Sectoral Technical and Economic Cooperation' (BIMSTEC). It is a relatively new grouping of countries around the Bay of Bengal, including Bangladesh, Bhutan, India, Nepal, Sri Lanka, Myanmar, and Thailand. Speaking at its first summit meeting, India's prime minister said that BIMSTEC is a 'collective and effective forum for giving full expression to the widely felt need to rediscover the coherence of our region based on the commonality of many linkages around the Bay of Bengal'. It is India's hope that this organization can play the important role of a bridge between the countries of South and South-East Asia, and this would also place the vast north-eastern region of India firmly in the centre of this bridge. Here, again, a Free Trade Area lies at the core of BIMSTEC activities.

ENERGY SECURITY FOR SOUTH ASIA

Cooperation in the energy sector figures prominently on the BIMSTEC agenda. This is understandable given the enormous potential of developing and exploiting to mutual benefit the rich hydropower and hydrocarbons (especially gas) reserves in the region. India has announced its intention to host a conference of energy ministers in 2005 with a view to evolving a regional framework for energy cooperation. For too long, and utterly detrimental to the peoples of the South Asian region, India's smaller neighbours have looked upon India with degrees of apprehension, fear, and suspicion (most times unwarranted), and a fear of domination by it. The key objectives of all that has been said earlier is to once again reassure India's neighbours and to anchor this assurance in a virtuous web of cross-border, socio-economic and commercial linkages. India's appeal is that it can be looked upon as an opportunity; where its size and growing economic strength would become an asset rather than a liability in dealings with its neighbours. Numerous non-economic, psychological, and other factors contributing to negative mindsets need to change if South Asia is to join the mainstream of the several beneficial developments in Asia, underlying subregional, regional and trans-regional cooperation.

The various initiatives in the Bay of Bengal region must of necessity be complemented by others surrounding the maritime and littoral areas of the Arabian Sea extending to the Gulf regions. The vast improvement in the understanding between India and Pakistan could contribute to a political environment where mutually beneficial, cost effective, and secure connections in the energy sector could be undertaken. Involving India and Pakistan as growing end-users, pipelines carrying oil and gas from Iran in the west, Turkmenistan, and other Central Asian countries through

Afghanistan have now become more distinct possibilities than in the past. To realize all this it is necessary for the same changes in mindsets referred to earlier.

CONCLUSION

To conclude, it is relevant to quote from an address in New Delhi by the Foreign Minister of Thailand, Surakirt Sathirathai, on regional cooperation for growth and property. 'Asia's strength,' he said, 'should not depend on the lopsided prosperity balance. It may be the fact for the time being that East and South-East Asia are growing faster than other parts of Asia but we must not let them run away with their economic growth and prosperity. . . . That is why Thailand recognizes the importance of South Asia. Thailand recognizes the necessary linkages between South and Southeast in order to create inter sub-regional partnership[s].' The importance of South Asia, not just some of its individual member countries, to the world at large would be greatly enhanced if the region as a whole is perceived as engaged constructively in realizing the goals so clearly laid down at Islamabad.

CHAPTER 4

Comprehensive Security in South Asia: A View from Bangladesh

FAROOQ SOBHAN

To speak of comprehensive security in South Asia today means looking beyond the state-centric view of security, which traditionally focuses on military security or conventional security. In South Asia, as elsewhere in the world, it is accepted that military security by itself cannot ensure the security of the individual. In order to ensure any kind of meaningful security, a more broad-based or comprehensive approach has to be adopted. Comprehensive security in South Asia therefore should cover—in addition to military security—environmental, economic, energy, and human security. Above all, comprehensive security should encompass both the security of the state as well as of society and the individual. Issues such as poverty alleviation, malnutrition, illiteracy, disease, scarcity of water, unemployment, and the safety and welfare of the individual and the society he lives in, should constitute the cornerstone of comprehensive security in South Asia.

In addition, several other issues such as smuggling, arms trafficking, drug trafficking, the trafficking of women and children, and the activities of insurgents or terrorists also have a direct impact on security in the region. All these activities seriously undermine the security of the region. This broad-based approach to security should also cover within each of the region's countries issues such as peaceful coexistence among religions, languages, and ethnic groups. Equally important are the quality of governance, the strength, effectiveness, and efficiency of institutions, the law and order situation, the degree of corruption, the need to provide adequate space and opportunity to every community in the region to prosper free of any form of discrimination, and the promotion of an effective democracy in the country, with the maximum degree of decentralization, where human rights are up held, in particular the rights of women and children.

The third dimension of comprehensive security in South Asia is the key issue of South Asia's relations with the rest of the world, in particular with the major powers, as well as with individual states in the region and collectively with all the countries in the region. Of special importance are the relations of individual states in the region with each other, in particular with India, since all the South Asian countries share borders with India. The security environment in the region has been dominated by Indo–Pak relations, which have had a multi-dimensional impact on the security and stability of the region for the past fifty-seven plus years. Simultaneously, the growth and development of SAARC, and the implications of this on the security outlook in the region, needs to be addressed. Equally important are the perceptions of civil society in the region and the interaction and dialogue between civil societies and governments.

The end of the Cold War and the break up of the Soviet Union had a profound impact on South Asia. It brought an end to the Cold War in South Asia and to the rivalry of the major powers for influence in the region by siding with either India or Pakistan. 11 September (9/11) and its aftermath, and prior to that the nuclear tests carried out first by India and then by Pakistan, ensured that South Asia, for the very first time, became a region of priority concern to the United States, the sole remaining superpower. Today, for the first time in five decades, the US enjoys good relations with both India and Pakistan. The rapid economic growth of India in recent years, the growing influence of the Indian diaspora in the US, and its leading role in the IT sector, have encouraged the White House to view India as an emerging power. At the same time, Pakistan has become a key strategic ally in the US led war against Al Qaida and its allies. Europe, although comparatively a much less significant factor in the region, also maintains cordial relations with both India and Pakistan. Russia, which used to be a major player in the region, saw its influence decline substantially. China, which for years had followed a pro-Pakistan policy, has shifted gears to pursue a more balanced policy, based on developing and strengthening relations with all the countries in the region.

Three critical and inter-related questions emerge. First, how should the countries in South Asia view the US's security policies in the region? Second, what can three countries do, in the region, to change these policies? And specifically, what should South Asia be doing to strengthen its own security?

Since 9/11, the US has concentrated all its attention on winning support in the region for the 'War against Terror'. This has influenced US policy towards all the countries in the region, in particular towards India and Pakistan. But the US perspective on security has been to pursue a conventional or traditional approach to security, central to which have been military or strategic objectives. The US has thus neglected to take a comprehensive view of security in South Asia. Very little attention has been given to human security, environmental security or to the host of inter-related issues mentioned earlier. This one-dimensional approach to security has placed the states of South Asia in an awkward situation. Thus, while all the states in the region enjoy the best of relations with the Bush administration, the Bush foreign policy has resulted in the US becoming extremely unpopular throughout the region. It is to be hoped that, the US's security perspective on South Asia, following Mr Bush's re-election, will undergo a change and the importance of comprehensive security will be recognized in the South Asian context.

The US should encourage and promote human development throughout the region. It should extend duty-free access to all the countries of South Asia with immediate effect; and in the case of LDCs this should be done unconditionally. The creation of jobs, female empowerment, and the promotion of education are the best ways of tackling the twin problems of poverty and terrorism, since one breeds the other.

In order to facilitate a better understanding of each other's concerns, the governments of South Asia should take the initiative to propose annual consultations along the lines of the ASEAN regional forum with the US. Other dialogue partners should be

China, Japan, Russia and the EU. In order to prepare the ground for such a dialogue, a Track II process can and should be initiated in the region without delay.

Apart from promoting trade, special attention should be given to encouraging US investments in the region. Enormous opportunities exist for investment in infrastructure projects, particularly in the energy sector. South Asia could rapidly become self-sufficient in energy instead of an energy deficient region. The leading role played by India in the IT sector can, with the help of India, be expanded to cover the region as a whole. The strong links between India and the US should also be further expanded and strengthened to cover South Asia as a whole. The key to adopting a regional approach to comprehensive security is to develop a cooperative approach to both the understanding and the strengthening of comprehensive security in the region. This cooperative approach can be achieved only through strengthening and expanding regional cooperation in the region at the inter-governmental level through SAARC, and also thought a host of other South Asian inter-governmental initiatives, such as the South Asia Regional Forum which can be a stand-alone initiative.

But a cooperative approach to strengthening comprehensive security in South Asia will also require civil society in each country to play an extremely proactive role. Civil society includes the private sector, the business community, NGOs, think tanks, universities, academics, the media, economists, environmentalists, retired government servants, in fact every possible segment of society. Indeed one of the success stories in the region during the past twenty years has been the active role of each of these groups within each country and also within the region. Perhaps it is time to think in concrete terms of a two-tier South Asian parliament. One chamber will be of elected representatives, while the second chamber will be made up of representatives of all segments of civil society.

In the meantime, it will be of vital importance to promote a regular dialogue and interaction between the governments and all segments of civil society in the region. There has to be a strong partnership between the governments and civil society on all aspects of the regional cooperation agenda. Such dialogues should be institutionalized and held at regular intervals. This is already happening to some extent. It has now been accepted that at the time of the annual SAARC Summit, the SAARC Chamber of Commerce and Industry will be invited to make a presentation to the Council of Ministers. This practice needs to be further expanded. At each inter-governmental meeting, in particular those held at the ministerial level, civil society representatives should be invited to make a presentation. An annual South Asia Business Summit should be held along the lines of the World Economic Forum at Davos. All SAARC heads of government should attend this business forum, where there will be strong participation not simply from the business community but from civil society as a whole.

At the 12th SAARC Summit in Islamabad in January 2004, the SAARC Social Charter was signed. It could perhaps be argued that the Social Charter constitutes a commitment to promote comprehensive security in South Asia and to do so on the basis of a cooperative approach. The SAARC Social Charter is an ambitious document. The challenge lies in translating the broad principles for social development that it embraces into specific time-bound targets with an effective mechanism or mechanisms to monitor implementation. This monitoring exercise could be the dual responsibility of the annual SAARC Summit as well as a South Asia Coordinating Committee, which will be made up of representatives of government and civil society. This Coordinating Committee, which should meet once every three months and be supported by a strengthened SAARC Secretariat, should present its report directly to the Summit every year.

I have given special emphasis to the SAARC Social Charter because its effective implementation would constitute a major step forward in strengthening cooperative and comprehensive security in the region. The framework agreement for a South Asia Free Trade Area (SAFTA), which will come into force in 2006, was also signed at the Islamabad Summit, endorsed the report of the Independent Commission for Poverty Alleviation in South Asia (ICPASA). SAFTA could pave the way for not merely a free trade area but for economic union as well. The key to success, as in so many other cases, lies with India. If India could find its way to opening its markets to all exports from the other countries in the region as a prelude to the SAFTA negotiations, a common market could be achieved in a relatively short period of time. While the primary responsibility for alleviating poverty in South Asia remains a national task, there is scope for implementing regional initiatives. Expanding trade and alleviating poverty are both crucial to promoting both economic and human security in the region.

Enhancing economic and human security in South Asia will require serious investment in developing the regions human resources, improving particularly the quality of vocational training. Good governance, accountability, and transparency are relevant and important for every country in the region. The countries can all help each other through exchange of information about best practices. Some thought can also be given to the establishment of an independent commission in the region, which would publish, along the lines of the Human Development Report, a report on governance which could cover a host of inter-related issues including human rights violations, the extent of corruption in each country of the region and the effort of both government and civil society to tackle this problem, the law and order situation, progress in poverty alleviation, and a host of other subjects. This annual report would require the full cooperation of the government and a number of government agencies. Such a report could cover all aspects of comprehensive security. This is indeed an ambitious task but one that needs to be undertaken if we, the people of South Asia, are serious about strengthening regional cooperation and thus strengthening all aspects of security in the region.

To sum up, strengthening regional cooperation is the key to strengthening comprehensive security in South Asia. This can be achieved through a variety of mechanisms and institutions. For each of these (mechanisms and institutions) to be effective, it will not only require close cooperation between the states and civil society in each country, but also on a regional basis. To demonstrate the region's commitment to strengthening comprehensive security, it is necessary to endorse specific goals and targets, which, in turn, should be closely monitored in a credible and effective way.

CHAPTER 5

Comprehensive Security in South Asia: A Pakistani Perspective

GHANI JAFAR

THE SETTING

The South Asian security scenario appears more confounded today then it was before the region's emergence as a grouping of seven sovereign states in the post-War era. So, what else is new on the global scene? one may well ask. The entire international order structured by the victors of the Second World War in the form of the UNO has, no doubt, been made all but irrelevant. But such a retort would still miss the point.

In the first place, contemporary South Asia enjoys the dubious distinction of being the one and only region in the post-Cold War world that has failed to put in place even a basic institutional framework for underscoring the collective security of its seven constituent states. To factor in SAARC and all that in this context would at this stage at least, betray an exceptional naivety.

If that characteristic of South Asia is not enough today, the confusion is compounded mainly by researchers, academics and analysts, who are given mostly to knee-jerk reactions to the daily dose of mercurial developments in these defining moments of global history in the post-9/11 era without taking into account the bedrock of geopolitical and, more importantly, geoeconomic determinants. There is a crying need for the perspective to be clarified.

Let us take a closer look at the core Pakistan–India relationship. It would, traditionally, have gone without saying that comprehensive security in South Asia is not only influenced but also determined to a large extent by the given state of relations between these two largest South Asian states. Not necessarily so anymore. For in more recent times, specifically with the former Prime Minister Vajpayee's celebrated proffering of the 'hand of friendship' to Pakistan at Srinagar in the summer of 2003, New Delhi has consistently pursued a two-track policy vis-à-vis its immediate neighbourhood, whereby, in sum and substance, Islamabad's coequal sovereignty is allowed greater space by the former than is the case regarding the other five South Asian states.

Such an approach is, however, seriously flawed in terms of its fallout on prospects of comprehensive South Asian security. That disregards nothing more profound than a contemporary truism: Shakespeare's descriptive of the world's being a stage—in the extended sense of a common platform for societal as also global interaction—has never been as true as it has come to be in the post-9/11 era.

While being a geographical, geopolitical, geo-strategic and—as already highlighted—geo-economic entity in itself, South Asia is anything but an archipelago of seven-odd island states detached from the rest of the planet; to say nothing of the even more preposterous proposition that Pakistan and India can, in disregard of the concerns of their five smaller neighbours, kiss, make up, and be content that security would reign in the region.

As for the central Pakistan–India equation, there have of late been increasing signs coming from New Delhi to suggest its readiness to resume the historic turnaround initiated by the outgoing Prime Minister, Atal Behari Vajpayee in the characteristically hostile relationship. It would thus be sufficiently sound to proceed here on the assurance that the determinants that decided the change of tack in both Islamabad and New Delhi in the first place would, sooner rather than later, be fully in place again in India also.

What are the factors contributing to the new direction? Are they mostly internal in the South Asian context of the bilateral relationship or are they propelled by extraneous influences/pressures? Is it the state, and considerations of statecraft, that is providing the driving force, or is it the two respective societies? These are the basic questions that would need to be answered.

THE NEW BEGINNING

The history of the acrimony between Pakistan and India is too elaborate and well known to be recounted here. Suffice it to say that the two countries, ever since their emergence as independent entities in 1947, have continued to view each other in mutually antagonistic frameworks. At the same time, the roots of their acrimony can be traced back in history—ancient or modern, depending upon the given viewpoint—to communal religious differences (supposedly irreconcilable) that led in the first place to the partition of the subcontinent into the Muslim-majority Pakistan and the Hindu-majority India by the departing British colonial power in August 1947.

It should thus be clear at the outset that nothing short of a basic change in the societal mindsets of the two nations can hold a promise of structural readjustments in the inter-state relationship from the positions of seemingly well-entrenched hostility to those of peaceful, amicable coexistence by the neighbouring South Asian states. That, in short, sets the stage for the present study.

Finally, by way of introductory remarks, the cut-off dates for the purposes of outlining the shift in Pakistan–India relationship needs to be mentioned. Again, the relevant historical record could provide any number of past developments involving the two countries to serve as the starting point. Nevertheless, it is roughly from the late-2002 start of the process of the thaw between Islamabad and New Delhi that the present study will begin, going on to the breakthrough achieved in the improvement of the bilateral relationship by the leaders of the two countries in early January 2004 during the SAARC Summit Conference in the Pakistan capital, Islamabad.

The choice of the dates is anything but arbitrary. The period thus selected represents, in the first place, the topically pertinent phase for a review of the subject at the present stage. However, its added significance lies in the fact that, by all available accounts, Pakistan–India bilateral developments encompassed between October 2002 and May 2004 furnish such a consistently progressive movement towards improvement in the relationship as is not to be found at any time in the past.

Indeed, if anything, the peace momentum has continued to gain strength. To that extent, therefore, the formal agreement for the resumption of the structured dialogue between the two countries signed by Prime Ministers Jamali and Vajpayee on 6 January 2004 represents a watershed in India–Pakistan relations, whose beginnings can be traced back to the tentative opening made in that direction in October 2002.

In fact, the first real chance of a historic breakthrough between the two sides began exactly three years earlier, on 12 October 1999, when providentially, those with the last say in the given situation of each country assumed power at both New Delhi and Rawalpindi/Islamabad. The ultimate wielders of political authority among the hard core Indian nationalists—the BJP—and those with the same credentials in Pakistan—the armed forces—came to form the government. Atal Behari Vajpayee became the Prime Minister of India and General Pervez Musharraf, Chief of the Army Staff, the 'Chief Executive', in Pakistan. (The only difference being that the Indian Prime Minister had returned to office after calling early elections.)

In retrospect, neither took long before coming to terms with harsh realities. That does usually happen with the exercise of responsible power. The disrupted process of composite dialogue was not only resumed but also led to an agreement on the approach for a resolution of the Kashmir question at the Agra Summit in July 2001, which, in the event, was scuttled by those in India who had the luxury of not bearing state responsibility in personal terms. Thereafter, Vajpayee lost the initiative to his deputy, Lal Krishna Advani; whereas General (now President) Pervez Musharraf, far from being subjected to any impediment, continued to gain both authority and credibility at home and abroad.

Epochal as the 9/11 was the hard core of the *Hindutva* lot among Vajpayee's coalition government, led by L.K. Advani came initially to have delusions that they could deal with Pakistan once and for all in the mode of a superpower by pre-emptive strikes and extra-territorial judicial writ. The gamble failed. Pakistan was able to deter Indian aggression on the one hand, and US military intervention on the other. Vajpayee stood vindicated. India announced the unilateral withdrawal of troops from the international border on 16 October 2002.

Pakistan, meanwhile, had come a considerable way along democratic transition. Elections to the National Assembly had been held on 10 October 2002. Those were judged as generally fair and free by both the Election Commission of Pakistan and the international community. Prime Minister Zafarullah Khan Jamali assumed office in November 2002 after being elected as the leader of the house by the National Assembly. Nevertheless, it understandably took the two countries time to pick up the pieces of the peace structure being put in place by them, which, as we have seen, was shattered by the misreading of Pakistan's situation by some in New Delhi.

THE 'HAND OF FRIENDSHIP'

The so-called 'hand of friendship' to Pakistan was first extended by Prime Minister Vajpayee at a public meeting he addressed in Srinagar on 18 April 2003—six months after the start of the de-escalation process.

The public statements of the two Prime Ministers as reported by the media, together provided as promising a start to the process of reconciliation between Pakistan and India as could have been expected of the two long-estranged South Asian neighbouring states:

> Saying that the gun was no solution to any problem, the Prime Minister, Atal Behari Vajpayee, today began his two-day visit to Kashmir with a call for friendship with Pakistan but said it should be extended from both sides. He also reiterated the Centre's [New Delhi's] promise to hold talks with the people of Jammu and Kashmir and assured complete support to the State Government.
>
> At a massive public meeting . . . Mr Vajpayee said his government had made efforts to build a harmonious relationship with Pakistan. 'As Prime Minister of the country I wanted to have friendly relations with our neighbours and I went to Lahore, but it was returned with Kargil. We still continued and invited General Pervez Musharraf to Agra but again failed,' said Mr Vajpayee.
>
> 'We are again extending a hand of friendship but hands should be extended from both the sides. Both sides should decide to live together. We have everything which makes us to have good relations,' Mr Vajpayee

said. This was the time to change the map and 'we are busy in Delhi towards that and we need to live together'.

Making a reference to Iraq, Mr Vajpayee said the war should have been averted, as 'I believe the gun is no solution to problems'. It would only kill people and would not solve any problem. The time had come to change Kashmir's fate. 'Sitting in Delhi we are concerned about Kashmir,' Mr Vajpayee said amid a thunderous applause.

Without naming any separatist or militant group, he reiterated New Delhi's promise to hold a dialogue on both internal and external problems. 'Not only our doors but also our hearts are always open for you. You (can) come to us with your grievances,' he said, adding 'no guns but only brotherhood can solve the problems'.[1]

The then Pakistan Prime Minister wasted no time in responding to his Indian counterpart's proffering of the 'hand of friendship'. In responding to a journalist's query regarding Mr Vajpayee's offer the same day as it was made in Srinagar, Mir Zafarullah Khan Jamali reiterated the long-held position of his country being ready for the resumption of official dialogue with India:

In Islamabad, Prime Minister Mir Zafarullah Khan Jamali reacted positively to Mr Vajpayee, saying: 'We welcome it; we appreciate it.' Speaking to reporters in Parliament, Mr Jamali said Pakistan had always said talks were the only way to resolve issues, including the Kashmir dispute. 'On the main issue (of Kashmir), Pakistan's stand remains the same. But once talks start . . . there could be flexibility from both sides,' he added.[2]

President General Pervez Musharraf further strengthened the newfound hope of improvement of relations with India in his first reported response to Vajpayee's offer the following week. Having been bitten once by the sorts of Advani at Simla, President Musharraf's welcome to the Indian gesture was understandably cautious:

President General Pervez Musharraf on Thursday welcomed Indian Prime Minister Atal Behari Vajpayee's initiative for resumption of talks between India and Pakistan, and hoped that it was a genuine gesture. He said: 'I do not want to say anything more. It is a good beginning. Nobody has won and nobody has lost. Both have won. Frankly, I think Mr Vajpayee's gesture is genuine, and I hope that it is genuine.'

Speaking at a meeting with newspaper editors and senior journalists here [in Islamabad], he said Prime Minister Zafarullah Khan Jamali did the right thing by responding to the offer of talks promptly. 'I see light and we must go forward on this.'[3]

The United States, too, was quick in adding its 'resounding endorsement' to the Indian Prime Minister's peace move. In his despatch from Washington, *The Times of India* correspondent dealt at length with the continued US interest in and encouragement of the Pakistan–India peace process:

India and Pakistan could soon be talking again. American persuasion that India should hold talks with Pakistan despite continuing cross-border terrorism, while admitting Washington's own failure to force Islamabad to stop the violence, appears to be bearing fruit.

On [a] day of rapid developments on the diplomatic front, Washington first acknowledged its lack of success in holding Pakistan to its commitment on infiltration and cross-border terrorism. Hours later, in the face of this important admission, Prime Minister Vajpayee offered an olive branch to Islamabad and disgruntled Kashmiris in course of his speech in Srinagar, saying only talks and not guns could resolve the issues. . . .

But the remarks were met with an immediate and resounding endorsement from Washington. 'We could not agree more with the statement and we welcome the Prime Minister's words,' the State Department said in a statement.

Washington's admission on Pakistan and priming of India came in several interviews senior administration officials gave this week ahead of a proposed fire-fighting visit to the region by US Deputy Secretary of State Richard Armitage.

In remarks on a new Turner Documentaries film 'Avoiding Armageddon' and interviews to a raft of Indian television channels, State Department's policy chief Richard Haas admitted as much that US pressure on Pakistan was not working, but suggested strongly that India should still talk to Pakistan.[4]

US 'PRESSURE'

Several other news reporters, commentators, and analysts—both within South Asia and outside the region—also credited the United

States for the reinitiation of the peace process. Not to let go of an opportunity to add dramatic flourish to their despatches, which has increasingly become the norm for western mediapersons in particular, the *Reuters* report on Vajpayee's Srinagar public address went so far as to suggest that the Indian Prime Minister had somehow immediately felt obliged to offer friendship to Pakistan by the US announcement of Armitage's imminent trip to the region: 'Mr Vajpayee's comments came hours after US officials said Deputy Secretary of State Richard Armitage may visit India and Pakistan in the next several weeks.'[5]

That, surely, took the joke too far. The United States has, no doubt, continued to take active interest in the resolution of all disputes between Pakistan and India; all the more so since the two countries went nuclear in May 1998. But the fact also remains that both Islamabad and New Delhi have throughout this period not obliged the United States at the expense of their respective perceived national interests. Kashmir was—and remains—central to the prospects of lasting peace between the two nuclear powers in South Asia.

If anything, the then US President, Bill Clinton, minced no words while describing the situation in the former state of Jammu & Kashmir as posing the most serious threat to the world before embarking on his South Asian tour in March 2000 with the express intent of helping to resolve the differences between Pakistan and India:

WASHINGTON: US President Bill Clinton has said he believes the simmering Kashmir imbroglio is the most dangerous situation in the world, exacerbated further because both India and Pakistan now possess nuclear weapons. . . .

In an interview with the *CBS* 60 Minutes II programme. . . . Clinton said despite the demise of the Cold War 'we still have to deal with these traditional threats'. 'That's why . . . the Kashmir issue is perhaps the most dangerous one in the world today because you've got two nuclear powers there who are somewhat uncertain about one another and we have to work hard to avoid that,' he said.[6]

The United States did indeed continue to 'work hard' to bring about a rapprochement between Pakistan and India, centred on a negotiated settlement of the Kashmir issue. Washington would make no secret of its active interest in this regard. In its place, Islamabad, too, would go on reiterating its readiness to resume the dialogue process with New Delhi 'at any level, any time and anywhere' to address all outstanding issues between them including the 'core' question of Jammu & Kashmir. The Indian political leadership, however, took its time in responding to these overtures.

Without recounting the details of all these developments, which do not belong here, what does remain relevant is the Agra Summit meeting between President General Pervez Musharraf and Prime Minister Atal Behari Vajpayee in July 2001, as also the failure of those renewed negotiations. In retrospect, would those given to crediting the United States with making the two leaders meet at Agra also hold Washington responsible for the fiasco that the summit meeting turned out to be?

The Agra Summit failed due to factors internal to Indian politics and the political leadership of the time. As has been well documented, the 'hawks' within the Indian cabinet had at the last moment practically sabotaged the signing of the agreement between the Pakistani and Indian heads of government, President General Pervez Musharraf and Prime Minister Atal Behari Vajpayee.

As for US interest in South Asian peace and stability, it has continued unabated despite the change from the Democratic to the Republican administration in January 2001. In her remarks to the Senate Foreign Relations Committee on 17 May 2001, Christina B. Rocca, the then acting Assistant Secretary of State for South Asian Affairs, highlighted such a continuity of US approach to the region:

> Even a cursory look at the region makes it obvious why we have strategic, political and economic interests throughout South Asia. . . . The nations of South Asia cover the spectrum of the United States' most vital interests in the world today: on the negative side, we face terrorism, the spread of weapons of mass destruction and drug trafficking. . . .
>
> On the positive side, we have long-standing friendships, a chance to promote democracy and truly amazing economic opportunities. The fact that President Clinton visited South Asia's three largest nations last year, and that President Bush and his senior officials have already been

in contact with regional leaders is more evidence of South Asia's growing importance to the United States. . . .

As for US relations in the region, allow me to start with India. The Bush Administration will continue the policy of substantive bilateral engagement. The past few years have seen the beginning of a transformation in our relationship with the world's largest democracy. Now is the time to complete that transformation. . . .

In the case of Pakistan, ours is a friendship of long standing, and one that must be sustained and enhanced. . . . Pakistan is an important regional power ***and*** an important Islamic power. For those reasons and so many more, the Bush Administration is committed to working through difficult economic, political and social challenges now facing Pakistan. . . .

Where we can cooperate, in areas such as counter-narcotics, we must continue. Where we do not cooperate optimally, for example on Afghanistan, we must work harder to show Pakistan the shared threat we face from the regime in Kabul.[7]

Then came 9/11, adding a new urgency for Washington to both secure Pakistan's support for the war against terrorism in Afghanistan and advance South Asian stability. The then US national security adviser, Condoleezza Rice dilated upon both these dimensions in her testimony before the National Commission on Terrorist Attacks Upon the United States (the 9/11 Commission) on 8 April 2004:

More importantly, we recognize that no counterterrorism strategy could succeed in isolation. As you know from the Pakistan and Afghanistan strategy documents that we have made available to the commission, our counterterrorism strategy was a part of a broader package of strategies that addressed the complexities of the regions.

Integrating our counterterrorism and regional strategies was the most difficult and the most important aspect of the new strategy to get right. Al Qaeda was both a client of and a patron to the Taliban, which in turn was supported by Pakistan. Those relationships provided Al Qaeda with a powerful umbrella of protection and we had to sever that. This was not easy. Not that we hadn't tried.

Within a month of taking office, President Bush sent a strong private message to President Musharraf urging him to use his influence with the Taliban to bring bin Laden to justice and to close down Al Qaeda training camps. Secretary Powell actively urged the Pakistanis including Musharraf himself to abandon support for the Taliban.

I remember well meeting with the Pakistani foreign minister, and I think I referred to this meeting in my private meeting with you, in my office in June of 2001. And I delivered what I considered to be a very tough message. He met that message with a rote answer and with an expressionless response. America's Al Qaeda policy wasn't working because our Afghanistan policy wasn't working. And our Afghanistan policy wasn't working because our Pakistan policy wasn't working.

We recognized that America's counterterrorism policy had to be connected to our regional strategies and to our overall foreign policy. . . . Our new approach to Pakistan combined the use of carrots and sticks to persuade Pakistan to drop its support for the Taliban. And we began to change our approach to India to preserve stability on the continent.[8]

Thus, preservation of stability in South Asia became a key element in the United States' overall approach to the region in the post-9/11 scenario; and Kashmir, needless to say, had for a long time been perceived by Washington as posing a real and present threat to peace in the world. The point to be noted with regard to the present study, however, is that despite such a heightened US interest in the normalization of relations between Pakistan and India, the two South Asian powers, still felt free to fashion their mutual ties not on American dictation but as each one considered best in terms of its individual national interests.

As already noted, the attack on the Indian Parliament in December 2001 marked the beginning of a phase of incremental loss of all goodwill between the two countries, leading to a protracted military stand-off the likes of which had not been seen along the Pakistan–India air, land and sea borders over the previous more than half of a century of their uneasy relationship. The United States—as also all the other major regional and global powers—did no doubt remain highly proactive in trying to defuse the situation, but, again, both Pakistan and India dealt with the crisis on their own respective terms till they found it best to de-escalate the situation in late 2002.

President George Bush was quite right in recalling, as he did on 21 April 2004, the role his country (together with the UK) had played throughout this period; but neither of the two sides in confrontation had gone to war for reasons that were entirely their own. It nevertheless remains pertinent to cite the US President in this context:

WASHINGTON, April 22: President George Bush has said that America's shuttle diplomacy prevented a war between India and Pakistan three years ago. '2001 was the year that we had shuttle diplomacy to convince Pakistan and India not to go to war with each other,' said Mr Bush while addressing the Newspaper Association of America's annual convention here on Wednesday.

He referred to the events that took place in the summer of 2001, when India deployed hundreds of thousands of troops along Pakistan's border following a terrorist attack on its Parliament building in New Delhi. Pakistan responded with similar deployments.

With media reports suggesting that both sides might also have moved nuclear weapons to strategic locations, the Bush administration feared that the tensions could lead to yet another war between South Asia's two nuclear rivals.

To prevent the war, Mr Bush said, the United States and Britain sent several senior officials to New Delhi and Islamabad to defuse tensions. The emissaries included US Secretary of State Colin Powell, British Foreign Secretary Jack Straw and Mr Powell's deputy Richard Armitage.

Powell went, and then Straw went from Britain, and then Armitage went, and then whoever his equivalent is from Britain went, with the idea of kind of talking everybody down,' Mr Bush said.

The shuttle diplomacy, he said, not only reduced tensions between India and Pakistan but also paved the way for further improvement, and now, quite the opposite, they're talking with each other in a positive way.

Mr Bush hoped that the ongoing talks would allow the two neighbouring states to get some sticky issues resolved, for the sake of world peace and stability in that part of the world. He said both India and Pakistan had made some progress in resolving their disputes and offered to work with them to bring stability to that region.[9]

It was against such a backdrop of the Pakistan–India equation and the global response to it, that Prime Minister Atal Behari Vajpayee extended his much celebrated 'hand of friendship' to Pakistan in Srinagar on 18 May 2003. Islamabad, as mentioned earlier, wasted no time in responding positively to the move.

POST-9/11 IMPERATIVES

The new-found global role of the United States had a sobering effect on many nations and leaders around the world. Vajpayee betrayed the same when he was obliged to satisfy the MPs, understandably confused by the sudden change in their government's tone and tenor toward Pakistan. After all, only a few months earlier (on 18 May 2002), that the Deputy Prime Minister, L.K. Advani, had sought—and had been spiritedly given—a virtual carte blanche by them to wage war against Pakistan. A report by the special correspondent of *The Telegraph*, Kolkata, was eloquent about the difficulty faced by Vajpayee on this count:

> New Delhi, May 2: Sending out a clear signal for renewing talks with Pakistan, Prime Minister Atal Behari Vajpayee today told Parliament he wanted to restore diplomatic, civil aviation and sporting links between the two countries.
>
> 'It has been decided to appoint a high commissioner to Pakistan and to restore civil aviation links on a reciprocal basis,' Vajpayee said in a statement read out in both Houses on his phone conversation with Pakistan counterpart Mir Zafarullah Khan Jamali on Monday.
>
> 'The third round of talks with Pakistan will be decisive and the last dialogue with the country in my lifetime,' Vajpayee said in an emotional outburst in the Rajya Sabha later. . . .
>
> In Parliament, the Opposition welcomed the peace initiative but demanded to know what had pushed Vajpayee into taking it. 'The answer ... lies in the changed international situation. The world is unipolar and gravitating towards one centre of power. We do not want any one nation to become the sole pivot of power,' he said.
>
> Vajpayee also hinted that the US-led war on Iraq had impacted his decision. He has been suggesting off and on that one lesson to be learnt from the war is that unless nations resolved differences bilaterally, external intervention could be expected.
>
> 'There are some nations which have taken it upon themselves to decide the future of other nations,' Vajpayee said.
>
> Replying later to legislators' queries in the Rajya Sabha, Vajpayee said, Jamali had invited him to Pakistan but he had turned down the offer. 'The Prime Minister suggested resuming sporting links. . . . I emphasised the importance of economic cooperation, cultural exchanges, people-

to-people contacts and civil aviation links. We agreed that as a beginning these measured could be considered.'

Underlining that Jamali had condemned terrorism, he said: 'We have repeatedly expressed the need to create a conducive atmosphere for a sustained dialogue which requires an end to cross-border terrorism. . . .'

Vajpayee made it clear not all his 'friends' appreciated the gesture. In an oblique reference to critics in the *Sangh Parivar* [Hindu hardliners], he said: 'In the eyes of my compatriots, I am in the dock for opening a channel of communication with Pakistan.'

But his tone was confident and hopeful that the future would see easing of tensions. 'The road ahead is bumpy. But I do not see darkness,' he said.[10]

Vajpayee's counterpart in Pakistan, Prime Minister Jamali, echoed the same understanding in an interview with an Indian television channel a couple of weeks later:

New Delhi: Prime Minister Mir Zafarullah Khan Jamali says he is confident that new peace efforts will put an end to his country's five-decade hostilities with India. 'Let me say I am very confident,' Jamali said in an interview with India's state-run television, *Doordarshan*. 'Things will work out,' the Premier said.

. . . Jamali said he agreed with Indian Prime Minister Atal Behari Vajpayee that governments in New Delhi and Islamabad have to think about their differences in light of developments in Iraq.

Vajpayee told Indian Parliament earlier this month that he launched the peace initiative with Pakistan after seeing how the United States overruled the United Nations and attacked Iraq. 'Yesterday, it was Afghanistan. Today, it is Iraq. What is tomorrow?' Jamali said.

He said the only way for India and Pakistan to ensure that they are not made targets in future is to shed hostilities and forge friendly ties. 'Try to be one compact bloc . . . a situation where no one dare touches you. One must have a sense of feeling that we stand together as far as the region is concerned,' he said and added: 'And that can be done only if we are at good relations with each other.'[11]

POLITICAL CONSOLIDATION

Further developments over the next year in this key component of comprehensive South Asian security—the Pakistan-India relationship, that is—were clearly infused with that core imperative of regional peace and security as voiced by the democratic leaders of the two countries in May 2003.

Pakistan, as seen earlier, had been cautious in its initial response to Prime Minister Vajpayee's 'hand of friendship' at Srinagar on 18 April 2003. As noted earlier, President Musharraf's said: 'Frankly, I think Mr Vajpayee's gesture is genuine, and I hope that it is genuine.' Nevertheless, it was then Prime Minister Jamali's turn to make the first substantive move towards the de-escalation of the situation along the volatile Line of Control (LoC) in the part of Jammu & Kashmir occupied by India. In his address to the nation on the completion of his first year in office (on 23 November 2003), Jamali announced the unilateral cessation of hostilities on the LoC which had over the previous years seen an almost daily toll of military as well as civilian casualties.

That ceasefire is in place till today. The military, as well as the political, import of Pakistan's initiative here is of no small significance. The military dimension of the cessation of hostilities between two traditionally adversarial neighbours, and along the sector that lies at the root of the socio-political discord between them, is self-evident. However, what still escapes recognition in general is the political weightage of the development in the given context. For, firing across the LoC has had a crucial relevance to India's long-held charge of Pakistan's complicity in what the former refers to as 'cross-border terrorism'.

In other words, it was allegedly Pakistan who would provide firecover for infiltrators, and India would, it maintained, act only in response. Islamabad, of course, would describe India's firing and shelling across the LoC as unprovoked. Regardless of the veracity of either side's account, however, the fact remains that even if Pakistan was indeed involved in facilitating the crossing over of the supposed 'terrorists' to the part of Jammu & Kashmir under India's administrative control, Islamabad has for the past year now effectively not resorted to any such alleged activity.

Again, the passage of a year is not just the completion of so many days, weeks, and months but, more to the point, the coming and going of the four seasons; most crucially, summer. For the Indian case had been that if the LoC remained quiet during the long winter months, no thanks to Islamabad, the deep and treacherous snow in the passes in the mountainous terrain would provide a nearly impregnable natural barrier. There are many sides to the argument. Those are best left alone for now.

The next milestone after Jamali's ceasefire announcement of November 2003 was laid by his then Indian counterpart, Prime Minister Vajpayee, in a landmark address he gave in New Delhi only a couple of weeks later on 12 December 2003:

> Making out a strong case for rejecting conflict and embracing co-operation, the Prime Minister, Atal Behari Vajpayee, said today that South Asia needed the wisdom to emulate the experience of regional organisations in other parts of the world devoted to economic integration. Addressing a conference organised by *Hindustan Times*, he set India's tone for the coming South Asian Association for Regional Cooperation Summit in Islamabad by stressing that hostility only stunted economies, inhibited trade and retarded progress.
>
> 'As we develop greater economic stakes in each other (in South Asia), we can put aside mistrust and dispel unwarranted suspicions. We will also develop mutual sensitivity to each other's concerns and promote more of our common interests . . .' he said.
>
> If legitimate trade was developed, the region could jointly tackle smuggling, drug-trafficking, money-laundering and other trans-national crimes, which flourishes in the region because of mutual rivalries and inadequate coordination. Once we reach that stage, we would not be far from mutual security cooperation, open borders and even a single currency.
>
> Mr Vajpayee said that those who thought this seemed 'unrealistic and utopian' were, perhaps, being unnecessarily cynical. 'Let us remember that the world did not anticipate the sudden end to the Cold War or the collapse of the Berlin Wall. No one thought that apartheid South Africa could be transformed bloodlessly into Mandela's Rainbow country. . . .'
>
> Each one of these developments, he said, flowed from objective factors in the global environment, but actually occurred because of some 'enlightened and responsible decisions' by people at the helm of affairs. He asserted that the people of South Asia, businesses and organisations were waiting to interact with one another. 'We can sense this impatience in the outpouring of popular sentiment after our initiatives. The increased travel between India and Pakistan of Parliamentarians, businessmen,

artists and sportsmen show[s] the intense desire for amity and goodwill. We have to respond to this desire by seeking every possible way to banish hostility and promote peace.'

Mr Vajpayee sounded a note of warning as well. 'If we in South Asia look back objectively at the experiences of our freedom struggles and of our nation-building, the one stark lesson that stands out is the imperative of forging a unity based on our commonalities.'

Whenever we have dissipated our energies in internal squabbling, external forces have come in to sort out our differences and stayed on to exploit our resources. We should never create the possibility of reliving these historical differences in new forms and on different fronts.

Collective regional interest was an expression of enlightened self-interest and the peace dividend lay in converting South Asia's potential into a vibrant reality. Our region is heir to a centuries-old tradition of tolerance, pluralism and creative interaction. We need to recapture this ethos in the modern context.

In the post-Cold War world of globalisation, countries around the world are increasingly focusing on regional economics. Political disputes have been resolved diplomatically or quietly deferred for tackling at a more opportune time....

Mr Vajpayee pointed out that despite geographical proximity, intra-South Asian trade amounted to less than 5 per cent of our total foreign trade.[12]

That, in short, was the backdrop to the SAARC Summit in Islamabad in January 2004, when Pakistan and India agreed formally to restart the long-adjourned process of composite dialogue.

It fell to John Cherian of *Frontline* to capture the import of the moment: 'For the first time in the history of SAARC, a Pakistan premier did not mention the Kashmir dispute. The words 'cross-border' terrorism' did not figure in Vajpayee's speech.'[13]

SOCIETAL CHANGE

The following few months of the bilateral relationship till the 2004 change of government at New Delhi in late May 2004, brought in their wake unprecedented progress at a staggering pace between the people and societies of India and Pakistan which, in the considered view of some analysts of the issue, has laid the strong and stable enough foundations of regional peace, security and stability, not to be uprooted by those in these parts and elsewhere with a stake in the conflict.

Although there are any number of instances that can be cited to illustrate the attitudinal sea change—which, incidentally, is going on regardless of the change of government in May 2004 at New Delhi. One arena in which the two neighbouring peoples would fight the hardest is cricket as is evident from an *Associated Press* report in January 1999:

Hours before Pakistan's cricket team was to fly into India for its first tour in more than a decade, police in the western city of Bombay on Thursday arrested 14 radical Hindus for attacking the office of the Indian cricket authority, police said. The 14 included five senior leaders of the right-wing Shiv Sena party [one among Prime Minister Vajpayee's ruling coalition], which has vowed to disrupt the cricket tour. The Pakistani team was to fly into India later Thursday to begin preparations for the tests. Pakistan plays a junior Indian cricket team in the central Indian city of Gwalior on Saturday.

The Shiv Sena opposes any attempt to improve political relations with Pakistan, saying the neighbouring nation arms and trains militants fighting in Indian-held Kashmir, a Himalayan region over which both nations have fought two wars. Pakistan says it provides only moral support to the insurgents.

In the southern city of Madras, a youth belonging to a fundamentalist Hindu group doused himself with kerosene and set himself ablaze Wednesday night. He was hospitalised with burns over 80 per cent of his body and was in critical condition, doctors said Thursday. Police also arrested 100 activists of the Shiv Sena in the city, the site of the first five-day test beginning January 28.

Riot police ringed the M.A. Chidambaram Stadium in Madras and set up barricades on roads leading to it. In Bombay, the Shiv Sena leaders and others arrested were charged with rioting, assault, destruction of property and trespassing, joint police commissioner Parvinder Pasricha said. If convicted, they each face up to two years in prison, he said.

Police said the activists were among 70 men who attacked the office of the Board of Cricket Control India on Monday, destroying furniture and cricket trophies. The cricket authority announced it would move to

Calcutta because of the attack. 'Our investigation continues. We will continue to follow some leads,' Pasricha said.

Shiv Sena denied that its members had attacked the cricket headquarters in Bombay. Last month, Shiv Sena activists dug up the cricket pitch in New Delhi where the second India–Pakistan test match will be played from 4–8 February. Shiv Sena chief Bal Thackeray has vowed to disrupt the Pakistanı tour. 'We are still opposed to the match and we will prevent the Pakistanis from playing in India,' he told a public meeting Wednesday night. Nationally, Shiv Sena is a fringe group. But it shares power in Maharashtra state, of which Bombay is the capital, with Prime Minister Atal Behari Vajpayee's Bharatiya Janata Party.

Shiv Sena activists have threatened to disrupt the cricket matches by setting fire to themselves or letting loose poisonous snakes in the stadiums. The India–Pakistan cricket series has won support from the main opposition Congress party, which staged rallies in Bombay and New Delhi on Wednesday to protest the Shiv Sena campaign.

Political tension has kept the Indian and Pakistani teams from visiting each other's homelands for a decade. They have not played against one another in either country since Pakistan toured India in 1987, when Pakistan won the series 1-0.

The two have faced each other outside the subcontinent, including matches in Canada and the United Arab Emirates. Cricket is the most popular sport in both countries, which were separated at independence from Britain in 1947.[14]

As mentioned by the *AP* report, the Indian cricket board moved to Kolkata after the demolition of its Mumbai office. The choice of the West Bengal capital, also the venue of an India–Pakistan match during the tour, may have been influenced by the city's traditionally civilized culture. However, big surprise was in store for all interested parties. The rioting by the spectators became so serious when they saw victory going to the visiting side that all 70,000 of them had to be forcibly ejected from the stadium by the police, and the match was played before empty stands. Thereafter, India, banned all cricket fixtures with Pakistan, either on each other's soil or anywhere else in the world, thus barring all ground interaction between the two sides.

Finally, L.K. Advani and his fundamentalist associates gave way. The Indian team got the home ministry's permission to tour

Pakistan which, finally, materialized in April 2004, even as India was going through a protracted phase of parliamentary elections. M.N. Panini, with the Centre for the Study of Social Systems, Jawaharlal Nehru University, New Delhi, observed on the series in *The Hindu*:

In contrast to the India-Pakistan matches in the past, the current series exuded bonhomie. There is, of course, the tension of the game and passions are no doubt aroused, but a remarkable feature has been the manner in which the bonhomie overwhelmed sharp partisan positions that the game generates.

During the one-day matches, cameras zoomed in on spectators carrying both Indian and Pakistani flags and hugging each other after the game, irrespective of a win or loss. The flood of reports on the hospitality extended to both the Indian team and visiting Indian spectators suggest that, at the people-to-people level, decades of hostility have given way to warm friendship.

Indian visitors are discovering that the jingoism that dominated the discourse between India and Pakistan ever since Partition [of the subcontinent, in 1947] has evaporated, bringing to [the] surface common bonds that tie the cultures of both the countries. Certainly, this new bonhomie reflects Entente in the State-level political relations between India and Pakistan in the last few months.

The current cricket series has generated a groundswell of opinion favouring peaceful resolution of disputes between the two countries and dampening hostilities that used to erupt so often in the past. Even Bal Thackeray, the Shiv Sena leader, endorsed the current series.[15]

The bonhomie pointed out by the contributor of *The Hindu* feature cited above, is mutual to the two societies, and continues to be demonstrated to this day. Evidence for both those premises was furnished by the crowd behaviour during the cricket match played between the two sides in Kolkata, again, in November 2004. The event at the Eden Gardens, full to its 1,00,000 capacity, was an exmaple of sportsmanship to both by the spectators and by the players which would put many a competing side in the so-called 'civilised world' to shame. That, despite the fact that the visitors inflicted a humiliating defeat on the home side.

Perhaps, an even more telling field is that of cinema. Big-money ventures, as the popular Indian movies are, their producers always keep a watchful eye on the prospective box-office earnings while selecting themes for investment. They make what sells. And what is selling these days in India and Pakistan? The answer has, again, come only recently. In a story entitled 'Pakistanis no longer Bollywood baddies', Mike Collett-White of *Reuters* reported from Mumbai, 'Bollywood'—the Indian counterpart of Hollywood—on 14 November:

> Pakistanis, once portrayed in Indian movies as extremists and terrorist sponsors, are morphing into Bollywood heroes.
>
> Actors, producers and directors believe Bollywood, followed religiously by Pakistanis as well as Indians, has the power to help bring the divided countries closer together. . . .
>
> Those [India-Pakistan] relations have begun to improve over the past year, as India and Pakistan embarked on a glacial peace process that has seen transport links reopened and the two cricket-mad nations batting it out on the pitch.
>
> But the central issue of Kashmir, which is disputed by the nuclear neighbours, has yet to be resolved.[16]

CONGRESS GOVERNMENT

Getting back to the political dimension of the subject in hand, the tables were turned on Vajpayee's BJP by the Indian electorate; but primarily due to the latter's rejection of the party's *Hindutva* agenda—and not on grounds of abhorrence for the peace process.

For peace with Pakistan was not the issue in the 2004 elections in India. The Congress party, which won this time round, had done everything but fault the policy shift made by the ruling BJP in this regard during electioneering by the former. The then opposition was, if anything, one step ahead of the Vajpayee government in the quest for peace.

In Pakistan also, there was a change in the person of the prime minister some three months after the replacement of Vajpayee by Manmohan Singh. But in contrast to India, the election of Shaukat Aziz as the leader of Pakistan's lower house of Parliament, the National Assembly, in late August 2004, and his being appointed Prime Minister, after the resignation of Mir Zafarullah

Khan Jamali from office did not involve any change of the party in power. That was and still remains the Muslim League (Quaid-i-Azam Group) headed by Chaudhry Shujaat Hussain.

There has thus been a broad continuity in Pakistan's core internal and external policies ever since the military intervention in October 1999. The contours of the policy and its nuances have, no doubt, undergone any number of adjustments in these interesting days of the post-9/11 era. That, however, is not to understate the basic change in Pakistan's internal power reality after the assumption of the extra-constitutional office of the 'Chief Executive' by the Chief of Army Staff General Pervez Musharraf.

Regardless of the ways and means of the transition between 12 October 1999, when General Pervez Musharraf became Pakistan's Chief Executive, and 20 June 2001, when he assumed the office of President—bold acts a matter of controversy with, mostly, his opponents at home to this day—the cold fact in terms of power politic is that the military commander has represented that continuity in the national policy.

There has been no matching continuity in the case of India. In terms of South Asian security, the most marked element of the change of government in New Delhi in May 2004 has been the ouster from power of the *Hindutva* brigade. As already pointed out, India and Pakistan had the best credentials for establishing a durable framework of regional peace, security and stability while the centre of authority in both countries remained with their respective 'fountainheads' of power. That historic chance is now lost.

That does not ipso facto mean that the entire peace process will be detailed. The key question here is regarding the bases on which the positive change in the bilateral relationship was premised in the first instance. If those are compellingly strong, the improvement will not only endure but will be further consolidated in the days ahead.

The clear perception of the regional security imperative for South Asia subsequent to the US occupation of Iraq in March 2003—which has since been described as 'illegal' by the UN Secretary General as well—by the leadership of the two countries, has already been cited in the words of the then Prime Ministers, Vajpayee and Jamali.

Despite the lack of progress made by the United States in establishing its writ over Iraq, and in the face of the former's casualties now running into four figures, President Bush has received an unambiguous electoral mandate for a second term in office for 'more of the same' in his handling of national and international affairs. The responsibility of exercising state power in this age is bound to dawn on the new Congress party government at New Delhi as well.

There has, however, been no such indication forthcoming from New Delhi ever since Manmohan Singh took over as the Prime Minister. What has emanated from the Indian capital instead are two broad trends: In the first place, India's policy towards its Western neighbour lacks cohesiveness, without which those at the helms of policy in any entity lack the authority to decide on matters of war and peace. That somewhat confused state of affairs should not be confusing to the watchers of the Indian scene.

'*HINDUTVA*' BAGGAGE

What we have out there is a technocrat Prime Minister fully alive to the dictates of peace, but encumbered by some of the Congress baggage he has been bequeathed by the last regime of the party as far back as the mid-1990s. As the then Finance Minister, Manmohan Singh was, no doubt, a pillar of the then P.V. Narasimha Rao government, but politics has never been quite his cup of tea. His profile on Indian government's official website refers correctly to him as 'a thinker and a scholar'. The descriptive goes on:

> In what was to become the turning point in the economic history of independent India, Dr Singh spent five years between 1991 and 1996 as India's Finance Minister. His role in ushering in a comprehensive policy of economic reforms is now recognized worldwide.
>
> In the popular view of those years in India, that period is inextricably associated with the persona of Dr Singh. In his political career, Dr Singh has been a Member of India's Upper House of Parliament (the Rajya Sabha) since 1991, where he was Leader of the Opposition between 1998 and 2004 [during the Vajpayee years].

On the dot, again; but hardly the credentials to captain the vessel in the turbulent and murky waters of Indian governance. His signal service to the homeland notwithstanding, Manmohan Singh, is 'only' a Jat of the land-cultivating third-lowest Vaisyha caste from Punjab in the racist *Hindutva* scheme of things that, ironically, has once again come to the fore in the person of certain officials at the commanding heights of the incumbent Congress part of the government.

Working outside the realm of India's democratic and otherwise fully functional institutions, the official role of some of these individuals cannot be understated; one was currently the national security adviser to the Prime Minister, and another, is the current foreign minister. And, that is where the second broad trend of New Delhi's current approach to Islamabad, referred to earlier, comes in.

This disastrous approach of the 'Indira Doctrine' of the late 1980s at the height of the Cold War was, essentially, a page out of *Kautiliya Arthashastra*, wherein the divine Brahmin commands the 'Righteous' rulers' duties to include, among a host of others, to always follow the 'Sixfold Interstate Policy':

> The king who is endowed with personality and the material constituents of sovereignty and on whom all right policy rests is called the conqueror. That which encircles him on all sides and prevails in the territory immediately adjacent to his is the constituent of the circle of states known as the enemy. . . .
>
> When he [a neighbouring prince] is in difficulty, he should be attacked; when he is without support or has weak support, he should be exterminated. In contrary circumstances (that is, when he is strong or has strong support, he should be harassed or weakened.[17]

It remains uncertain as to how much of a spoiler's role Messrs Dixit and Natwar Singh would, in the event, be able to play, but neither of them makes any secret of their palpable difficulty with coming to terms with the times. They continue to push their terribly misplaced haughtiness through both the South Block-linked pen-pushers in the media and in their own personal conduct.

One particular piece carried in its 27 August 2004 issue by *The Hindu* raised particular concern among all those who were looking for a continuity in the peace process in South Asia subsequent to the change of government at New Delhi. Written by the well-informed correspondent of the newspaper, C. Raja Mohan, it was as faithful a reproduction of the *Kautiliyan* regime as could be published in presentable political science diction.

C. Raja Mohan was indulgent enough to grant both Pakistan and China the status of India's immediate neighbours that are, in the words of the *Arthashastra*, 'strong or have strong support', and hence entitled to merely being 'harassed or weakened'. No such licence for Nepal, Bangladesh or the Maldives, all of whom were judged by him to be either 'in difficulty' or 'without support/ having weak support'; hence, worthy of being attacked if not exterminated: 'India might have no option but to develop a pro-active policy to encourage internal political change within the subcontinent. That is part of the burden of being a responsible power in the international system.'

He was chillingly unsparing of Nepal in particular: 'India's muscle-flexing on Nepal has only helped postpone the final denouement in the once tranquil Himalayan kingdom now trapped in a brutal civil war. India will need a lot more than the commitment to use force to defend order in Nepal.

'It will have to address the sources of the deepening crisis in Kathmandu. New Delhi should combine its will to intervene militarily in Nepal with a whole range of other policy instruments to get all the three elements in Nepal—the monarchy, political parties, and the Maoists—to resume the stalled dialogue on fundamental political and social change.'

As for Bangladesh and the Maldives, C. Raja Mohan said: 'In Bangladesh, too, India must press the two main political parties to end their bitter rivalry, which has allowed the growth of extremist forces in that country. And in the Maldives, New Delhi must warn President Gayoom to either shape up through democratisation or ship out.'

So as to leave no doubt where C. Raja Mohan was coming from, he went just a bit too far by advocating the heady 'Indira Doctrine' of Dixit–Natwar of the 1980s:

> . . . the Nepal crisis has brought back into focus the question of India's use of force in the neighbourhood. Since its military intervention in Sri Lanka during the late 1980s, India has been extremely cautious in committing its troops to defend its security interests in the immediate

neighbourhood. Prudence on use of force is always a sensible policy. But to suggest it will not be considered at all, as the recent Indian foreign policy tended to, is not wise.[18]

Thus, in one stroke, C. Raja Mohan would rubbish the regional peace momentum as 'unwise'. One cannot argue with this view of wisdom. Nor for that matter with the kind of insensitive diction both the National Security Adviser and the Foreign Minister would habitually employ ever since assuming office with reference to crucial and sensitive dimensions of comprehensive security in South Asia.

The following is a sampling from just one day, 13 November 2004:

PTI, New Delhi, November 13: The national security adviser, Mr J.N. Dixit today slammed the Hurriyat Conference for insisting on talking to Pakistan high commissioner here and not to Union Home Minister, Mr Shivraj Patil, saying 'We can't have this high-horse spirit. Let Pakistan talk to their own Kashmiris and we will do the same. Why should we respond to Pakistan's insistence that talks should be held in their territory and at their insistence,' he said in a hard-hitting interview to *Tehelka* weekly.

Known for candid speaking, Mr Dixit, a former high commissioner to Pakistan, said Umer Farooq, acting chairman of Hurriyat, had met Pakistan President, General Pervez Musharraf in Amsterdam and 'the Pakistan high commissioner is a permanent host to them'.[19]

Natwar Singh had this to say:

The composite dialogue is progressing satisfactorily . . . so far there has been no back-tracking or setback except what the prime minister has stated that President Musharraf must live up to his January 6 announcement that he will not permit his country's territory to be used for terrorist attacks on India or any other country.

Mr Natwar Singh recollected that Gen Musharraf had last year made an 'objectionable speech' at the UN to which then Prime Minister Atal Behari Vajpayee had replied.

'This year, the general made a speech which we could accept . . . there was no verbal exchange. His speech set the tone for the meeting between the two leaders,' Mr Natwar Singh said, referring to the talks held between the Indian premier and the Pakistani president on the margins of the General Assembly.[20]

The three targets of the Dixit–Natwar duo referred to above would all belong, indeed, to the especially 'despicable' category of 'outer barbarians' who are not even worthy of inclusion in the key caste system of the Brahmanic racist scheme: 'It is almost impossible for a Hindu to regard himself otherwise than a member of some particular caste, or species of Hindu mankind. Everybody else who disregards Hindu *Dharma* is an "outer barbarian" (*mlechha*) no matter how exalted his worldly rank or how vast his wealth may be.'[21]

That mindset of the Hindu faith as described by one of the most credible historians of his time has certainly undergone a lot of change, most drastically in India's recent past, especially since the transformation of the country's economy by Manmohan Singh in the early 1990s. The liberalization process, coupled with the globalization of the economy, has led to a rapid increase in the Indian middle class that has both the sense and the financial means to stand tall before the Brahmanic overlords.

THE BALANCE-SHEET

We have to allow political space to the sagacious Jat from the land of the five rivers in appreciation of the tremendous pressures he has to bear as the prime minister of a nation in the midst of a socio-economic transition. That, in one's view, explains what appear to be twists and turns in his policy pronouncements in the area of regional peace and stability.

There has, no doubt, been no dearth of such confusing statements coming from Prime Minister Manmohan Singh. But one would still uphold the necessity of taking a larger contextual view of things rather than jumping at each disturbing sign.

One should not forget that the verbosity of some at New Delhi notwithstanding, unprecedented progress in substantive terms continues to be made by the India–Pakistan peace process in both the official and the societal realms. The process of composite dialogue goes on apace.

Pakistan's Prime Minister Shaukat Aziz is due to arrive in New Delhi within a matter of days from now where, according to Foreign Minister Khurshid Mahmood Kasuri, he would discuss

President General Pervez Musharraf's broad—but concrete—suggestion of 25 October 2004 for a peaceful solution of the Kashmir dispute[22] to the satisfaction, above all, of the long-suffering people of what was once the paradise on earth.

Meanwhile, for the first time in fifteen years, since the start of the insurgency in the part of Jammu & Kashmir controlled by India, New Delhi announced the withdrawal of unspecified number of troops from the region. It was also reported on 16 November 2004, that an official meeting held in New Delhi had decided to start the troop pull-out process the next day.

Let us also not lose sight of the progress already achieved by the two sides on this key question of South Asian regional security—indeed, stability—at the highest level during the first interaction between President General Pervez Musharraf and Prime Minister Manmohan Singh in New York where both had gone on the occasion of the UN General Assembly's opening session for the year 2003:

> NEW YORK, September 24: After a historic, hour-long meeting in New York on Friday, Indian and Pakistani leaders issued a joint statement that recognized Kashmir as an issue and agreed to explore all possible options for a peaceful settlement.
>
> 'I sincerely believe that today is an historic day and we have made a new beginning,' said Indian Prime Minister Manmohan Singh as the two leaders emerged from the meeting room with a tired but contended look on their faces.
>
> 'And I feel confident that despite the difficulties on the way, I and President Musharraf will together work and succeed in writing a new chapter in the history of our two countries,' he said.
>
> Mr Musharraf agreed. 'I hope that this augurs well for the future of Indo–Pakistan relations,' he said.
>
> The two leaders also addressed the issue of Jammu and Kashmir and agreed that possible options for a peaceful, negotiated settlement of the issue should be explored in a sincere spirit and purposeful manner,' said the joint statement that President Musharraf read out after the meeting.
>
> The statement, although an important diplomatic document in itself, was more noticeable for what it omitted than what was said. The most notable omission was that of the Indian claim that Pakistan was encouraging cross-border terrorism in Kashmir.

The document also emphasized the need for 'a peaceful negotiated settlement' of the 56-year-old dispute, a phrase Indians strongly objected to in the recent past, insisting that Kashmir was their internal problem.

But in the joint statement, the emphasis was on accommodating, rather than confronting, each other. The language, and the tone, both reflected this desire as both sides avoided terms that had complicated problems in the past.

The discussions were held in 'a constructive and frank spirit' and the two leaders reiterated their commitment to continue the bilateral dialogue to restore normalcy and cooperation between India and Pakistan, the statement said.

They agreed that confidence-building measures of all categories, under discussion between the two governments, should be implemented keeping in mind practical possibilities.

The two leaders, according to the statement, agreed to maintain the spirit of the Islamabad declaration issued after an equally historic meeting between President Musharraf and former Indian Prime Minister Atal Behari Vajpayee in January that set the current peace process rolling.

In the spirit of the Islamabad statement, they agreed that CBMs will contribute to generating an atmosphere of trust and mutual understanding so necessary for the well-being of the peoples of both countries.

The document also reflected the desire of the Pakistani leader to go beyond 'hackneyed positions' on Kashmir and make a fresh start, as he said at the News Conference on Thursday.

... Mr Musharraf contributed to creating a friendly ambience for the talks by presenting Mr Singh a painting of his native village in Pakistan, an album of his childhood friends and a report card from the village school where Mr Singh had studied before migrating to India after the partition.

'*Aapnay mera dil moh liya* (you have won over my heart),' said the Indian Prime Minister after receiving the gifts. 'I was only checking who got better marks in mathematics,' joked the Pakistani president.[23]

THE SONIA FACTOR

Finally, in terms of the current Indian domestic power equation, perhaps the person of the Congress party chief, Mrs Sonia Gandhi, provides the best guarantee for the advancement of the prospects of regional peace, security and stability in South Asia. She seems to have paid back the *Hindutva* brigade in the same coin by putting up the Jat as the head of the government when the former persisted in falling so low as to refuse to accept the honourable lady as a citizen of the 'Secular', 'Democratic', 'Socialist' 'Republic' of India. Or perhaps, it is just another case of Divine Retribution! At any rate, the clear-headed widow of the late Prime Minister Rajiv Gandhi has come out strongly, in political terms, by opting not to become the prime minister. She also has a lot of living memories of the racist mindset of the followers of Manu.

It is unlikely that she would not recall the bitter past on this count. When her late husband, Prime Minister Rajiv Gandhi, started steering India in the new direction of regional peace and security soon after coming to power in 1988, his patriotic credentials also came to be questioned by the C. Raja Mohans of the time, epitomized by the late former editor Girilal Jain.

This particular individual had then hit such depths as to allude in a piece of newspaper writing to Rajiv Gandhi's father, the late Prime Minister Indira Gandhi's husband, the late Mr Feroze Gandhi, as not being a proper Indian as he was a Parsi and, hence, a *mlechha* by definition.

That experience seems to have redoubled her determination to see the dream of Rajiv Gandhi through to realization. She made just such a manifestation by choosing the heights of Kargil to send out a message of peace at a public meeting on 30 September 2004. The venue and the wording were both very meaningful:

NEW DELHI, September 30: The Indian government would take every step needed to peacefully resolve the Kashmir issue with Pakistan, Congress party leader and chairperson of the ruling United Progressive Alliance (UPA) Sonia Gandhi said on Thursday.

She told a public meeting at Kargil that the composite dialogue process with Islamabad would not only continue but also be strengthened to establish peace. 'The UPA government will take every step to resolve the Kashmir issue through dialogue and reconciliation,' *Press Trust of India* quoted Ms Gandhi as saying on her first visit to the Line of Control after the UPA government assumed office in May.

Ms Gandhi is expected to visit Pakistan in December, but officials say she has not yet confirmed the final dates. She said the recent meeting between Indian Prime Minister Manmohan Singh and President Gen Pervez Musharraf in New York was a step towards establishing peace in the region. War between the two countries had brought nothing but havoc, she declared.

Describing [the] people of Kargil as soldiers without uniform, Ms Gandhi said they had witnessed a turbulent period and rendered numerous sacrifices during the Kargil conflict.[24]

Since the publication of this report by the *Dawn* correspondent there has been further confirmation, this time from the Pakistan high commission sources, of her plan to visit Pakistan next month. By doing that, Mrs Sonia Gandhi, as the first—and top—leader of the incumbent Indian government, would do doubt go a long way to the consolidating the bilateral peace process: 'The president of the Indian National Congress, Sonia Gandhi, according to the Pakistan High Commission sources in New Delhi, has accepted a formal invitation by Islamabad for a visit. She is due here some time in December as a goodwill gesture for the advancement of the peace process that, both sides feel, is going on satisfactorily.'[25]

SHARED STAKES

Together with the societal and political dictates of regional peace and security that have been touched upon in the earlier sections, there are at the same time bright prospects of a cross-national energy network coming in place sooner than later. That, all said and done, would serve as a more durable structure of stability than the otherwise mercurial times may guarantee.

For when two or more nations of South Asia come to have a shared stake in each other's economic lifeline in the form of energy, there would, by the same token, emerge a common stake in each other's stability. The signs on this crucial count are more encouraging today than they have ever been in post-colonial South Asia.

What remained a 'pipedream' during the Vajpayee era—thanks to the likes of C. Raja Mohan—is fast becoming a reality in the shape of the project to transmit gas from where it is in abundance, Iran—to where there is a terrible need for the energy resource—India—across Pakistan, of course.

One has not recalled C. Raja Mohan without good reason in this context as well. An extract from his writings in *The Hindu* dated 26 January 2003 throws ample light on why it took India ten long years to agree to the project. In short, New Delhi remained adamant in trying to radically alter the geopolitics of the region:

NEW DELHI January 25. In a move that could radically alter the geopolitics of the region, India and Iran today agreed to step up work on transport projects that link the subcontinent with the Persian Gulf, Afghanistan, Central Asia and Europe.

The projects announced today by the visiting Iranian President, Syed Mohammed Khatami, and the Prime Minister, Atal Behari Vajpayee, as part of a new road map to strategic cooperation, would increase the leverage of India and Iran in the Great Game for accessing the landlocked resources and markets of Eurasia.

Ever since the Partition in 1947, Pakistan had blocked India's access to Afghanistan and beyond. The new transport corridors through Iran could liberate India from the geographic constraints imposed by the division of the subcontinent.

The transport links reinforce Iran's claim as the natural gateway between Eurasia and the Indian Ocean littoral. An early completion of these transport corridors could give Iran an edge over Pakistan which wants to control access routes and energy pipelines from land-locked Central Asia.[26]

It was perhaps beyond the imagination of the closed minds that open minds could change more readily than 'geopolitics'. The to-the-point, short joint declaration issued at the end of the meeting between the Pakistan President and the Indian Prime Minister in New York made a specific reference to the transactional gas pipeline project in terms signifying not just India's whopping energy-deficiency but also the desirability of early implementation of the scheme 'for the welfare and prosperity of the people of both countries'.

Small wonder, then, that 'both the ministers [of oil and gas in India and Pakistan] have invited each other for talks but the dates and venue are yet to be finalised'. That is from a report carried by *Dawn* on 8 November 2004, which goes on to state: 'Foreign

Office sources told *Dawn* on Sunday that Indian Minister for Petroleum and Natural Gas Mani Shankar Aiyar has written two letters in a week to his Pakistani counterpart about the proposed talks.'[27]

Mani Shankar Aiyar, a friend of the late Prime Minister Rajiv Gandhi, has made no secret of his keenness to carry the project through to completion. An earlier report in the same newspaper, on 7 October 2004, was eloquent in this regard:

NEW DELHI, Oct 6: India's Petroleum and Natural Gas Minister Mani Shankar Aiyar said late Tuesday that New Delhi was seeking to move forward on energy cooperation with Islamabad in the wake of last month's summit between leaders of India and Pakistan.

Though Mr Aiyar said no specific meetings on energy cooperation had yet been set between leaders of the two countries, India was considering the possibility of selling diesel to its neighbour.

He also said a pipeline linking India to Iran's massive gas fields through Pakistan could be a key to ensuring the country's energy security. 'If we are seriously fossil-fuel deficient, we will need to have an alternative,' said Mr Aiyar. 'General improvement of atmosphere could facilitate some types of contact' between India and Pakistan, he said, referring to the proposed pipeline.

The minister said he remained personally 'bullish' on India–Pakistan relations. But he said that legal and commercial security was essential for projects in energy to move forward. 'There are a huge number of issues' that need to be resolved, said Mr Aiyar.[28]

Such being the scenario in South Asia today, it is doubtful that any country in the region would still prefer to see the glass half empty. Even if it fills drop by drop, at least the next generation will live to enjoy it, if and when the galss does get filled.

NOTES

1. Shujaat Bukhari, 'PM extends hand of friendship to Pakistan', *The Hindu*, Srinagar, 19 April 2003.
2. 'Vajpayee offers talks, Jamali welcomes', *Reuters*, *Dawn*, 19 April 2003.
3. 'Musharraf welcomes Vajpayee's initiative', Special Correspondent, *Dawn*, 25 April 2003.

4. Chidanand Rajghatta, 'US welcomes Vajpayee's talks offer to Pakistan', *The Times of India*, 19 April 2003.
5. 'Vajpayee offers talks, Jamali welcomes', *Reuters*, *Dawn*, 19 April 2003.
6. Aziz Hanifa, 'Kashmir conflict, most dangerous: Clinton', *IANS*, *The Times of India*, 30 December 1999.
7. http://usembassy.state.gov/islamabad/wwwh01051803.html
8. http://www.9-11commission.gov/hearings/hearing9/rice_statement.pdf
9. Anwar Iqbal, 'Shuttle diplomacy prevented Indo–Pakistan war: Bush', *The News*, 23 April 2004.
10. 'Envoy returns with hand of friendship', Special Correspondent, *The Telegraph*, Kolkata, 3 May 2003.
11. *The News*, Islamabad, 21 May 2003.
12. Amit Baruah, 'Let's reject conflict, says Vajpayee', *The Hindu*, New Delhi, 13 December 2003.
13. John Cherian, 'Looking ahead', vol. 21, no. 2, URL, http://www.flonnet.com/fl2102/strories/20040130006301200.htm (Cover Story)
14. http://www.turkishdailynews.com/old_editions/01_22_99/Sport2.htm
15. http://www.thehindu.com/thehindu/mag/2004/04/25/stories/2004042500420200.htm
16. http://www.reuters.co.uk/newsPackageArticle.jhtml?type=entertainmentNews&StoryID=620728§ion=news
17. Wm. Theodore de Bary (ed.), *Sources of Indian Tradition*, vol. I, New York and London: Columbia University Press, 1958, p. 247.
18. http://www.hinduonnet.com/thehindu/thscrip/print.pl?file=2004082701661000.htm&date=2004/08/27/&prd=th&
19. http://www.navhindtimes.com/stories.php?part=News&Story_ID=11142
20. http://www.dawn.com/2004/text/top5.htm
21. http://www.tribuneindia.com/2004/20041115/main1.htm
22. Vincent A. Smith, *The Oxford History of India*, Karachi: Oxford University Press, 1981, p. 62.
23. http://www.dawn.com/2004/09/25/top5.htm
24. http://www.dawn.com/2004/10/01/top11.htm
25. http://www.dawn.com/2004/10/28/top11.htm
26. http://www.hinduonnet.com/thehindu/2003/01/26/stories/2003012604420800.htm
27. http://www.dawn.com/2004/11/08/top6.htm
28. http://www.dawn.com/2004/10/07/ebr3.htm

CHAPTER 6

Bangladesh–India Relations: Recent Trends

MOHAMMAD HUMAYUN KABIR

INTRODUCTION

A study on the relationship between Bangladesh and India, characterized by both conflict and cooperation, assumes importance for several reasons. First, there is the need to adequately appreciate the general framework in which the two countries operate in relation to each other. The regional and global perspectives are to be taken into account here. Secondly, there have been certain changes in the politico-economic spheres in both Bangladesh and India. It is imperative to examine these dynamics currently obtaining so far as they impinge on the relations between the two countries. And lastly, some new trends are observed in the foreign policies of Bangladesh and India. It is crucial to highlight their impact on the relationship between the two countries.

Now, how recent is recent? For our purpose in this study, by 'recent' we mean the time frame since the early 1990s. And since the study is on 'Comprehensive Security in South Asia', as such, foreign policy has to be understood as part of the comprehensive security of a country. Comprehensive security has been defined as 'the pursuit of sustainable security in all fields (personal, political, economic, social, cultural, military, environmental) in both domestic and external spheres, essentially through cooperative means.'[1] What is notable here is that the definition has three elements; first, it emphasizes the content of comprehensive security as an overarching, organizing concept. Secondly, it provides for the process to facilitate security management in comprehensive terms at the sub-national, national and regional levels. And thirdly, the definition incorporates an approach to security, that is, security by what means—cooperative, not competitive, means.

The study has five sections, including the introduction. The second section deals with the permanent features that characterize Bangladesh–India relations. It also highlights the intervening factors that only at times tend to influence the relations between the two asymmetric neighbours. The third section examines the issues of conflict between Bangladesh and India, while the fourth section focuses on the strategic dissonance developing between the two countries. The fifth and last section highlights some issues of cooperation between Bangladesh and India.

THE 'GIVENS' AND THE INTERVENING FACTORS IN BANGLADESH–INDIA RELATIONS

The givens in Bangladesh–India relations are the asymmetry in size and power, the locational factor, India's upper riparian status, and the big-power small-power syndrome. The intervening factors are India's regional policy and the issue of regime compatibility.

To begin with, just a few words on the foreign policy of Bangladesh seem to be in order, as it relates to the country's security and to the fact of living next to a giant neighbour. The fundamentals of Bangladesh's foreign policy are laid down in the Constitution of the Republic. Article 25 of the Constitution of Bangladesh states;

> The State shall base its international relations on the principles of respect for national sovereignty and equality, non-interference in the internal affairs of other countries, peaceful settlement of international disputes and respect for international law and the principles enunciated in the United Nations Charter. . . . The State shall endeavour to consolidate, preserve and strengthen fraternal relations among Muslim countries based on Islamic solidarity.

Indeed, the foreign policy of Bangladesh, an economically and militarily weak country, is the first and second line of defence.

For understandable reasons, India's size and power and the Indo-centric geographic layout of the region of South Asia engenders in Bangladesh a big-power small-power syndrome vis-à-vis India. This generates certain perceptions, attitudes, expectations, and policy preferences in the smaller neighbour. While Bangladesh and India share as many as fifty-four rivers, India being the upper riparian, and economically and technologically more advanced, is in an advantageous position. This also puts the lower riparian, Bangladesh, in a number of difficult situations, affecting the country's relations with India.

The intervening factors in the relationship between Bangladesh and India are the regime compatibility and India's regional policy in South Asia. There is a belief in Bangladesh that India tends to prefer a certain party to be in the government in Dhaka. There is also a perception there that a non-Congress government in India is friendlier to Bangladesh. This means that Bangladesh–India relations are understood to be warmer under certain kind of governments in these countries, and will pass through a cold phase under certain other regimes. However, this has been changing in both the countries over the last decade or so. The Gujral Doctrine was welcomed by many of India's South Asian neighbours, as it contained New Delhi's political/diplomatic overtures towards those countries regardless of reciprocity from them. This also seems to be changing, to the chagrin of the smaller neighbours.

As mentioned earlier, Bangladesh–India relations witness both strains and goodwill and warmth, as reflected in conflict and co-operation between the two countries. We now turn to some of these issues.

ISSUES OF CONFLICT

Some of the issues that generate conflict between Bangladesh and India are:

- Border Issue
- Trade Issue
- Push-in Issue
- Alleged Insurgent Training Camps in Bangladesh
- Export of Bangladeshi Gas to India
- Transit Issue
- Common Water Resources Management

Border Issue

Allied issues like border demarcation, border fencing by India, the Teen Bigha Corridor, enclaves, etc., are not new, but what is interesting to note is the changing position of India on the ratification of the 1974 Mujib–Indira Border Agreement. India is yet to ratify the agreement, while Bangladesh did so immediately after its signing. As the agreement involved ceding territory, India started dilly-dallying on the pretext of the case being sub judice, as one citizen from the Indian state of West Bengal filed a writ petition against India's handing over of a tiny patch of its territory to Bangladesh. Indian courts took about two decades to decide on a verdict; that the Indian Constitution did not have to be amended for such mutual transfer of territory. Only 6.5 km of land boundary remains undemarcated between Bangladesh and India. India now says that the ratification of the 1974 Border Agreement is subject to completion of the boundary demarcation between the two countries. This tendency to procrastinate on the part of India creates bad blood in Bangladesh, preventing the blossoming of relations between the two close neighbours.

Trade Issue

The staggering gap in the trade balance between Bangladesh and India is not new. What is relatively new, even in this age of economic liberalization and market economy, is New Delhi's denial of access to Bangladeshi goods to the Indian market by way of imposing an array of tariff and non-tariff barriers.

Push-in Issue

India claims that there are a large number of illegal Bangladeshi migrants in India. This number widely, and wildly, varies—from 1 million to 19 million, scattered all over the country but concentrated mostly in the bordering states of India as also in Delhi and Mumbai. The criteria for identifying these people remain obscure and there are many in India itself who oppose the methods. Bangladesh denies the existence of such illegal Bangladeshi migrants in India and, therefore, there is no question of taking them back. India is now making vigorous attempts to push in people whom it calls illegal across the border into Bangladesh. India is engaged in this exercise in a big way, making the bilateral relationship rather bitter. Remarkably, Indian attempts usually coincide with the nature of the relationship with Bangladesh, with the centre–state relationship in India, with the approaching of elections in India, particularly in the states bordering Bangladesh, etc.

Alleged Insurgent Training Camps in Bangladesh

India alleges that Bangladesh offers shelter and training to rebels who are waging insurgencies in India's north-east. It is alleged that there are as many as 195 training camps inside Bangladesh territory. The number of camps on the Indian list keeps on increasing with every meeting between the chiefs of the para-military forces and the home secretaries of the two countries. It is ridiculous that these suggested camps include some cantonments and the academic institutes. Bangladesh denies the existence of such training camps. It is believed in Bangladesh that the camp issue is a convenient whip in India's hand to occasionally beat Bangladesh with. The whipping frequency and intensity is now gathering pace, it seems.

Export of Bangladeshi Gas to India

Energy-hungry India is extremely eager to get gas from Bangladesh, while the latter is hesitant to export it to its giant neighbour. The issue is at best controversial in Bangladesh. The exact quantity of gas in Bangladesh is not known and most of the country does not have access to it. In fact, while Bangladesh buys gas at a high price in dollars from foreign companies exploring for gas in the country. While domestically the use of gas is debatable, the export of it to India becomes politically sensitive and even explosive. India's persistent insistence on gas export makes the situation a lot worse.

Transit Issue

India wants transit through Bangladesh territory to connect its mainland in a big way with its seven isolated north-eastern states. As India views it, this will facilitate the development of and communication with the north-east and guarantee access to Chittagong port. Bangladesh has misgivings about Indian intentions. It is not convinced about the economic benefits that might accrue from granting transit facilities to India, and Dhaka remains concerned about the security implications and strategic underpinnings of the transit project of India. It is a most sensitive issue vitiating relations between Bangladesh and India.

Common Water Resources Management

For Bangladesh this is the most important and sensitive issue, as the life and living in the country depends on the water resources that flow from upstream India. The issues here are the sharing of these common resources, flood forecasting, harnessing the resources for the economic development of the two countries, maintaining the ecosystem and the navigability of the watercourses, clean water, etc. Bangladesh and India are only addressing the problem of sharing the water of the common rivers, mainly of six including the Teesta River. Over the last seven years, there have been many meetings at the political, official, and technical-expert levels over the problem of sharing the water of these watercourses. So far little progress has been made. Hopes in Bangladesh were high concerning the Teesta. Even here, the JRC level and the expert-level meetings held in the last two-three months could not make any breakthrough, as the two sides still tend to differ over the formula for sharingthe waters of the Teesta and over the quantum of water required for the river itself. Things took a grave turn with the news of India's river-linking project. Bangladesh, which has experienced the effects of the Farakka Barrage, is deeply concerned about the implications of it.

There are some strands in the foreign policies of both Bangladesh and India, observed since the 1990s, which reflect certain strategic dissonances in the interests and worldviews, and which have implications for their respective national security perceptions.

ISSUES OF STRATEGIC DISSONANCE

India's Nuclear Doctrine

Bangladesh is concerned by the nuclearization of South Asia, regardless of the debate whether nuclearization has stabilized or the security situation between India and Pakistan or not. India's nuclear doctrine professes that it will not use nuclear weapons against non-nuclear weapons' states. This laudable intention has been much compromised by the provision that the deadly weapon will be used against non-nuclear states aligned with other nuclear powers. This 'alliance' relationship will obviously be determined by New Delhi, thereby putting any non-nuclear states on India's potential hit list under certain scenarios. This position of India on the use of nuclear weapons is not lost on Bangladesh.

Indo–US Relations

The ever-expanding and deepening relationship between India and the United States is as such not a menace to Bangladesh. However, two factors need reflection—the Bush Doctrine of Preemptive Strike and US insistence on the export of gas from Bangladesh to India. There is a perception in Bangladesh that, having been emboldened by the US actions in Afghanistan and Iraq with impunity, India might feel tempted to do the same in any part of South Asia and be able to get away with it. As regards gas export, the American position smacks of a cruel preference for economic benefits to the imperatives of the political sovereignty of a nation.

Indo–Israeli Ties

Despite protestations to the contrary and despite the fact of a new, Congress-led coalition government in New Delhi India's ties with Israel are growing. Bangladesh being what it is, and given its policy towards the Middle East, Dhaka will look at this new thrust in India's West Asia policy with unease.

Sino–Indian Relations

It is not unusual for Bangladesh to attempt to cultivate extra-regional great powers with a view to redressing the power imbalance between Bangladesh and India. China has been one such power for Bangladesh to build as a counterpoise vis-à-vis the giant neighbour. The Sino–Indian relationship over the last several years seems to have blunted the opportunity for Bangladesh to rely on borrowed strength. China now seems inclined to advise Bangladesh to settle issues bilaterally with India.

Indo–Pakistan Relations

Under the Gujral Doctrine, Pakistan was to be isolated while the other South Asian neighbours of India were to be engaged for mutual benefits. This policy gradually made a shift to engaging Pakistan under the BJP-led NDA government, and it has gathered momentum under the Congress-led UPA government of Prime Minister Manmohan Singh. India's smaller neighbours are not nervous or concerned about the Indo–Pak rapproachement, but they are carefully observing the events and processes while assessing if they might lose or benefit from the normalization of Indo–Pak relations.

Bangladesh's 'Look East' Policy

Over the last couple of years, Bangladesh has been pursuing a policy of 'Look East'. Relations have indeed improved with the countries of South-East and East Asia, particularly with Myanmar, Thailand, Singapore, Vietnam and South Korea. This created certain misgivings in India, as this policy strand of Bangladesh's foreign policy was interpreted as being pursued at the expense of Dhaka's relations with New Delhi. In reality, it was a misinterpretation of facts. Bangladesh just wanted to diversify its foreign policy options and directions, without being prejudicial to the interests of any particular country.

India's Strategic Interests in Bangladesh's Internal Affairs

According to the Indira Doctrine, enunciated by late Prime Minister Indira Gandhi in 1983, India has its 'legitimate' interests not only in the foreign policies of its South Asian neighbours, but also in their domestic stability. This was blatantly evident in the wake of the grenade attacks on the Awami League party rally and the assassination attempt on the leader of the opposition in Bangladesh, Sheikh Hasina, on 21 August 2004. Views expressed in India, particularly in the print media, were too belligerent. In sum, the Government of India was advised by some to invade Bangladesh to stabilize the situation there. This reminds us in Bangladesh not only of the Sri Lanka situation in 1983 but also of the Bush Doctrine of Preemption. This does not bode well for cementing relations between neighbours.

However, Bangladesh–India relations are not only of conflict, these have also witnessed phases of cooperation.

ISSUES OF COOPERATION

Bangladesh embarked on a policy of economic liberalization in the early 1990s. Though not India-specific, this policy has helped India by facilitating large-scale Indian exports to Bangladesh. Bangladesh is now the sixth-largest trading partner of India.

The CHT Peace Accord

A peace accord was signed between the Government of Bangladesh and the PCJSS in early 1997 to put an end to the tribal insurgency in the Chittagong Hill Tracts (CHT) of Bangladesh and bring peace and development to the embattled region of the impoverished country. The accord was possible due to the positive role played by India. It is recognized that without Indian advice to the CHT rebels and the cooperation extended to the Bangladesh Government, the accord probably would not have been signed.

The Ganga Water Treaty

A thirty-year treaty on sharing of the waters of the river Ganga was signed between Bangladesh and India on 2 December 1996.

It is not an ideal treaty but it is a long-term commitment and is a good beginning for cooperation on a wide range of water-related issues between the two countries.

Indian Investment in Bangladesh

Although the closest of neighbours, Indian investment in Bangladesh has not been significant so far. However, the climate has brightened of late. The giant Tata Company of India has very recently offered to invest in Bangladesh as much as 2 billion US dollars in the steel, cement and power generation sectors. If the deal comes through, this would be the largest single foreign investment in Bangladesh. Perhaps much more investment will follow from India and also other countries.

This only goes to show how the concept of regime compatibility does not seem to be holding true anymore in terms of the relationship between Bangladesh and India. There is indeed ample scope for cooperation between the two countries. Having a friendly India with mutually beneficial ties should be a healthy security policy of Bangladesh. Similarly, a stable and prosperous Bangladesh on the eastern flank of India is a sensible security policy for the regional giant. The foreign policies of the two countries need to be geared to these ends.

NOTE

1. Council for Security Cooperation in the Asia Pacific (CSCAP), memorandum no. 3: The Concept of Comprehensive and Cooperative Security, 1995.

CHAPTER 7

Indo–Lanka Relations: Recent Trends

JEHAN PERERA

The signing of the Ceasefire Agreement between the Government of Sri Lanka and the Liberation Tigers of Tamil Eelam (LTTE) in February 2002 would count as by far the most important overall development to have taken place in the past two decades in Sri Lanka. Similarly, the role played by the Government of Norway in facilitating the peace process, and the rapid internationalization of the process, would count as the most important foreign-policy related development. This study will approach the recent trends in Indo–Lanka relations through the prism of these two developments.

At present, the major development in Indo–Lanka relations concerns the signing of an Indo–Lanka Defence Agreement. Signing a defence agreement with India appears to be one of the few matters on which there is bipartisan political agreement in Sri Lanka. Former Prime Minister Ranil Wickremesinghe also discussed the matter with his Indian counterpart, former Prime Minister Atal Behari Vajpayee in New Delhi in October 2003. An Indo–Lanka Defence Agreement was part of the grand design of an 'international safety net' that the former Sri Lankan Prime Minister sought to put in place. This was a countervailing factor to the concessions he was making to the LTTE on the ground following the signing of the Ceasefire Agreement of February 2002 with that separatist organization.

The proposed Indo–Lanka Defence Agreement seeks to bring India's military dealings with Sri Lanka under one framework. It seeks to systematize the military training, sale of military equipment, and the sharing of information that already takes place between the two countries. India is now by far the biggest trainer of Sri Lankan military personnel. The proposed defence agreement would, however, see an increased role for India as a supplier of military equipment to Sri Lanka. But perhaps the most significant aspect of the combined impact of formalizing the Indo–Lanka military cooperation would be that Sri Lanka would enter into the realm of having a 'special relation' with India, which would clearly bring the country within the Indian sphere of control.

So far the only publicly pronounced unhappiness shown by any party to the proposed Indo–Lanka Defence Agreement has come from the LTTE and Tamil political parties. During the tenure of the former prime minister Ranil Wickremesinghe, the LTTE's chief ideologue, Anton Balasingham voiced his apprehension that 'A military pact with India would encourage the Sinhalese political leadership to take a hardline belligerent attitude towards the Tamils and eventually destroy the mutual trust between the estranged communities which is a crucial factor necessary for the consolidation and promotion of peace.'[1]

The mainstream Tamil media, which has been closely echoing the LTTE's views on matters that affect the overall strength of the Tamil polity in Sri Lanka, has also taken a strong stand against the signing of the Indo–Lanka Defence Agreement. One newspaper editorialized that 'India would have to clarify whether the pact was aimed at scuttling the struggle of Sri Lanka's Tamils for substantial autonomy based on their right to self determination'. Another commentator accused India of 'fishing in troubled water of Sri Lanka to establish its economic and military hegemony over the entire island'.[2] This Tamil apprehension is that the defence agreement would lead to a strengthening of the Sri Lankan government's military capacity and hence reduce its willingness to yield or be politically accommodative to the LTTE's negotiating position.

Most Sri Lankans, on the other hand, do see India as a bulwark against the LTTE and against Tamil separatism. It is believed that India would never permit the division of Sri Lanka into two states because this could inspire similar separatist sentiments in India, particularly in the Indian state of Tamil Nadu. However, there is also a need to be sensitive about India's domestic pressures which could lead to India ignoring appeals from its troubled neighbours. Both the government and the people of Tamil Nadu have, in the not-so-distant past, been openly supportive of the Tamil struggle in Sri Lanka. In May 1999, when the Sri Lankan government appealed for assistance from the Indian government to halt an LTTE military offensive in the north, no material assistance was forthcoming. As the well-known maxim of international relations goes, states do not have permanent friends but only permanent interests.

UNFORTUNATE HISTORY

The Indian role in fostering the civil war in Sri Lanka is an unfortunate one. In the early 1980s, India trained, armed, and provided bases for Tamil militants to attack the Sri Lankan government forces. A former diplomat and political columnist, K. Godage, has written that 'Indian military strategists at that time, led by a strident Indira Gandhi, seem to have decided that Lanka was drifting away from India's sphere of influence and should be brought within the defence perimeter. The ethnic conflict in Lanka afforded India the opportunity to intervene.'[3]

Godage further says, 'The destabilization of Sri Lanka was made easier by the attitude of the [Sri Lankan] government and Sinhala people who were not inclined to concede to the Tamil minority rights which they claimed for themselves. As the level of insurgency intensified, India not only gave refuge to Tamil militants, but helped them with arms, training and money. The magazine *India Today* in an article titled "Ominous Presence" filed by correspondent Shekhar Gupta identified the training camps and gave a detailed account of what the Indian authorities were doing to destabilize Lanka.'[4]

The late J.N. Dixit, who was ambassador to Sri Lanka at that critical time and was foreign policy adviser to the Indian Government explained the Indian involvement in Sri Lanka in the following terms. 'Tamil militancy received support both from Tamil Nadu and the Central Government not as a response to the Sri Lankan Government's military assertiveness against its Tamils, but it was also a response to (Sri Lankan President) Jayewardene's orchestrating military intelligence presence of the US, Israel and

Pakistan in Sri Lanka. The assessment was that these presences would pose a strategic threat to India, as they might encourage fissiparous movements in the southern states of India'.[5]

Clearly, the geopolitical context within which India intervened in Sri Lanka was largely its concern over its security interests. As stated by Godage, 'The Panikkar doctrine (named after K.M. Panikkar) emphasized the importance of the Indian Ocean for the defence of India. According to Panikkar, this vulnerability made it necessary for Lanka or Ceylon to become an integral part of India's defence structure. The British had kept out other imperialist powers from the Indian Ocean to protect their interests. The perception was that India considered itself the successor to the British Raj and therefore sought to use the same principle to incorporate other states and keep external forces from the Sub Continent.'[6]

The continuing relevance of the Panikkar doctrine is also borne out in a commentary by V. Suryanarayan, a professor and director of a research institute in India. He quotes a report of September 1997 by the Maritime Intelligence and Counter Piracy Operations Centre that Sri Lankan waters had become 'extremely dangerous areas for maritime traffic'. He observed that 'If effective steps are not taken, the LTTE will expand its geographic space as well as range of operations, posing a threat to South Asian security'. He also recommended that 'New Delhi should develop the political will to pursue courses of action that promote India's national interests. India should work with the objective of neutralizing the (LTTE) Sea Tigers at the earliest opportunity'. He concludes that 'What Sardar K.M. Panikkar wrote in 1944 on the strategic significance of Burma applies very much to Indo–Sri Lanka security linkages today: "The defence of Burma is in fact the defence of India and it is India's primary concern, no less than Burma's, to see that its frontiers remain inviolate."'[7]

THE CEASEFIRE

It is a truism that all wars must end one day. However, prior to the signing of the Ceasefire Agreement of February 2002, it seemed that Sri Lanka was doomed to an indeterminate and long-term period of civil war. It was a war fought with escalating intensity and at tremendous cost to both sides. A few examples would suffice to give an indication of the costs of war. In the year that preceded the ceasefire, the economy regressed by a negative 1.4 per cent, the first time ever in the post-independence period. The downturn in the economy followed an LTTE attack on Colombo's international airport which destroyed most of the country's civilian air fleet. Also, in May 1999, the LTTE succeeded in overruning the second-largest military base in the Jaffna peninsula which was manned by about 8,000 soldiers. This attack brought the LTTE to the outskirts of Jaffna city, the main northern city.

In this context of rapidly escalating costs, the stoppage of the war through the signing of the Ceasefire Agreement came as a major and welcome surprise. But the compromises it entailed on the side of the Sri Lankan government were correspondingly high. Some of them would be the explicit acknowledgment that a significant part of Sri Lankan territory had fallen under the rule of the LTTE, and awarded the Norwegian facilitators to give rulings on the lines of control between the two sides.

As a part of its counter-strategy to negate these compromises, which could jeopardize Sri Lanka's security and sovereignty, the government sought to canvass an international safety net for itself. India was a primary focus in the Sri Lankan government's search for international allies. The Sri Lankan Prime Minister's first visit abroad after signing the Ceasefire Agreement was to India, where he met with his counterpart. Subsequently, the Prime Minister, as well as the top ministers involved in the peace process, paid several more visits to India.

During that period, the government-controlled media editorialized on the importance of Indo–Lanka ties in facilitating a solution to the ethnic conflict. An editorial written four months after the signing of the Ceasefire Agreement stated; 'Prime Minister Ranil Wickremesinghe's current visit to India, his second to that country in the past six months, freshly underscores India's continuing importance to the Lankan peace process'. But even in that tribute to India there was an uneasy undertone. 'India has continuously pledged its support for a negotiated and just political settlement in Lanka's conflict and it is unlikely to deviate from this position. However it would be appropriate to inform India about the rationale behind our major moves, lest our intentions be misunderstood.'[8]

INDIA'S AMBIVALENCE

However, despite these and other Sri Lankan efforts to woo India into supporting the peace process, India's ambivalence towards it has been marked. While India has issued several messages of support for the peace process, the Indian government has shown no interest in getting directly involved in it. For instance, India declined to play a major role in the Tokyo donor conference of June 2003, attended by over forty countries and forty international agencies, at which Norway, Japan, the United States and the European Union were appointed as co-chairs.

Today, with Sri Lanka's peace process stalled after the election of a new government in April 2004, there is much speculation about the Indian role. The new government has sections within it that have advocated that India should replace Norway as the facilitator. There is a strong belief that India is behind these moves. 'The JVP's continuing protests against many aspects of the peace process using several front organisations and acting as an opposition within the government is suspected by many as manipulations of India'.[9]

The roots of Indian ambivalence towards involvement in Sri Lankan affairs can be traced back to the Indo–Lanka Peace Accord of 1987. The events that unfolded from this agreement had tragic consequences for both countries. What began as an Indian exercise in power mediation and problem-solving diplomacy ended in a new war, albeit one fought between the Indian army and LTTE. The Indian Peace Keeping Force was eventually asked to leave by the Sri Lankan government with its mission incomplete. This was followed by the subsequent assassinations of former Prime Minister Rajiv Gandhi and the Sri Lankan President R. Premadasa as a consequence.

After the ill-fated Indo–Lanka Accord, the Indian attitude towards the Sri Lankan ethnic conflict has been a hands-off one in terms of the public sphere. India has restricted itself to the issuing of statements of concern about Sri Lanka's territorial integrity and the protection of the rights of all communities. These statements have been generally welcomed by the Sri Lankan government and anti-LTTE groups. But there has been no direct Indian intervention even when such intervention has been requested by the Sri Lankan government. To quote an editorial:

> Since the Indian military intervention in 1987, Sri Lanka has been bending over backwards to please New Delhi with regard to the battle against terrorism, foreign policy and defence. Friendship with India has been a cornerstone of our foreign policy, it being held that antagonising India was the main cause for the events of 1987. While India's hostile attitude towards this country has changed very much for the better from what it was in the eighties, and there is constant repetition that India 'supports the unity and territorial integrity of Sri Lanka', in tangible form regrettably Indian support has not amounted to very much.[10]

The most outstanding example was the appeal made by the Sri Lankan government to India in May 1999 when the LTTE during a military offensive, brought them to the verge of capturing the northern capital of Jaffna. The Indian response was to offer humanitarian assistance in the form of evacuation of the Sri Lankan army from Jaffna if the need arose. However, this desperate situation did not arise. The Sri Lankan military was able to halt the LTTE offensive, and even partially reverse it, with new weaponry hastily airlifted from Pakistan and the Czech Republic.

INDIAN LIMITATIONS

A lesson to be gleaned from the experience of May 1999 is that India is not prepared to directly intervene in Sri Lanka in a situation of military conflict. If Jaffna had fallen to the LTTE, it would have been in possession of a most important political asset in its campaign for a separate state. India's constraints as a military ally is only one reason why Sri Lanka should be judicious in signing a defence agreement with India when it has no external enemies. A comparison with other defence-related agreements that India has signed, such as with its other neigbours Bhutan and Nepal, would reveal that India tends to demand a high price in terms of exclusive relations.

Sri Lanka has only to look at its own Indo–Lanka Peace Accord that was signed in 1987. Letters exchanged between the leaders of the two governments summarized Indian concerns about Sri Lanka's independent foreign policy where it touched on India's geopolitical concerns. They stated that 'both Sri Lanka and India reaffirm the decision not to allow our respective territories to be used for activities prejudicial to each other's unity, territorial integrity and security'. Indian concerns at that time pertained to the use of Sri Lanka's ports and airwaves by foreign powers.

The issue of Indian conditionalities when it comes to the signing of military-related agreements with itself has surfaced once again over the repairing of the military airport within the military complex at Palaly in the Jaffna peninsula. Media reports indicate that the Sri Lankan Government has been considering an Indian request to grant India sole user-rights over the airport along with Sri Lanka, thereby creating a special relationship which would exclude all other countries. In return India has offered to repair the airport as a gift from India.[11]

The Sri Lankan experience in May 1999 raises the question whether accepting such a condition would be in the best interests of Sri Lanka. Also, as a democratic government seeking a negotiated settlement of the ethnic conflict, there is a need for the government to seriously consider the protests that emanate from Tamil society which is a part of the polity whose sentiments need to be respected.

The problem for India is that its past experience in Sri Lanka, and in particular its antagonistic relationship with the LTTE, has made it difficult for it to directly participate in the peace process. As currently structured, the peace process is about legitimizing the military gains of the LTTE and also legitimizing the LTTE as a political actor. But it is certainly reasonable to believe that India would not be happy to have a neighbouring state which is headed by those who assassinated one of its Prime Ministers. India's extradition request to Sri Lanka regarding the LTTE leadership, and its ban on the LTTE following the assassination of Rajiv Gandhi, pose insurmountable obstacles to any role that India could play as a third party in such a peace process.

NEW PHASE

The problem for Sri Lanka, however, is that India's inability to participate in the peace process led to an estrangement of India from the peace process and to concerns that India could actually be a major impediment to the entire process. A glimpse of this problem was seen when a question was asked on the floor of the Indian Parliament a short while after the signing of the Ceasefire Agreement in Sri Lanka. The question was whether the extradition request to Sri Lanka still stood, and the answer given by the Indian Government was that it did. This incident was seen in Sri Lanka as a deliberate Indian move to put the LTTE on notice that the international recognition it was receiving through the peace process would not change certain basic realities.

India has also shown its unhappiness with the growing internationalization of the Sri Lankan peace process. The letters exchanged between Prime Minister Rajiv Gandhi of India and President J.R. Jayewardene of Sri Lanka in July 1987 as an adjunct to the Indo-Lanka Peace Accord summarized Indian concerns about Sri Lanka's foreign policy at that time. Its clauses stated, among others, that 'Trincomalee or any other ports in Sri Lanka will not be made available for military use by any country in a manner prejudicial to India's interests'. Also that 'Sri Lanka's agreements with foreign broadcasting organisations will be reviewed to ensure that any facilities set up by them in Sri Lanka are used solely as public broadcasting facilities and not for any military or intelligence purposes'.[12]

Although much has changed in the realm of international relations since the signing of the Indo-Lanka Peace Accord, and India's global relationship with the United States has been transformed, it can be believed that India's concerns about geopolitical matters in its neighbourhood remain, albeit to a lesser degree. Although both the Sri Lankan and the Norwegian Governments have taken public pains to keep India briefed on developments in the peace process, there has been a cosmetic element to them. India has been unable to prevent the internationalization of Sri Lanka's peace process. What started as an exclusive Norwegian initiative in 2000 has now grown into a process that officially includes Japan, the United States, and the European Union.

These three international actors, all of them global superpowers, now have a continuing role as co-chairs of the Tokyo Donor Conference which set benchmarks for the peace process and which pledged a massive total of USD 4.5 billion for four years. India's unhappiness at Japan's political and economic role in the peace process has been reported in the media. The challenge for Sri Lanka is to assuage India's security and geopolitical concerns even as it strives to harness international assistance to resolve its ethnic conflict and develop its economy. There is need to ensure transparency in Sri Lanka's dealings with foreign powers and to ensure a peace process in which there is constant consultation with India.

There are some important reasons why India would wish to play a bigger role in the Sri Lankan peace process. The first would be to reaffirm its diplomatic dominance over the South Asian region. The active diplomatic role being played by Norway in the Sri Lankan peace process could signal an increased international role in intervening in conflict resolution processes in South Asia as a whole. In fact, due to the continuing Indo–Pakistan tensions over the Kashmir issue, the United States has tried to play a conflict resolution role between the two countries.

It is reasonable for India, as the big power of the region, to be apprehensive about the entry of so many other big powers into a region it considers its own backyard. Of all the world's leading powers it is India that has the greatest direct interest in Sri Lanka. Keeping out the world's big powers from the South Asian region would be only one of its interests. Another would be in respect of the final settlement arrived at in Sri Lanka. There is no doubt that what happens in Sri Lanka will be closely studied by those who wish to forge a new polity in India itself. The peace settlement in Sri Lanka, and the new parameters of the constitutional arrangement, could be proposed as a model for some of India's own internal conflicts.

It would be in India's longer-term interest to obtain for itself a positive role in the Sri Lankan peace process. However, if India is to play a constructive role in Sri Lanka, it should find itself a role which would be welcomed by all sections of the polity, by ensuring a win-win solution for every one of them. Unfortunately this is the genius that India has failed to show in the past in its dealings with Sri Lanka. The still evolving Indo-Lanka Free Trade Agreement could be the centrepiece of a new relationship based on mutual economic benefit for the two countries and their diverse peoples.

NOTES

1. Ranga Kalanasooriya, 'Indo-Lanka Deal: Defence or Military Industry Pact?', *Daily Mirror*, 22 October 2004, p. 8.
2. 'Indo-Lanka Defence Pact Comes in for Criticism', *The Island*, 27 October 2004, p. 1.
3. K. Godage, 'Historical Continuities', in '*Securing South Asia*', a symposium on 'Advancing Peace in the Subcontinent', September 2002.
4. Ibid.
5. J.N. Dixit, *Assignment Colombo*, Colombo: Vijitha Yapa Bookshop, 1998, p. 329.
6. Ibid.
7. V. Suryanarayan, 'Tigers—Threat to Indian Security', *The Island*, 31 July 2004.
8. *Daily News*, 11 June 2002.
9. Kesara Abeywardena, 'Embattled Government in War Talk', *Daily Mirror*, 28 August 2004, p. 9.
10. Editorial, *The Island*, 11 June 2002.
11. Sunil Jayasiri, 'Government rejects India's bid for Palay', *Daily Mirror*, 11 November 2004, p. 1.
12. Dixit, *Assignment Colombo*, pp. 360-1.

CHAPTER 8

Indo–Pakistan Relations: Latest Trends

NAJAM RAFIQUE

Most informed opinions across geographical divides agree that if relations—to whatever form they exist in the present circumstances—between India and Pakistan were to collapse irreparably, the South Asia region would stand on the verge of a nuclear conflict. The notion has gained even more credence with the growing phenomenon of 'terrorism' that has permeated across the globe. While the history of Pak–Indo relations over the last fifty-seven years marked by their obstinate 'official' stands on issues left over following the great partition, and punctuated by three wars, may have given credence to that particular view, the common mass who form the over one billion total in the region still continue to hold on to a vision of a better future than a nuclear holocaust.

Today, even the officials on both sides of the Wagha realize the need for 'flexibility' on official positions on certain core issues that have plagued relations between the two states. No less than the president of Pakistan, General Pervez Musharraf has reiterated the call for flexibility at innumerable forums, and the need to move away from traditional positions when it comes to the question of dealing with the core issue of Kashmir. For Kashmir is seen as the one issue on whose settlement would rest the foundations of the relations between the two estranged neighbours.

At the start of the new century, when peace talks between India and Pakistan stalled during the Agra Summit of 2001, both sides were disappointed and pessimistic about the future. Then in April 2003, the Indian Prime Minister, Vajpayee made a speech offering the 'hand of friendship' to Pakistan. Over the next eight months, officials ferried messages back and forth between Vajpayee and General Musharraf, who came to see a possibly unique opening to end a half century of enmity. The issue gained momentum with Vajpayee's decision to attend the 12th SAARC Summit in Islamabad in January 2004, where the two leaders agreed to start the process of a composite dialogue. This was preceded by a number of CBMs as both India and Pakistan, moving cautiously, were now at least talking about steps to improve relations between the two countries. (We shall look at some of these steps later and take stock of the process of the 'composite dialogue'.)

It would seem, finally, that both countries realize the necessity of resolving their long-standing problems and will rebuild a relationship which has continually broken down in the years past.

THE MECHANICS OF CURRENT PAKISTAN–INDIA DETENTE

In the spirit of turning the adversarial relationship around, witnessed during the 12th SAARC Summit, the foreign secretaries of Pakistan and India held their first formal talks in February 2004 in Islamabad. The talks were part of the Pak–India rapprochement that has been witnessed in the flurry of people-to-people contacts across the Wagha. During those talks, both sides agreed on the basic 'roadmap' for a composite dialogue process:

1. *March/April 2004:* A meeting took place between the DG Rangers and the Inspector-General of the Indian Border Security Force (BSF).

   The Inspector General of India's BSF, J.S. Gill, and Pakistan's Maj. Gen. Hussain Mehdi of the Pakistan Rangers met in March in Lahore and signed an agreement aimed at curbing cross-border smuggling, drug trafficking and illegal immigration.

   In April, Pakistan proposed the hosting of expert level talks on nuclear CBMs between Pakistan and India on 25–26 May. The talks were held on 20 June, following a postponement by India, and focused on nuclear crisis management, including a ban on further tests and preventing the accidental or non-authorized use of nuclear weapons. Views were also exchanged on respective security concepts and nuclear doctrines.

2. *May 2004:* Talks on drug trafficking and smuggling were held.
3. *May/June 2004:* The foreign secretaries of Pakistan and India agreed to hold talks on Kashmir, CBMs and Peace and Security, in New Delhi.

   Two days of talks between the foreign secretaries of Pakistan and India concluded on 28 June 2004. This was the first meeting between the foreign secretaries after a gap of six years, the last foreign secretary level talks were held in 1999. Both sides agreed on various confidence building measures which include: a hotline between the foreign secretaries; advance notification of missile tests; reopening of consulates in Mumbai and Karachi; restoring the staff strength at their respective High Commissions to 110, and the release of fishermen held in each other's water. The foreign ministers also agreed to meet in the third week of August to review the progress achieved in the composite dialogue before the meeting of the foreign ministers.
4. *July 2004:* Talks on issues such Siachen, the Wullar Barrage/ Tulbul Navigation Project, Sir Creek, terrorism, economic and commercial cooperation, and friendly exchanges between the two countries were held.

   Mr Ajay Vikram Singh who replaced A.K. Bhatnagar as the new Indian defence secretary in the first week of July 2004 is scheduled to discuss a coterie of issues with his Pakistani counterparts sometime in the first week of next month. Both sides will be holding talks on six different subjects including Siachen, and prepare a report for bilateral dialogues between the foreign ministers.
5. *August 2004:* The foreign ministers of the two countries meet. The results of their composite dialogues are given in Table 8.1.

The fact that experts from both the sides are now talking about conflicts ranging from Kashmir to Siachen, to Wuller Barrage and the Sir Creek is by itself a positive indication that both countries

TABLE 8.1: COMPOSITE DIALOGUE—RESULTS

S.No.	Agenda	Date/Venue	Status
1.	Meeting DG Rangers & Indian Border Security Force	March 2004, Lahore	Agreement signed aimed at curbing cross-border smuggling, drug trafficking and illegal immigration. The two sides also held talks on 15–16 June 2004 on the smuggling issue.
2.	Meeting between nuclear experts on nuclear CBMs	20 June New Delhi	Inconclusive
3.	Foreign Secretaries Talks	27–28 June New Delhi	Inconclusive
4.	Wullar Barrage/Tulbul Navigation Project	29–30 July Islamabad	Inconclusive
5.	Promotion of friendly exchanges	3–4 August New Delhi	Inconclusive
6.	Siachen	5–6 August New Delhi	Inconclusive
7.	Sir Creek	6–7 August New Delhi	Inconclusive
8.	Terrorism & drug trafficking	10–11 August Islamabad	Inconclusive
9.	Economic & commercial cooperation	11–12 August	Inconclusive

want to prevent the outbreak of the fourth round in their version of the South Asian Cold War. Like all disputes, the process of settlement can be laborious, especially between neighbours who, 'hate each other's guts', but the very fact that Islamabad and New Delhi now have the confidence to talk and seek ways for dealing with issues that in the immediate past would have threatened an all out war on their borders is a hopeful sign.

The foreign ministers of India and Pakistan met in New Delhi on 5–6 September 2004, to 'review' the nine-month old process of the composite dialogue. While there was no major breakthrough on the core issue of Kashmir, both sides agreed to continue and move into the second phase of the process with talks scheduled in the next few months on nuclear and conventional weapons; coast guard cooperation; discussions on the launch of a bus service between Muzaffarabad and Srinagar and restarting a train service; and technical-level talks (in Oct.–Nov.) to revive the Munabao–Khokhrapar rail link. For the first time, both have now also agreed to open up to group tourism

UNOFFICIAL LIST OF PROPOSALS EXCHANGED BETWEEN INDIA AND PAKISTAN AS PART OF THE COMPOSITE DIALOGUE

On Kashmir

1. Relocate forces from the Indian side of Kashmir, including Siachen
2. Repeal 'draconian' laws
3. Reduce human rights violations
4. Establish Srinagar–Muzaffarabad bus link
5. Open the Jammu–Sialkot route
6. Permit cross-border trade at selected points
7. Allow interaction at selected points between people on both sides of the LoC
8. Permit pilgrimages on both sides to shrines
9. Promote cultural interaction and cooperation
10. Explore cooperation on issues such as management of environment, forestry resources, etc.

In the latest moves on Kashmir, President Musharraf has suggested various proposals for debate within Pakistan on the issue. Among the various options for discussion, he has suggested dividing Kashmir into seven zones instead of treating it as one whole political unit for the purposes of eliciting the views of the Kashmiris, Indians, and Pakistanis. Five of these zones would be in India—the Valley, Rajauri, Jammu, Kargil and Leh—and two in Pakistan—Azad Kashmir and the northern areas. These he suggested should be further identified, demilitarized, and their status changed. The Valley may be given under the joint suzerainty of both India and Pakistan. Other options include independence, joint control or UN mandated territory.

These ideas merit serious consideration and examination in order to resolve the dispute that has held one-fifth of humanity hostage over the last fifty-seven years.

On CBMs

1. Establish new communication links between the two navies and air forces, re-establish links at Division/Corps Commander level, specifically Leh and Kargil–Gilgit, Baramulla and Kupwara–Murree, Rajouri–Jhelum, Srinagar and Nagrota–Rawalpindi and Jammu–Sialkot
2. Upgrade, dedicate and secure the communication links between the DGMOs and establish a hotline between the two foreign secretaries
3. Establish communication links between the Indian Coast Guard and the Pakistan Maritime Security Agency
4. Develop links between the armed forces through exchange of visits by naval ships, seminars between academic and research institutes dealing with strategic and defence-related issues, exchanges between defence training establishments; friendly sporting tournaments and joint adventure activities between the two militaries such as the exchange of military bands
5. The DGMOs of the two countries could meet periodically, followed by an annual meeting between the two VCOAS
6. Restore the strength of respective high commissions to 110
7. Re-establish consulates general in Karachi and Mumbai
8. Release all apprehended fishermen

On Commercial and Economic Cooperation

1. Pakistan should grant MFN status to India
2. Grant transit facilities to each other's goods on a reciprocal basis
3. Open the Attari–Wagha land routes for trade
4. Promote investment in joint ventures
5. Participate in trade fairs/exhibitions
6. Tackle piracy of Indian music and films in Pakistan

7. Lay down optical fibre cable from Attari to Lahore
8. Facilitate counterpart arrangement between mobile operators
9. Allow Indian companies in telecom projects in Pakistan
10. Allow multiple airlines to operate scheduled services
11. Allow air connectivity with India to designated carriers of Pakistan
12. Amend the 1974 Protocol on Resumption of Shipping Services to allow third country flagships/vessels to lift India/Pakistan bound cargo; also allow flag carriers of both countries to lift cargo for third country from each other's ports
13. Supply petroleum products from India to Pakistan and extend diesel pipeline to Pakistan
14. Commercial cooperation in the CNG sector
15. Participation of Indian companies in on- and off-shore production activities
16. Harmonize customs procedures and valuation
17. Cooperation between SEBI and Securities and Exchange Commission of Pakistan
18. Cooperation in the field of Information Technology
19. Bring out a joint commemorative stamp, and exchange philatelic exhibitions
20. Open branches of nationalized banks in each other's country
21. Collaborate in post-harvest technologies
22. Cooperate in the water resources sector

On Promotion of Friendly Exchanges

1. Exchange of artists, writers, poets, musicians, painters, and sculptors
2. Liberalize visa regime for performing artists, film personalities, and liberalize visa regime through grant of one-year multiple visas to bona fide businessmen; grant of Exempt from Police Reporting (EPR) visas to journalists, artists, students, scholars, businessmen, persons working with multinational companies, senior citizens (65 years and above)
3. Invitation to theatre groups from Pakistan and India

4. Exchange of exhibitions, paintings, sculpture, photographs, handicrafts, musical instruments
5. Exchange of publications, recorded music, slides
6. Interaction between national museums
7. Participation in book fairs/exhibitions in each other's country
8. Cooperation between libraries
9. Joint seminars in the field of elementary education
10. Interaction between the University Grants Commission and the Higher Education Commission of Pakistan
11. Joint workshop in the field of medicinal and aromatic plants
12. Cooperation and exchange between institutions of excellence
13. Exchange of youth delegations
14. Exchange of sportspersons, teams and coaches
15. Remove ban on Indian TV channels in Pakistan
16. Remove ban on Indian newspapers and periodicals
17. Hold film festivals
18. Annual seminars between groups of journalists
19. Delhi Transport Corporation (DTC) and Pakistan Tourism Development Corporation (PTDC) could start group tours
20. Both sides to exchange lists of civilian prisoners in each other's custody and initiate their release
21. Offer consular access to jails
22. Pakistan requested to make another effort to trace and release the recorded 54 Indian POWs
23. Increase the size of pilgrim groups

All these proposals are significant in themselves, and indicate that India and Pakistan have now passed the stage of serious tension and their relations, although far from normal, are better than the post-December 2001 period. Significantly, on 5 July 2004 in a departure from the past, and under the umbrella of SAARC, India allowed a group of Pakistani boy scouts to attend a scouts' function in Gulmarg, close to Srinagar. This is being seen as a step further in the CBMs. It has also been suggested by India that the LoC in Kashmir should be turned into a line of peace and tranquility. Meanwhile, Pakistan has suggested that the two countries should evolve mutually acceptable modalities for discussing Kashmir, and how to engage and associate Kashmiris in the process. Pakistan has also suggested fixing a timeline for these discussions. However, India seems hesitant to put a timeline for accepting the best options and solutions for resolving contentious issues that most certainly will be discussed again and considered for mutually acceptable implementation by the two countries.

While irritants over the Baglihar hydropower project have almost been ironed out, both India and Pakistan have yet to move forward in certain difficult security areas and facilitate easier visa regimes, improve economic relations, and ease tough posturing over Kashmir. Moreover, unlike in the past, the current process of composite dialogue has survived the government changes in the two countries, reflecting an expanding consensus across the borders to move the peace process ahead. As in Pakistan, so also in India, peace with the former was an undisputed issue among the main contestants in the most recent general elections. Both the BJP and the Congress party, and also other important regional players including the Left, campaigned for reconciliation with Pakistan. On the other hand, the Musharraf administration has kept its commitment to pursue dialogue. Consider, for example, Musharraf's four points on resolving Kashmir: recognize Kashmir as the core issue; dialogue; flexibility; and finding alternatives to traditional positions. Also, the leading components of Mutahida Majlis-i-Amal (MMA) such as JUI, and the PPP–Parliamentarian in Alliance for the Restoration of Democracy (ARD) have been more or less supportive of the process. It remains to be seen how far the domestic adversaries will rise above their political expediencies in allowing a negotiated settlement of bilateral disputes, including Kashmir.

Thus far, both India and Pakistan have shown willingness for a sustained and serious dialogue, and both sides have responded positively to nuclear CBMs, including a proposal by India for a common nuclear doctrine floated by its external affairs minister, Natwar Singh. Pakistan has also suggested similar expert-level group meetings in the areas of conventional CBMs. Several conventional CBMs are in the pipeline, which need follow-up action including an MoU between the Maritime Security Agency of Pakistan and the Indian Coast Guard.

Although differences remain over issues such as troop reduction and a permanent mechanism to sustain ceasefire along the LoC, with a comprehensive and sustained framework of CBMs in place across frontiers, these would not be difficult to bridge if the political leadership remains engaged in building an all-round momentum towards mitigating apprehensions.

These new initiatives are sound in themselves and should not be allowed to fall victim to the mistrust between the governments that has prevented successful implementation in the past. The overall atmosphere that prevailed during the present round of talks has raised a great deal of optimism. Moreover, the media, both in Pakistan and in India, minus the usual rhetoric of the vernacular press, showed a degree of responsible reporting. The officials of both India and Pakistan have shown a professionalism that many previous encounters lacked. There were no abrupt conclusions of talks and no walkouts by either side. Both have in fact managed to impress on the outside world that despite the lack of any concrete progress in these talks, there is still a possibility of some breakthrough in future talks.

The easing of tensions provides an opportunity to reassess and revitalize the role of CBMs in normalizing relations. The new approach does not require a sweeping shift, but detailed mechanisms to address disputes. The people in and outside the region hold their breath for peace in South Asia, as the train of dialogue in South Asia moves slowly along. But with the growing feeling of bonhomie, even as the 'hawks' across both sides of the Wagha continue to hope for an end to the dialogue process, people can only pray, that *inshallah*, this time the train will reach its station, minus the massacres so reminiscent of the Partition in 1947. The 'spoilers' on both sides of the Wagha divide should by no means be provided with ammunition for raising tensions and putting pressure to end the dialogue process. Such a scenario would be disastrous indeed.

Under the present circumstances, when the very sanity of nations is in question, there is some relevance to the timeline formula, and India must not fritter away this opportunity. As we look at our shared continent, the poisoning of our environment; the distortion of our economies; the erosion of our sovereignty;

the suppression of social justice; the escalation of militarism and terror stagger the mind. India and Pakistan can, as they have for the last five decades, choose to ignore these or decide to correct the wrongs through concerted action. None of our problems are susceptible to old panaceas, worn-out slogans like Islam in danger or Hindu supremacy and bankrupt approaches. New approaches, new outlooks, and new thinking have to be the order of the day. We can kill each other or choose to live together. One can only hope that both will choose to do the latter. This can only be done by recognizing our common destiny, by focusing on similarities and accepting differences and redirecting energies towards securing a better future. In this endeavour, the progeny of Gandhi, Jinnah and Nanak must not prove to be lacking.

Indeed, the very fact that India and Pakistan have chosen to engage in a dialogue process is an indication of the maturity of the political process between the two sides. But one must not expect instant results for an end to decades of belligerency. The fact that the composite dialogue process has not broken down is by itself a big achievement, and there is still a lot of give and take to come, and it is going to be part and parcel of the dialogue process before the final outcome.

CHAPTER 9

Media–State Relations in South Asia: A General Overview with Particular Reference to India

NARAYANI GANESH

THE NATURE OF THE MEDIA–STATE RELATIONSHIP IN SOUTH ASIA

The media in South Asia was, till very recently, dominated by a problem peculiar to this region. By and large, the media here tended to be an extension or reflection of the state and its ceremonial activities. Look at the events that hogged prime space in the print media or prime time on state-owned television news channels. They were so predictable: the arrival or departure of the head of state to or from a foreign trip; rote speeches delivered at state functions; press releases issued by government departments; and reports of the annual statements of public sector undertakings and the five-year plans were what the readers and viewers were inflicted with. Even newspaper editorials read like speeches from the pulpit, doling out advice directed almost exclusively at the government.

Today, particularly in India, the question often raised in journalism classrooms is: Let's say you were a reporter covering the prime minister's speech and the *bandobust* (security) for him disrupted normal life; would your report deal in large part with this disruption of everyday life or would it focus on the prime minister's speech that was full of platitudes? Those journalists who are intrepid or candid enough to say they would focus on the disruption are in the new mould that is gradually emerging as more responsible and professional reflectors of ground realities.

The engine of this change is the social and economic middle class that has preoccupations with issues relating to civic life as distinct from political life or life of the state. It is this middle class —of which most have neither clear-cut political preferences nor even an interest in politics—that forms the main constituency of a free media. Issues such as emancipation of women, education, health, consumer protection, and environmental impacts are gradually overtaking the emphasis given to statements of political leaders. With this change comes a change in perspective that the media has with the state for a healthier, more dynamic relationship between the two.

Wherever the media in South Asia is either browbeaten or compromised to disseminate information that is largely an elaboration of state-related activity, there is need for soul-searching and introspection—both by the media and by the state. With the exception of India and maybe Sri Lanka—the two South Asian countries where parliamentary democracy has survived the worst possible threats to it from both within and without—the media in the region needs to move away from placing undue emphasis on statements of political leaders. Instead, more space and attention should be given to the people–centric issues mentioned earlier. In fact, the media should go further and also highlight issues that impact us not just directly but also indirectly. We need to take the theory of the butterfly effect seriously, that anything that happens anywhere in the world can affect anything anywhere in the world.

The relationship between the media and the state should be a healthy, dynamic one; they should see themselves as neither adversaries nor buddies. This is possible only if both parties play the roles they were meant to play. The media should reflect the success or failure of the state in serving the people rather than serve as the state's mouthpiece. For the state's sole reason for existence is not its self-glorification; rather, it is to serve as an instrument of governance, carrying out its responsibilities as facilitator in assuring safety and security and executing the day-to-day administration of the country.

Why the Media Sometimes Compromises its Role as Reflector of Reality?

WHEN THE STATE MUZZLES THE MEDIA

Governments often go to the extreme by muzzling the media in order to garner support for themselves; to present a sanitized version of the goings-on in the country to the citizens of that country and to the international community. However, this can only be a temporary tactic as neither force nor information suppression can be sustained for long.

On 26 June 1975, following the Allahabad High Court judgement that declared the then Prime Minister Indira Gandhi's election invalid, Mrs Gandhi declared a state of internal emergency under Article 352 of the Constitution. The media was forbidden from criticizing the government, as this was seen as being subversive and unpatriotic, and this went on for nineteen months till the emergency was lifted. Today, all those who believe in the freedom of expression have discredited both the emergency and the journalists who wholeheartedly supported it.

What should a responsible journalist do in instances where the state has been accused of human rights violations in certain areas? In the interest of national security, should there be self-censorship by the media in such circumstances? This might have made sense at one time but today, in the era of satellite television, the Internet and global information networks, such self-censorship—or indeed, state-induced censorship—becomes utterly meaningless. The foreign media which is as accessible as the local media today, will make what we might try to hide from readers or viewers available to them.

Besides, reportage of human rights violations, even efforts to play down incidents of violence that are either sought to be concealed for a while or under-reported for fear of sparking widespread panic and violence, are not possible today. For instance, in the Indian context, the tragic and violent killing—of both former Prime Minister, Indira Gandhi and later, her son Rajiv Gandhi—were first reported by the foreign media before the regional media reported on them. Even the extent of the casualties and human suffering following a natural calamity like the Gujarat earthquake of 2001, or the state-abetted post-Godhra riots in 2002, were all reported first by the foreign media and only then followed by regional media reports. So, clearly, any delay in information dissemination locally is no guarantee that things will remain under wraps till the situation is under control. In fact, it will work to the contrary, as blanking of information can cause more harm than good, creating crises of confidence leading to more panic.

The Indian media, however, has shown exemplary courage and spirit in unearthing the truth about the Chittisinghpora controversy. The media exposed the killing of five innocent civilians by security forces in Jammu & Kashmir. The security forces had claimed that the five were foreign militants who in fact were responsible for the massacre of thirty-five Sikhs in the region in 2000. The recent turmoil in Manipur in north-eastern India has received extensive media coverage by way of special reports, opinion articles, and editorials, generating a huge debate about the necessity or otherwise of continuing with the Special Armed Forces Act in the region. Post-Godhra Gujarat coverage delved into every little detail, raising important questions and exposing the way the state had overstepped its limits. The Indian media went about its business in a fearless manner, even at the risk of offending the state.

In Kathmandu, a curious thing happened. Maoists killed Tekendra Raj Thapa, correspondent of Radio Nepal and human rights activist, two months after they had kidnapped him, on 17 August 2004.[1] The local media reacted by blanking out all news of Maoist activity. Was the media right in blocking from public view what was happening on the ground? And by doing so, how would it help in resolving the conflict? And why is the life of a journalist more precious than that of the nearly 10,000 people who have died in Nepal over the last ten years since the Maoist movement gained momentum?

COMPULSIONS OF MISPLACED PATRIOTISM DURING TIMES OF WAR/TERRORIST ATTACKS

What is the responsibility of the media during times of war or terrorist attacks? Isn't it the patriotic duty of the media, one would ask, to wholeheartedly support the government in times of such national emergencies?

During the 1999 Kargil conflict, the bodies of some Indian soldiers were sent to Delhi from the front. Many sections of the Indian media reported that the enemy had mutilated the bodies of the soldiers. However, there were other journalists who claimed that this was mere propaganda aimed at stirring up patriotic emotions.[2] These few journalists—more the exception than the rule—were accused by many of their colleagues, friends and relatives of being less than patriotic. The ethical question that arose was: to whom did the professional journalists owe primary loyalty, to the profession that earned them their livelihood, or to the state? If the journalists failed to do their duty—in this case, in the name of the state—could not the same state require this of the journalists at some later date to suit its own purpose?

In 1998, following the nuclear tests carried out by India in Pokhran, anyone who questioned the legitimacy or ethics of the tests was dubbed anti-national by the ruling Bharatiya Janata Party (BJP). The media therefore is constantly walking a tightrope—between facing the danger of being branded unpatriotic/anti-national and that of sanctifying anything in the name of nationalism and patriotism. Post-9/11, this is what happened even in the United States, where the media was emotionally blackmailed into tempering down reports for fear of being seen to be unpatriotic. Similarly, in the case of the US invasion of Iraq, pacifists and anti-war activists were accused of being insensitive to the plight of the young US soldiers who were operating in punishing conditions.

That is why media–state relations should transcend the here and now to take stock of larger long-term issues in order to bring the right perspective into reporting and governance. A debate involving policy makers, people, and the media only ends up degenerating into specifics of time and place, personalities and geographical boundaries. With globalization and communication networks shrinking the world into one geographical entity and one big community, isolated arguments on security, terrorism or even globalized businesses are completely irrelevant. Macro perspectives are crucial to formulating micro policy.

GOVERNMENTS GO TO WAR, NOT PEOPLE

Recently, journalist Amrith Lal, visited Jammu in the state of Jammu & Kashmir, to do a story on the plight of the refugees there. These refugees are not the Kashmiri Pandits who fled the Kashmir valley in the wake of the militancy that flared in 1989. They are from villages close to the Line of Control (LoC) separating Azad Kashmir from the Jammu region. With constant shelling from either side damaging their homes, and their agricultural land rendered dangerous with landmines, these villagers were forced to leave their homes, much against their will, and seek refuge in camps in the township of Jammu. Amrith Lal laked to them and brought back their poignant story. Earlier, when their fields were not sown with landmines, the villagers would lie low when crossfire across the border carried on for many days, with both the Indian and the Pakistani armies taking aim at each other. After a point, villagers from both sides of the LoC would stride up to their respective armies posted there, and throwing up their hands, would declare firmly: *Bus, bahut ho gaya hai, ab hame apna kaam karne do.* (We've had enough of this nonsense; stop this right away and let us get on with the business of life.) And there would be a ceasefire, while the villagers resumed their daily tasks and visited each other across the border, without either official documents or passports to proclaim their 'national' identity. Many families in the villages on either side were related to one another through marriage or birth.

When the media highlights these kinds of people-to-people contact stories, it not only makes for interesting reading, it also reaffirms our faith in the Third Estate[3] and drives home the point that it is not people who go to war but governments.

THE MEDIA'S ACCESS TO INFORMATION AND THE FREEDOM TO PUBLICIZE IT

The dichotomy of maintaining the freedom of the media and preserving state security has led, in many instances, to stricter controls. How much information is good for public consumption and how far should a secret be preserved by the state?

The media in India enjoys much greater liberty and has access to more information than does the media in other South Asian countries. But it is closely followed by the media in Sri Lanka, and then by lesser degrees in Bangladesh, and Nepal. Despite the overtly undemocratic nature of the government in Pakistan, the media here has shown great resilience and initiative. An interview Najam Sethi, editor of *Friday Times*, gave to the BBC so enraged the Nawaz Sharief government that he was arrested and jailed.[4] He wasn't the only one; some others too who wrote exposes on corrupt government officials met with a similar fate. Very little information is available on Bhutan and the Maldives. The Indian media has access to and publishes details of the defence budget, for instance, whereas the media in Pakistan has access to barely a fraction of the entire defence report of Pakistan. So they can effectively only say whether Pakistan's defence budget has gone up or down but would have no details of what defence equipment is being purchased.

In India, the problem in the relationship between the media and the state is not that there is state control over information; rather, it is of the state's apathy to what the media reports. The media in India is free to report on any issue where information is freely available. The point to be pondered over is what is the extent of its impact on the way that the state functions?

After the 1999 Kargil conflict, a committee was set up under the chairmanship of defence analyst, journalist and former bureaucrat; K. Subrahmanyam. The Kargil Review Committee Report was put on the table of the Lower House of Parliament (the Lok Sabha) on 23 February 2000.[5] But till date, the House has not ventured to discuss its findings despite the media analysing the findings threadbare. So a free media in a free country has still to with the indifference of the state and, in many instances, even of the people.

A good example is the kind of investigative reporting carried out by Tehelka in India. The 2001 Tehelka expose saw several corrupt politicians caught red-handed by investigating reporters. But the result was that the investigative reporters and the media group had criminal cases slapped against them by a vindictive government. A conscientious journalist, in these circumstances, often suffers from existential angst. He might ask himself: Why bother to gather information and report it when the chances are loaded against such reports initiating positive action?

On the other hand, there are many instances of extensive media coverage and constant replay of crucial events and information spurring governments and people into action. Take the case of the Iraqi hostage crisis where armed militants threatened to kill three Indian truck drivers and others if their demands were not met. The twenty-four hour telecasting of the hostages, the hostage takers, the families of the hostages and community reaction definitely affected the quality and manner of the negotiations.

Even in a country like the United States, where the First Amendment confers unlimited freedom on the media, the media faced immense problems, post-9/11. The media was browbeaten into maintaining a very pro-government line, all in the name of patriotism and a united front against terrorism.

How South Asia Deals with Contentious Issues

Often, the South Asian media and states find themselves dealing with contentious issues—related to terrorism, strained bilateral relations and globalization—in a manner that suggests these are independent of one another. Often, armed conflicts, whether internal or external, are dealt with in isolation from all the other issues mentioned earlier, and so end up obscuring the larger picture. All these also involve issues of security.

Highlighting the prevailing security threat to the South Asian region after the nuclear tests conducted by India and Pakistan in 1998, Rashed Rahman, chairman of the board of governors of the Journalists Resource Centre in Pakistan, made a significant statement. He said that the arms race in the subcontinent had shifted the priorities of both governments from peaceful development to war. He pointed out that without drastic economic reforms in the agrarian and industrial sectors, along with a keen emphasis on human development, the lot of the people would never get better.[6]

The media in South Asia, where all seven countries are still grappling with the basic issues of development, can play the role of a catalyst by regularly highlighting life-affirming stories of individual and community-led efforts at bringing about improvements in local development. In the Indian context, there are several striking examples of how, by reporting these kinds of stories, the media helped disseminate positive information which led to greater awareness and development, often turning an inflammable situation, which would have compromised the security of the region, into one that fermented cooperation and progress.

In 1985, Indian social worker Rajendar Singh and his organization, Tarun Bharat Sangh, convinced the villagers in drought-prone Alwar district in Rajasthan, to revive traditional methods of water harvesting and storage. They began by repairing and restoring the old check-dams or *johads*, the traditional way of harvesting rainwater. Today, Alwar district alone has five hundred such functional *johads*. The water table has gone up and the land has become fertile, supporting the needs of the village. The experiment spread to other parts of water-starved Rajasthan, as well as to other states, a perfect example of how self-initiated development work at the grass-roots level—even with little or no state involvement—can help transform a society from deprivation to prosperity.[7]

So what is the connection between this story and the larger security issues in the South Asian region? There are two kinds of security threats—external and internal. If we take the examples of Nepal, the north-eastern parts of India, or even Kashmir or Jaffna and the surrounding areas in Sri Lanka, it becomes clear that internal unrest and rebellion are usually born out of conditions of extreme deprivation. When basic needs like food, shelter, health care and education facilities are either absent or scarce, unemployment and frustration drive people to take up force and rebellion as a means of survival. The state is given the heave-ho, and everything, including dispensation of justice, is taken over by rebel groups who set up parallel 'governments' of their own, however crude or violent they are in form and content. When such rebellion swells, the security threat snowballs and affects all aspects of civilian life and compromises national security as well.

That is why the media has a very important role to play in helping to defuse tension and in spurring development activity.

In the case of water harvesting in Alwar district, the media achieved something stupendous by turning the spotlight on the success of the villagers' efforts to revive waterbodies. It showed how a situation that could have become a hotbed of discontent and rebellion against the state and prosperous communities was transformed into action for self-recovery, progress, and prosperity. Media reports in fact 'incited' people of other villages to plunge into development activity rather than take to arms.

ROLE OF A RESPONSIVE AND RESPONSIBLE MEDIA IN THE CONTEXT OF GLOBALIZATION

The answer to many of the doubts professional journalists face in the South Asian region might lie in the marketing term 'glocal', an amalgam of the words 'global' and 'local'. By having a global perspective—by being sensitive to local sensibilities—the indigenous media can score over the international informational mega corps. Here again, the ability of the media to project the aspirations and reflect society's needs is important.

Nobel laureate and economist, Amartya Sen, famously pointed out that 'in the terrible history of famines in the world, no substantial famine has ever occurred in any independent and democratic country with a relatively free press'. Human rights campaigners took this to heart and they assert that the best way to prevent famine is to secure the right to free expression.[8] A free media could be one of the reasons why India has one of the lowest incidences of famine in the developing world. When deaths from hunger occur in remote areas, the government is forced to take action because the media blitz has a great impact on the people. To take this a step further, the elected representatives in government cannot really afford to ignore public opinion, which however remotely, affects voting patterns.

The media must get over its self-perception that it is somehow special by itself. If it is special at all, it is only because of the trust reposed in it by its constituency of readers, viewers and listeners. So the media's ultimate loyalty should be to this constituency—the forum of well-formed public opinion—that in a democracy has the ultimate potential to empower or disempower the media.

India's Prime Minister, Manmohan Singh, said: 'Everyday [*sic*] when I open the newspapers or when I tune into a channel, I am often disturbed by the messages we are transmitting. Have we no larger mission at hand? Of nation-building, of caring for the under-privileged....The challenge for a democracy like ours is to strike a balance between the possibilities of technology, the compulsions of the market, the passions of the audience and the interests of society and the nation.'[9]

The prime minister's remarks are relevant to those in the media who continue to project the state as the most important news-worthy element, at the cost of neglecting issues on the ground. But there are others in the media who choose to give front-page coverage to what Infosys chairman Narayana Murthy had to say about the future of information technology or employment options over government releases.

This kind of change in perspective comes when media persons realize the importance of highlighting development and private initiative, individual excellence and innovation, and stories of achievements in science and technology, environment and health, rather than confine themselves to being mouthpieces of the state. Reports on natural and man-made calamities, terrorism, conflict and economic ills are being increasingly juxtaposed with stories of how local initiatives helped the underprivileged in some areas overcome their problems.

NEED FOR CODE OF CONDUCT FOR THE MEDIA

Any kind of media—whether print, electronic, online, or radio—should evolve for itself a code of conduct that is predicated on the needs of its constituency guided by a spirit of enlightened self-interest.

In India, there was a time when many journalists allowed themselves to become permanent guests of the government by opting to live in houses given to them by the state on token rents. This was symptomatic of a culture of living off state handouts and junkets, despite the press being free and fair—the unassailable Fourth Estate that somehow props up the other three estates. Newspaper proprietors can play an important role here by facilitating not just housing and travel for motivated journalists, but also by making available options which include in-house training, earned sabbaticals and fellowships.

Over time, the media in India has evolved from being a hoary instrument of the freedom struggle to national conscience-keeper. Worldwide, the media has tended to be a faithful recorder of events and accidents. But there is a need to present trends and processes too. From dispenser of ideology to investigative journalism to becoming a friendly dispenser of news and views that include socio-economic issues and lifestyle changes, the media has indeed come a long way. But there is plenty of room for improvement.

It is in the media's interest to engage the state in both peaceful and troubled times, to be able to bridge the divide between the administration and the administered. A vibrant and free media that can continue to engage the state without getting compromised in the process is vital for evolving and creating a climate of comprehensive security in South Asia.

NOTES

1. *The Hindu,* 18 August 2004.
2. Siddharth Varadarajan, 'War and Dharma of a Journalist', *The Times of India*, 7 August 1999.
3. In today's context, the first, second and third estates would correspond to the ruling political class, the other privileged classes, and the rest of the population. In the nineteenth century, the three estates referred to the clergy, nobility, and peasantry.
4. http://web.amnesty.org/library, news service 089/99
5. http://nuclearweaponarchive.org/india/KargilRCC.html
6. Speech delivered by Rashed Rahman, Chairman, JRC, Pakistan at the South Asian Dialogue on Media, Peace & Development, 22–24 May 1999.
7. Rajendar Singh was given the Ramon Magsaysay award in 2001 for his pioneering work in water management.
8. 'Righting Wrongs', Global Agenda, *The Economist*, 16 August 2001.
9. Prime Minister Manmohan Singh's message on the occasion of the birth centenary celebrations of Ramnath Goenka, *Indian Express*, New Delhi, 28 August 2004.

CHAPTER 10

Religious Conflicts in South Asia: Their Impact on Security

PERVAIZ IQBAL CHEEMA

South Asia is confronted with grave security threats which are a product of many factors. Not only did the British in their hasty departure leave many inter-state conflicts unresolved, including festering border issues, but they also did not bother to look back and help the South Asians to secure the much desired resolution of their disputes. However, it is too late to put the entire blame on the British alone; the regional states have also exacerbated the existing complex situation. While many inherited conflicts still continue to affect the relationships, the policies of the regional states have also given birth to several new threats such as ethnicity, religious militancy and terrorism. This short study is divided in five sections. The first section highlights the four major sources of tension in South Asia; the second section outlines the major factors behind the rise of religious extremism, the next section provides an analysis of South Asian situations, the fourth discusses security debates; and the concluding section suggests a recipe for change. It needs to be mentioned here that the study is written in a generalized form, taking full cognizance of developments in most South Asian countries.

FOUR MAJOR SOURCES OF TENSION

South Asia is a peculiar region in many ways. It is an area where one witnesses simultaneous acknowledgement of operational complimentarity of interests as well as the existence of conflicting interests. That may be the reason why love-hate relationships frequently manifest themselves in one form or another. At the declaratory level, most leaders of the region have repeatedly asserted their utmost desire to work for peace, but at the practical level, the efforts have been viewed with suspicion and cynicism. Since the roots of the security problems are indigenous (both domestic and regional), the threat perceptions are sufficiently diverse to preclude a common approach. For India, the major sources of external threats are China and Pakistan despite the progress in normalization processes and the advent of regional organization. Similarly for Pakistan, and to a lesser degree for Bangladesh, Sri Lanka, and even Nepal, the main threat emanates from Indian policy pursuits. The Indian threat perceptions also include threats originating from outside the region.

Conflict and tension arose in South Asia mainly because of the hasty departure of the British who left many complicated and potentially explosive issues unresolved in the newly independent states of the region. The situation was further complicated when the apprehensions, not only exacerbated the existing sense of insecurity but also induced the leading states of the region to opt for divergent paths. In addition, the early linkage of regional interest with global developments cemented the adopted divergent pursuits within the region and also periodically caused a certain amount of adjustments among the powers involved like the US, SU (the former Soviet Union) and China.

Four major sources of tension have contributed considerably towards the perception formulation of the regional states; tension generated by the emergence of an asymmetrical power balance after British departure; tension due to the linkage between insiders and interested outsiders; tension caused by regional conflicts, and tension caused by domestic development and the emerging new threats such as religious militancy, sectarianism, ethnicity, terrorism, etc.

Undoubtedly the South Asians' regional perceptions have been, and in many ways still continue to be, greatly influenced by the unbalanced and asymmetric power structure that emerged after the departure of the British. The tyranny of geography manifested itself in such a way that whilst almost all the regional states acquired a common border with India, they did not enjoy physical proximity with each other. India is situated right in the middle of the region, blessed with large territory, a massive population, and endowed with enormous resources. Over the years it has built an impressive military machine. The towering Indian position in the region coupled with India's assertion to secure recognition and respect for its policies and its desire to establish a natural hierarchy, or hegemony as many often refer to it, within the region, generates apprehensions among the regional neighbours.

The tension generated by outsider involvement is likely to reduce. The constructive engagements of great powers could cause the total elimination of the tensions that are often credited to their presence. A great power's involvement in any region of the world is primarily due to two major reasons: to meet its global responsibilities; or to serve its own interests in the given region. The involvement of the great powers during the Cold War, was the product of their global objectives and South Asia was no exception. During the Cold War; the Americans perceived threats from the communist world and were feverishly engaged in enlisting players, friends and supporters for their own team. The local states that opted to join the Cold War alliance system were more influenced by regional compulsions and domestic reasons.

Following the end of the Cold War, the tragic events of 9/11, and the initiation of war against terrorism, the policies of the great powers changed and now appear to be more akin to what is called partnerships with a select group of nations. As far as the tension caused by regional conflicts is concerned, the South Asians will have to grow up and demonstrate maturity in resolving their regional disputes.

Among the regional conflicts the most important one has been the conflictual cobweb surrounding Indian–Pakistani relations. A good beginning was made when the Hizb-ul-Mujahideen offered a ceasefire in July–August 2000, which started a chain of events all aimed towards resolution of the ongoing Kashmir dispute. Admittedly, the process was interrupted by events like the attack on the Indian Parliament and India's consequent action of massive concentration of its forces on the Pakistani border, which evoked a somewhat similar reaction from the Pakistani side. The forces of the two countries were eyeball to eyeball for more than ten months. Eventually the Indians decided to withdraw. On 18 April 2003, the Indian prime minister offered to talk on contentious bilateral issues. This offer initiated a chain of positive developments, which led to the normalization of diplomatic relations, the restoration of communication and transportation links, the successful conclusion of the 12th SAARC Summit, and the initiation of the long-awaited dialogue on Indo–Pak contentious issues.

Periodic pressures emanating from internal dynamics confront the countries of the region with the ugly realities of realpolitik, influencing them to either accelerate efforts to seek resolution of the outstanding disputes/issues or face multiplied complex problems. The externalization of periodic internal problems could provide temporary relief, but in essence, it would further complicate the existing complex problems which would then need even more careful handling.

If the South Asians do not pay heed to the dictates of time, they are likely to be left behind. A major war in the region could cause havoc (because of the likely deployment of nuclear weapons) and destroy the region. It is not just the question of the retardation of growth, it would be total destruction. Even if nuclear weapons are not employed, a war would destroy the carefully groomed SAARC, retard growth, provide extreme disincentives for foreign investors causing their flight, and pave the way for increased religious militancy, ethnicity, sectarianism, drug trafficking, and terrorism to reach uncontrollable proportions.

The fourth source of tension is rooted in domestic developments and consequential policy pursuits. South Asia is a region which is blessed with a great diversity of religions and cultures. The long history of South Asia clearly indicates that almost all the great religions managed to gain some sort of foothold in the region. For years these religions continued to live side by side peacefully. However, with the arrival of the British, tensions between the followers of various religions began to appear. All religions suggest a code that aims to provide a divine source of strength and improve human behaviour. However, when the notion of imposition gains grounds, irritants surface which in turn tend to lead to conflictual situations. A simple glance at the history of South Asia will clearly show that while differences continued to be aired periodically religious conflict remained dormant and never acquired such dangerous proportions as to jeopardize state security.

RISE OF RELIGIOUS EXTREMISM: MAJOR FACTORS

Admittedly, the threats to regional security emanate from a combination of local, regional, and global factors, but in recent times religious violence has increased in South Asia. The advent and activities of the *jihadis* in Pakistan, the *Hindutva* ideology of the RSS and the activities of the Sangh Parivar in India, the separatist notions of the Tamils in the north of Sri Lanka, and ideologies such as the Maoist movement in Nepal, all reflect this trend. Religion-based nationalism, along with ideological extremism, has led to an alarming rise in violence.

Three main factors have given rise to religious conflicts/extremism in South Asia; the manipulation and effective exploitation of internal frictions by the outsiders, poor economic growth; and poor governance. A simple glance at Indian history clearly reveals that before the arrival of the British, there were hardly any major communal clashes within India. But after the British arrived religious clashes began to increase. Undoubtedly the British exploited the situation to their advantage, initially to establish the British Empire, later to sustain it, and at the time of departure, to ensure future dependence.

As mentioned earlier, an outside major power's involvement in any region is primarily the product of either the changes in the global environment or the changes in its policy pursuits devised to attain its interests. For small powers, the major consideration of forging closer ties with one or more major powers stems from a desire to sufficiently reduce the incumbent military imbalances and to accelerate its economic development. Ideological proximity and complementarity of interests often make it easier for both the major power and the small power to come closer to each other. The changing international environment and the emerging trends often cause adjustments and shifting loyalties in congruence with the dictates of emerging realities.

The second major factor that facilitates the rise of religious conflicts revolves around poor economic growth. Following independence, none of the South Asian countries maintained an impressive growth rate, though in recent decades India appears to be doing rather well. While the growth rate was poor, the population rate was impressive. Poor economic performance has given birth too many problems such as unemployment, malnutrition and other health problems, and income inequalities, along with the problem of the ever-increasing population. The decade of the 1990s saw a rapid rise in poverty. South Asia now has the dubious distinction of being home to more than 40 per cent of the world's poor surviving on less than one dollar a day.

By many accounts, the overall GDP growth rate in South Asia was not all that unimpressive during the 1990s yet it is the same decade in which poverty kept on rising. The average growth rate of South Asia was more than 5 per cent, though in the 1990s, the smaller regional states' performance was not at all that impressive. India's growth rate, however, was indeed impressive.

The third factor that appears to have contributed towards religion-oriented conflicts is poor governance. The inability to improve economic conditions and governments' tendencies to employ religious and ethnic cards to sustain their rule have increased the influence of religious extremists in South Asian societies. Some political parties indulge in manipulative politics. They are known to have links with extremists whom they support and protect as well as use whenever necessary. Violence is employed by militant groups as one of the effective means of manipulative politics. A combination of all these factors produces conflict situations and extremists in a society. Many of the ruling groups are known to have exploited the situation either to gain power or to sustain their rule.

ANALYSIS OF THE SOUTH ASIAN SITUATION

Almost all South Asian states have religious minorities but religions have not really caused an outbreak of a major war. It has always been a combination of various factors which also included religious contributions. Religious cleavages sometimes make the reconciliation path rather difficult. The era of typical religious wars such as the crusades is over and in modern times religion may be employed in conjunction with other developments or factors in order to make the best of the situation Admittedly, the establishment of Pakistan is sometimes attributed to only religious factors. It would be appropriate not to ignore other factors such as economic reasons or the contribution of Congress party leaders or British designs, etc., all of which substantively contributed and facilitated the advent of Pakistan.

Religions alone, in modern times, have not been a source of a major conflict, but the effective use of religions in conjunction with other operative factors has proved to be an effective instrument, especially in mobilizing the support of co-religionists or even to exploit the situation. The history of the region is replete with examples of religions being employed in order to attain stated or hidden objectives. Dwelling on religious exploitation facilitates policy pursuits.

The Soviet invasion of Afghanistan in 1979, was finally repulsed by the consequential US involvement along with the support of *jihadi* groups and Pakistan; but the hasty departure of the Soviets left Pakistan to face the dilemma of the growing strength of these militant groups, which in turn became a security threat in the post-Soviet withdrawal period. The subsequent use of religion in politics further complicated the situation. Similarly, the Iranian revolution and its consequential support of Shia groups in Pakistan and Bangladesh further exacerbated the situation.

The rise of *Hindutva* forces as a political phenomenon in India provided the much-needed support to militant forces resulting in the intensification of communal- and religion-based conflicts. The rapid rise of extreme Hindu nationalism not only resulted in periodic eruptions of violence but also provided the government with the opportunity to enact laws granting emergency powers. Over the years, a series of black laws like the Terrorists and Disruptive Activities Act (TADA), the Prevention of Terrorism Act (POTA), etc., were passed.

The conflict in Sri Lanka is a product of a combination of communal, ethnic, and linguistic factors, with majority–minority politics playing a key role. It becomes further complicated when one realizes that the religious divisiveness is along ethnic lines. The external factor also made its contributions.

In Nepal the case is slightly different as the country is facing an ideologically based extremism led by Maoists which is indeed a major security threat. Again, it was Nepal's communist party that proclaimed a people's war in order to seize power. However, close scrutiny indicates that the social and economic disparity between certain regions and classes is the real cause. A combi-nation of politico–economic and the incumbent socio-cultural factors enabled the Maoists to mobilize strength.

SECURITY DEBATES

The security situation is a product of both the internal and external sources. Perhaps the most important prerequisite for analysing any country's security problems is the identification of threats emanating either from external sources or from within. Threat is an environmental condition which makes one realize that one is likely to be deprived of one's coveted values and important possessions. 'The operative military doctrine and the existing forces posture are often designed to meet the perceived threats.' The main function of a military doctrine is to maximize the effectiveness of a state's military capabilities.

Security, essentially in negative terms, 'connotes the absence of real and perceived threats, whether stemming from external sources or internal turmoil or economic disparities and social inequalities to certain coveted values'. To deal with such threats effectively, nations seek power (political, economic, and military). Power can lead to prosperity and prosperity may generate more power. While this process is still somewhat continuous under the existing international political system in which states are theoretically sovereign independent entities, the traditional paradigms of security are undergoing transformation primarily because of many significant global developments along with the technological revolution.

Global developments of far-reaching consequences make it imperative to broaden the traditional concepts of national security in order to include areas like the rapid depletion of resources, increasing population, and environmental issues. For the developing world, two other areas need to be incorporated into the new definition of national security. With them, economic-related problems and social inequalities, along with the surfacing of ethnicity, religious militancy and terrorism, qualify for inclusion in the broadened concept of security. The expanded definition is usually referred to as the concept of comprehensive security. Etymologically, comprehensive security implies a satisfactory sense of security in all essential walks of life.

To attain comprehensive security one has to initially identify and evaluate the incumbent threats emanating from varied external and internal sources. Among the external threats, traditional threat to physical boundaries, injection of subversive ideas and insurgency movements, deprivation of essential goods upon which a nation is heavily dependent through blockade or sanctions appears to be prominent. Similarly, internal threats may emanate from economic, political, social, ethnic, and military sources. Among the threats that are frequently mentioned are illegal immigration, proliferation of small arms, drug trafficking, violence caused by ethnicity, communalism, widespread poverty, suppression of human rights, social and economic inequalities, etc. All of these developments could and have often resulted in destabilization which, in turn, may transform into a major security threat.

To cope with threats emanating from external and internal, military and non-military sources, different schools of thought have been promoting different approaches. Some advocate violent means while the others opt for more peaceful pursuits. One major group believes that the most effective means for dealing with perceived threats, especially external threats is via well-established institutions like the armed forces or the police. What about internal problems like revolution, subversion, and violent struggle for power, coups d'etat? Internal disorders range from ordinary crime to a full-scale civil war. It has often been observed that a minor internal disturbance snowballs into an acute international conflict situation reflecting the known characteristics of national security problems. At what stage should rulers undertake effective measures to deal with the situation. Should they wait and watch until the insignificant minor disturbance acquires a threatening magnitude or should they employ violent corrective means almost immediately? Minor disturbances are often the result of economic or social dissatisfaction.

The opponents of this group see heavy reliance upon the sole monopolies of sanctified means of violence (armed forces and police) as detrimental to the greater interest of the society. They tend to mistakenly project the institutions of armed forces and police as potential threats to the liberty of man in society. They advocate the obsolescence of military and other violent means and often stress that alternatives must be found to replace these traditional methods of national survival. While criticizing the sanctimonious means of violence, this group suggests that security must be perceived essentially in non-military terms such as the provision of education, employment, social welfare, housing, food, health and sanitation facilities. It seems to be a logical extension of an old idea that security lies in the defeat of the five major evils of society—Want, Disease, Ignorance, Squalor, and Idleness. Assuming that one has been able to get rid of all these evils of society and has acquired the much desired cultural refinement and economic prosperity, would it not then be right to assume that the principal concern in such a society would revolve around the preservation of what has been achieved? Experience indicates that economically prosperous and well-established states have also sought security in the traditional methods of building up their military machines. The military machine defends their coveted values, deters aggression, provides effective support for their political and diplomatic bargaining, gives them confidence, and serve as an index of their power and prestige.

Both schools seem to be obsessed with only one aspect, though a very important one, of national security, and therefore both are guilty of underplaying the other equally important aspects. The exponents of the armed forces are over-projecting the utility of the military. They are focusing on external threats exclusively, ignoring that threat which emanates from within. They tend to accord almost negligible respect to those aspects of security that stem from a lack of economic security or well-entrenched social inequalities.

A comprehensive approach needs to be employed, which would

include both violent and non-violent means. It must take into consideration the external and internal threats as well as the threats emanating from economic insecurity and social inequalities. Comprehensive security requires that a state should protect its citizens from external and internal dangers as well as provide economic and social opportunities with a view to improving the quality of life for its citizens. To deal with the external dangers emanating from aggression or the aggressive behaviour of another state, the development of the armed forces is often deemed necessary. But to deal with dangers originating from domestic sources, a much more comprehensive strategy is required, which would include the transformation of the traditional concept of security and opting for a balanced approach conceding appropriate importance to economic, social, and military elements. For developing countries to provide adequate economic and social security along with military security is indeed not an easy task. While deeply engaged in developmental pursuits, some developing countries have been able to go beyond the military security.

REMEDIAL MEASURES

Sharp regional disparities, along with social backwardness and with a sizeable population excluded from the economic, political, and social mainstream and deprived from enjoying the fruits of development, provide ample grounds for religious exploitation. Communalizing politics for political gains seems a popular instrument in South Asia. The religion card is often employed because of its effective influences in socially backward and economically deprived communities. The BJP's and the Sangh Parivar's persistent attempts to promote Hindu chavuinism caused a reaction among secularists and other religious minorities, which eventually resulted in facilitating the advent of a new regime. Similarly in Pakistan, the poor performance on the economic front and poor governance allowed sufficient space to religious groups to capitalize on it.

Being a man of optimism blended with realism, I feel the South Asians are likely to recognize the dictates of time and will opt for a more cooperative attitude than they have so far demonstrated.

Indeed it would require a concerted effort from all involved. Not only does governance need to be improved and the aspirations of the people accorded the respect they deserve, but also a steady improvement in the economic sector aimed to improve the quality of life for the people, is also needed to transform trends from extremism to moderation.

For obvious reasons regional conflicts should be subjected to an intense and sincere search for resolution. While there seems to exist among the countries of the region a recognition of being left behind if they do not resolve their regional bickering, the notion to get out of the complex issues on their own terms still persists. Thinking in regional terms and promoting the collective interests of the South Asian region could eventually provide the much-sought for solution.

CHAPTER 11

Military Confidence Building Measures in the India–Pakistan Context

SATISH NAMBIAR

A GENERAL PERSPECTIVE

Military Confidence Building Measures (CBM) are as old as conflict itself and were no doubt invoked in ancient and medieval times for the same reasons as they are invoked today: to provide a measure of reassurance to belligerents so as to prevent conflict from breaking out. And in the process, allow time and space for the initiation of talks, negotiations and discussions towards the resolution of differences. In some cases the momentum is driven by internal forces seeking change, and in others it is propelled by external actors who, for reasons of their own, do not wish to see conflict breaking out. Needless to say, the measures are most effective when initiated in combination with other moves in a wider framework of conflict resolution.

Modern CBMs in the international context are associated with the Cold War setting and are often cited as the basis for implementation within the India–Pakistan context. While there is little doubt that many lessons can be learnt from that experience, the India–Pakistan confrontation has a dimension that needs to be addressed in its own way. The nuclear status of the two countries introduces an altogether different dynamic to any earlier equation. In this context it is useful to examine what CBMs in the Cold War confrontation managed to achieve. While no one really knows the answer definitively, there is a general feeling the efforts were worthwhile. Some strategic thinkers are of the view that CBMs helped prevent war by stabilizing deterrence. Others argue that the CBM process was really a method by which the western bloc successfully influenced security thought in the Soviet bloc of countries, to its advantage as things turned out. There is another section of thinkers who argue that beyond a point CBMs impeded the prospects of reconciliation and peace because they induced a sense of complacency. Or, possibly, that there was hardly much point investing in the tortuous process of resolution of the disputes when there was reasonable assurance that stable peace would be ensured anyway. Even so, there can be little doubt that some benefits did accrue. Firstly, there was much interaction between various actors on both sides, which even if it did not always lead to solutions or agreements, afforded opportunities for understanding one another's points of view and quite often revealed convergence of positions. Secondly, there was occasion for introspection and review of one's own positions, assumptions, and strategic goals. And thirdly, there was an increased awareness that the other side's security was in many ways linked to one's own.

A HISTORICAL PERSPECTIVE OF THE INDIA–PAKISTAN SITUATION

Non-Military CBMs

In the India–Pakistan context, despite the depth and intensity of the antagonism between the establishments of the two countries and the fact that they have resorted to war against each other, there have been many initiatives for the maintenance of peace, promotion of better understanding, and some degree of co-operation at the official and non-official levels. In the immediate aftermath of a traumatic and bloody partition, a number of contentious issues were addressed satisfactorily, namely, the transfer of official assets, prevention of an even larger exodus of refugees, protection of the rights of minorities, property compensation to refugees, maintenance of places of worship, resolution of some territorial claims, and so on. The Indus Water Treaty is one of the most important non-military CBMs in place. There are other agreements like setting up a joint commission to strengthen good neighbourly relations and to promote co-operation in a number of areas such as economics, health, science and technology, sports, travel, tourism, and consular matters. Agreements have also been signed to ease visa difficulties and police reporting, open telephone circuits between selected cities, reopen the railway route in the Rajasthan/Sind Sector, end double taxation on each other's airlines, and so on. In August 1992, both countries agreed on a code of conduct for the treatment of diplomatic and consular personnel. This was reaffirmed by the foreign ministers of the two countries in July 1994. The Simla Agreement of 1972 and the Lahore Declaration of 1999 are landmark CBMs that incorporate non-military as well as military CBMs.

The unfortunate reality is that despite such an impressive array of non-military CBMs, actual implementation has been tardy and often overtaken by events like the Kargil war in mid-1999, the military mobilization on the border in 2002, or terrorist attacks against innocent civilians in various parts of India. It would appear that there is almost a deliberate effort by vested interests to undermine implementation. The real challenge therefore has always been, and will continue to be, to ensure that the CBMs agreed upon are protected from the compulsions of domestic politics in the two countries.

Military CBMs

The Karachi Agreement of 1949 may be classified as a military CBM because despite some basic infirmities it provided a sound basis for the resolution of misunderstandings on the then Cease Fire Line (CFL), at least till August 1965, when Pakistan sought to change the status of Jammu & Kashmir (J&K) through the infiltration of armed groups. In 1960, the two sides reached an agreement on the ground rules to be observed along the international border and this has generally held.

The terms of the Simla Agreement of 1972, following which the Line of Control (LoC) in J&K was delineated, had all the ingredients of an effective CBM, and generally held till 1989, when Pakistan-sponsored insurrection was initiated in the Kashmir valley. A telephonic communication linking the Directors-General of Military Operations (DGMO) of both sides was established and has been in regular use, particularly since 1987. This has stood the test of time and even in times of extreme tension proved useful. It has often been instrumental in preventing local situations from boiling over. Examples that can be cited from the present author's personal experience are the possible misunderstandings that were addressed during the conduct of Exercise Zarb-e-Momin in 1989–90 by Pakistan, and Indian troop deployment in 1990–1 in the Punjab to deal with the terrorist menace in that state. Similar communication links in the Baramulla–Murree and Rajauri–Kotli sectors were put in place but remained unactivated for various reasons.

In April 1991, both sides signed an agreement (negotiated by a defence delegation led by the present author) on prior notification of military manoeuvres at specific levels within certain distances of the border/LoC. This agreement also stipulated distances beyond which fixed- and rotary-wing aircraft may fly, and elaborated on the exchange of communication and signals by naval craft to avoid clashes at sea.

Nuclear CBMs

With the overt nuclearization in the subcontinent in May 1998, an altogether different dimension was added to the stand-off between the two countries. It is possibly a measure of the maturity of the leadership in both countries that CBMs in this vital area were addressed as far back as 1988 when the prime ministers of the two countries signed an agreement on non-attack on each other's nuclear facilities. This agreement was ratified in 1991, and requires an annual exchange of lists giving the locations of all nuclear-related facilities with both countries pledging not to attack the other's listed facilities. It is again of some significance that these measures agreed upon have been implemented even when relations between the two countries were otherwise under severe strain. A joint declaration on the prohibition of chemical weapons was concluded in August 1992, by which both countries agreed not to develop, produce, acquire, or use chemical weapons.

A memorandum of understanding signed by the foreign

secretaries of the two countries in the presence of the two prime ministers and appended to the Lahore Declaration of February 1999 envisaged the following:

- engaging in bilateral consultations on security concepts and nuclear doctrines to develop confidence-building measures in the nuclear and conventional fields,
- providing each other with advance notification of ballistic missile tests; an agreement on this has since been put in place and is being scrupulously observed by both countries,
- undertaking national measures to reduce the risks of accidental or unauthorized use of nuclear weapons, notifying each other of any accident, and establishing a communications mechanism for the purpose,
- continuing the unilateral moratorium on the conduct of nuclear tests.

CURRENT DIALOGUE AND INITIATIVES

After the rather turbulent and sometimes menacing situation in the aftermath of the terrorist attack on the Indian Parliament in December 2001, and the deployment of the armed forces of the two countries in a confrontation mode for almost a year, most observers and analysts of the subcontinent were no doubt encouraged by the initiative taken by the then Prime Minister of India, Atal Behari Vajpayee, to resume a political dialogue, and the reciprocal moves by both sides to effect a ceasefire along the LoC. Though the political process was placed on hold while the general elections were conducted in India, the ceasefire along the LoC continues to hold and has become a vital military confidence-building measure in itself. In many ways it really is a vindication of the view held by many over the years that, for any meaningful measures between India and Pakistan to succeed, the basis has to be bilateral.

The political process has gained momentum following the installation of the new dispensation in New Delhi, and a number of meetings have been held to pursue what is called a composite dialogue. A number of proposals towards better 'people-to-people' relationships are on the table. It is understood that 71 actionable proposals have been placed by India for discussion, ranging from mobile phone connectivity across the border to extending a diesel pipeline into Pakistan. On peace and security, the most important development has been expert-level talks on nuclear CBMs held in New Delhi on 19 and 20 June 2004. The joint statement issued at the end of these talks visualizes that

- The existing hotline between the two DGMOs would be upgraded, dedicated and secured.
- A dedicated and secure hotline would be established between the two foreign secretaries through their respective foreign offices to prevent misunderstandings and reduce risks relevant to nuclear issues.
- Both countries would work towards concluding an agreement with technical parameters on pre-notification of flight-testing of missiles, a draft of which was handed over by the Indian side.
- Each side reaffirmed its unilateral moratorium on conducting further nuclear test explosions unless, in the exercise of national sovereignty, it decides that extraordinary events have jeopardized its supreme interests.
- Both countries would continue bilateral discussions and hold further meetings to work towards the implementation of the Lahore MOU of 1999.
- Both countries would continue to engage in bilateral consultations on security and non-proliferation issues within the context of negotiations on these issues in multilateral forums.
- Both countries called for regular working-level meetings to be held among all the nuclear powers to discuss issues of common concern.

Since then, talks have been held on various issues including Jammu & Kashmir, infiltration across the LoC, terrorism, scope for the disengagement of forces on the 'Glaciers', and so on. As things stand, talks on these aspects have so far remained just 'talks'. There does not appear to have been much movement forward. The saving grace may be that there has been no breakdown or movement backwards.

Some of the other measures that are on the table in so far as military CBMs are concerned apparently include the following; a number of which have been on the table before but were never considered seriously:

- an agreement on peace and tranquility on the LoC; building on the current ceasefire,
- new communication links between the two navies and air forces; re-establish communication links at Division/Corps Commander level at Kargil–Gilgit, Baramulla/Kupwara–Murree, Rajauri–Jhelum, Jammu–Sialkot, and so on,
- communication links between Indian Coast Guard and Pakistani Maritime Security Agency,
- development of links between the armed forces through exchange of visits by naval ships; seminars between academic and research institutions dealing with strategic and defence related issues; exchanges/lectures/seminars between defence training establishments; friendly sporting tournaments and joint adventure activities between the two militaries; exchange of visits by military bands,
- periodic meetings between the two Directors-General of Military Operations and annual meetings between the Vice Chiefs of the Army.

THE WAY AHEAD

There can be little doubt that most ordinary people in India and Pakistan place great hopes on the success of the current initiatives. So also do the other countries on the subcontinent (the SAARC community), countries in the extended region (Southern Asia), and the wider international community. The stand-off between the two countries has not only stunted the growth of the two countries, but also impacted adversely on the potential for growth in the subcontinent and the region. Hence much is at stake in the process of reconciliation between the two countries.

Having stated that, it would be fallacious to ignore or underestimate the stake some vested interests have in ensuring that rapprochement between India and Pakistan does not succeed. It would require statesmanship of a very high order on both sides, and the unqualified support of the people of both countries, for the current process to be taken to a mutually satisfactory culmination. This is not beyond the realms of possibility. However ground realities will need to be recognized and appropriately factored into the dialogue processes so as to ensure that attempts at sabotage are pre-empted. This is particularly important if the military CBMs are to be effectively implemented.

It has been mentioned earlier that the decision by General Musharraf to order a ceasefire on the LoC with effect from 26 November 2003, and immediately responded to by the Indian establishment, has been one of the most significant military CBMs put in place between the two countries in recent years. It is pertinent to point out in the context of these deliberations that there is a strong section of the strategic community in India that takes the cynical view (not entirely misplaced) that the declaration of ceasefire by General Musharraf along the LoC in Jammu & Kashmir was a clever tactical move to enable the Pakistani forces to focus their efforts without distraction on dealing with the situation on the western front. It is no secret that the General is under severe pressure from the USA to undertake operations on the Pakistan–Afghanistan border against the Al Qaida and Taliban elements holed up in areas where they have strong support. Whether this move towards implementing a ceasefire was undertaken at the instance of the USA (which may also have put pressure on India to respond positively), is also a matter of some speculation. American interest and involvement is related to its desire for a stronger and more stable relationship with India and at the same time its need for assistance from Pakistan to deal with the Al Qaida and the Taliban. The declaration of a ceasefire is further perceived as a move to soften Pakistan's image as the fountainhead of *jihadi* terrorism and nuclear proliferation; to present itself as a reasonable and responsible state. That notwithstanding, the fact remains it is an effective military CBM.

Another aspect of some relevance is that there is great distrust of the Pakistani military led by General Musharraf within the establishment in India as also among the people at large. His role in the Kargil conflict and attempts in Agra to outsmart and score points over the Indian political leadership are still fresh in the memory of many in India. It is also of significance that the current initiatives are constantly commented upon by him as contingent on the resolution of the problem of Jammu & Kashmir. A recent report attributed to the General recently to the effect that once the Jammu & Kashmir question is resolved to Pakistan's satisfaction, the '*jihadi* elements operating from within Pakistan would have to wind up their activities and leave' only further hardens the position of the more cynical sections within India. For, as long as a position is taken that any moves for better understanding and rapprochement between India and Pakistan are totally hostage to the Jammu & Kashmir issue, there is little scope for progress; hence the scepticism about the current process among many in India. It is somewhat ironic, but true, that in any assessment, analysis or prognosis today, Pakistan and General Musharraf are more or less synonymous. That is not the case with India where neither the prime minister, nor the chief of the army staff has such unbridled authority and power. They are answerable to the establishment. It is in this context that an individual in the personality of General Musharraf becomes so important for the credibility of the process. We in India may draw some satisfaction from the fact that General Musharraf sees himself as Pakistan's man of destiny; and may therefore be prepared and willing to display statesmanship that someone with fewer pretensions would be reluctant to demonstrate. He seems to be determined to take Pakistan to its rightful place within the comity of nations. This he cannot do without coming to terms with the situation on the subcontinent; which really means ending or at least easing the confrontation with India. Unless of course he believes that he can be successful in breaking up the Republic of India or achieving parity with India politically, economically and militarily.

The way ahead therefore appears to lie in:

- Seizing opportunities for moving forward; without trying to outsmart each other or score 'brownie' points;
- Seeing if there are any lessons we can draw from the India–China experience, moving from the easy to the difficult, developing a vested interest in the stability of ties;
- Avoiding the rhetoric of animosity, isolating vested interests;
- Recognizing the reality of our nuclear status and the responsibilities it imposes on us; and
- Building people-to-people relationships.

CHAPTER 12

Intra-State Armed Conflicts in South Asia: Impact on Regional Security

SUBA CHANDRAN

DEFINING ARMED CONFLICT

This study is narrowly focused only on the armed intra-state conflicts in South Asia. While 'intra-state conflicts' is a vast subject including ethnic, environmental, economic, and social aspects, this study takes into account only those conflicts that have witnessed armed struggle between two or more groups.

Second, the study does not make any distinction on the basis of intensity of conflict. An *armed conflict* is defined as 'a contested incompatibility which concerns government and/or territory where the use of armed force between two parties, of which at least one is the government of a state, results in at least 25 battle-related deaths'.[1] A *major armed conflict* is defined as 'a contested incompatibility that concerns government and/or territory over which the use of armed force between the military forces of two parties, of which at least one is the government of a state, has resulted in at least 1,000 battle related deaths in any single year'.[2] An earlier definition of a *major armed conflict* described it as 'prolonged use of armed force between the military forces of two or more governments, or one of one government and at least one organized armed group, incurring the battle related deaths of at least 1,000 people during the entire conflict and in which the incompatibility concerns government and/or territory'.[3] For the purpose of this discussion, intra-state armed conflict is defined as an armed conflict between two groups of which one is the state, in which violence has been used by either or both parties resulting in human and material casualties.

Third, the study focuses primarily on ongoing armed intra-state conflicts. In South Asia, some of the armed conflicts have come to an end, while some lie dormant and others remain active. The analysis is limited to data on armed conflicts since 1991.

INTRA-STATE ARMED CONFLICTS IN SOUTH ASIA: SALIENT FEATURES

An analysis of armed intra-state conflicts in South Asia would reveal that, first, armed conflicts in South Asia have been primarily intra-state rather than inter-state since the 1950s. Since the late 1980s, South Asia has been witnessed a sudden growth in intra-state conflicts. When compared to intra-state conflicts, inter-state conflicts in South Asia in the last two decades were negligible or absent. The only inter-state armed conflict occurred between India and Pakistan during 1999. Besides 1999, there were two instances in which there were threats of an inter-state armed conflict, but due to various reasons, there were no open hostilities. Even at the global level, the armed conflicts were more at intra-state levels than inter-state. For example, according to a study, between 1990 and 2002, there were 58 major armed conflicts in 46 different locations, of which all but three were internal.[4] According to another study published between 1989 and 2003, there were 116 armed conflicts, of which 89 were intra-state, 20 inter-nationalized intra-state and 7 inter-state.[5]

Second, intra-state armed conflicts in South Asia are not monolithic in nature. They differ in their nature, causes of birth, intensity, etc. For example, the intra-state armed conflicts in Pakistan are related to terrorism, *jihad* and sectarianism; secessionism in Sri Lanka; left wing, terrorism, communalism, and secessionism in India; and left wing in Nepal. Even Bangladesh and Bhutan have witnessed armed intra-state conflicts in the recent past. The Maldives is the only country in South Asia that has remained free from any intra-state armed conflict.

Third, intra-state armed conflicts in South Asia do not have the same intensity in terms of armed violence since 1991. In most cases, the intensity waxed and waned throughout the period. However, in some cases, armed hostility continued without any major respite.

INTRA STATE ARMED CONFLICTS IN SOUTH ASIA: CRITICAL QUESTIONS

I. *Why are there More and Protracted Intra-State Conflicts than Inter-State Conflicts in South Asia?*

There have been more intra-state conflicts than inter-state conflicts at the global level, as has been seen earlier. The same trend was also reflected in South Asia. While there are many reasons for this trend, some are more crucial than others.

PROBLEMS OF NATION BUILDING

Invariably every state in South Asia is still in the process of nation building, a process that is complex and burdened with the presence of numerous actors with different demands and grievances—real and imagined. The states invariably, in the whole of South Asia, unfortunately considered themselves the successors of British India, and perceived these demands as threats to their legitimacy and instead of addressing them attempted state building rather than nation building. Instead of coopting the various groups into their fold in the nation-building process, states alienated them through confrontation. As William Zartman has phrased it eloquently; the internal conflicts emerge due to the 'inability or unwillingness of the government to handle grievances to the satisfaction of the aggrieved; that is they begin with the breakdown of normal politics'.[6]

MULTIPLE ACTORS WITH DIVERSE OBJECTIVES

Unlike inter-state conflicts, in most cases, there are more than two actors in any intra-state conflict. An agreement between two state actors engaged in an inter-state conflict where the stakes are high is likely to be resolved sooner. In an intra-state conflict, besides the state, there are other actors that are both political and militant. In the case of India, even the state is reflected in two entities—the federating unit and the federation. Jammu & Kashmir is a classic example of this. The 'state' is represented by the Union government and the state of Jammu & Kashmir. The governments in New Delhi and Srinagar at times had different objectives. The difference between these two has been reflected in so many cases. For example, in June 2000, the state legislative assembly passed a resolution demanding more autonomy for the state.[7] Though Atal Behari Vajpayee, the then Prime Minister of India commented that the resolution was within the framework of the Indian Constitution,[8] it was rejected at the subsequent Cabinet meeting.[9]

Besides the differences between the state actors, non-state actors are divided. In the case of Jammu & Kashmir, besides the mainstream political parties, there are other actors including the All Parties Hurriyat Conference (APHC) and the militant groups. The Hurriyat divided vertically into two factions after the split in 2003.[10] The two factions are now being led by Syed Ali Geelani and Moulvi Omar Farooq. The militant groups are also equally divided and there are three main groups—Lashkar-e-Toiba, Jaish-e-Muhammad and the Hizb-ul-Mujahideen.[11]

PROBLEMS OF DE-WEAPONIZING AND DE-MILITARIZING

The problems of the state and society in de-weaponizing and de-militarizing create an uncertainty factor about the post-conflict situation and opportunities amongst the non-state actors. In an inter-state armed conflict, the actors get back to their pre-conflict situation without disbanding and disarming, with their personal and economic security stable and safe. Unfortunately, in an intra-state conflict, where there are non-state actors involved, the problems of integrating them with the mainstream starts with an element of disarming and disbanding, which creates feelings of insecurity among them.

In South Asia, there are numerous cases in which an initial agreement with a non-state actor failed to materialize due to this factor. One of the reasons the government of Pakistan has failed to reach an agreement with the militants in South Waziristan is disarming and disbanding. Even in Sri Lanka, disarming was one of the main reasons why the LTTE resumed fighting after the July 1987 agreement between India and Pakistan.[12]

Besides, there are severe problems in dealing with the surrendered militants and this issues is acute in the Indian states of Assam, and Jammu & Kashmir. In Assam, a section of surrendered cadres of the United Liberation Front of Asom (ULFA) is called 'Surrendered ULFA' (SULFA). There are nearly 7,000 SULFA members in Assam, and the government is yet to come out with a comprehensive package to deal with them.[13]

The SULFA 'control the coal and transport syndicates, have indulged in large-scale extortion and intimidation, and usurped government tenders. Most of them have not cared to refund their bank loans. . . . It is alleged that the SULFA cadres played an important part in the former Asom Gana Parishad (AGP) government's "secret killings" policy to eliminate the relatives of the ULFA leadership; but they have proved to be a real menace now in the State.'[14] Even amongst the state security forces, there are differences over whether the SULFA needs to be completely disarmed and disbanded.[15]

In Jammu & Kashmir, the surrendered militants, known as *Ikhwans,* are today seen as a liability. According to a news report, 'local residents view them (the Ikhwans) with deep suspicion—some even with contempt—for switching sides. Mainstream parties sneer at their recent attempts into electoral politics. Even the Army admits their limited use.'[16] There were also reports accusing the *Ikhwans* of aiding in the search for new infiltration routes even after being appointed as Special Police Officers within J&K police.[17]

There was no standard policy towards *Ikhwans* in Kashmir. There are around 3,000 *Ikhwans,* being paid by the different security forces including the Army, BSF and J&K Police. The Army used to pay them each a monthly salary of Rs. 3,000 along with Rs. 5 lakh insurance, while the J&K Police used to pay Rs. 1,500 per month.[18] There was an attempt in December 2003 to convert these *Ikhwans* into a full-fledged Territorial Army battalion.[19] The decision was pending in the Cabinet Committee and Security in December 2003 and there have been no further reports on the outcome. Most of the *Ikhwans* were incorporated into the J&K's Special Operations Group (SOG), which was disbanded after Mufti Sayeed became the chief minister of the state. On the other hand, Mufti has also been advocating for a rehabilitation package for the surrendered militants, which would be entirely funded by the Union government.[20]

II. *Why do Intra-State Conflicts Wax and Wane in Certain Regions and Remain Constant in the Others?*

Invariably in most protracted armed conflicts, the intensity has never remained constant. Many factors contribute to the level of intensity and its sustenance.

IMPACT OF POPULAR SUPPORT

The popular support to an armed conflict could be overt and/or covert and also voluntary and/or forced. If the support is overt and voluntary, then the situation reaches dangerous proportions. The initial phases of militancy in Punjab, Jammu & Kashmir and Sri Lanka witnessed such overt and voluntary support; as a result the armed conflict was at its peak and the state had fewer options for restoring normalcy. Invariably, in all such cases in South Asia, this overt and voluntary support for the initial phase of militancy declined into covert and forced support for the armed movements.

Why does the initial overt and voluntary support decline into covert and involuntary? The primary reasons are, firstly, the people and those who are leading the armed conflict, after a period of time, realize the futility of such action against the state, which is well armed and also better equipped—economically and politically—to deal with the situation. Also, the initial romance of fighting the state dissipates once it is realized that the state is not weak enough to be demolished. The initial phases of militancy in Jammu & Kashmir and Sri Lanka witnessed this phenomenon. The leader of the JKLF, Yasin Malik and Javid Mir, were the first to realize the futility of an armed conflict with the Indian state, hence they came overground and started fighting politically. In Sri Lanka, many of the non-LTTE militant groups came overground by the second half of the 1980s.

Second, state response to the armed conflict in economic, political, and military terms also has an impact in reducing the overt and voluntary popular support to the armed conflict in its initial phase. The state, besides responding militarily also provides adequate economic and political space for the grievances to be met. The intelligence and counter-militancy efforts become more focused, making it difficult for the armed groups to operate freely. Coupled with this modicum of success on the military front, the state provides adequate space to the political groups and even militant groups to negotiate. The state, in certain cases, also rejuvenates its machinery, thus improving the standard of governance. When there is an improvement in the delivery mechanisms of the state in terms of governance, many of the local grievance are met; hence the local support for an armed conflict declines.

Third, the intra-conflict amongst the various armed groups in an armed conflict ultimately hits the local people. Both in Jammu & Kashmir and in Sri Lanka, the rivalries between the various armed groups had their own collateral damage, making the people realize that the militant groups were an immediate threat to their peace and security.

Fourth, over a period of time, most of the armed groups degenerate into nothing more than criminal groups with vested interests. The armed conflict is used as a means to further their ends and for any popular cause. When the militant groups resort to kidnapping and extortion from the local population, they become totally alienated from the people for whom they were allegedly fighting. In the north-east, there were numerous cases of militant groups engaging in extortion.[21]

STATE RESPONSE

Besides popular support, the response of the state is crucial in determining the longevity of an armed conflict and its intensity. In most cases, the beginning of an armed conflict and the popular support towards it appears from nowhere. The state after the initial shock wakes up to the reality and pursues a series of economic, political, and military measures. This economic, political, and military response has a crucial role to play in terms of sustenance of the armed conflict. If the state fails to use these three components in the right combination, then its efforts only increase the gap between it and the people, thereby increasing or sustaining the armed conflict. On the other hand, if the state succeeds in providing adequate space to the people while dealing successfully with the armed groups, the intensity of the conflict automatically comes down.

The states in many cases in South Asia, extended invitations to the armed groups for negotiations and to an extent have also succeeded in keeping them engaged in select regions in South Asia. This has had a direct impact on the intensity of the armed conflict, even if one principal group is engaged in the dialogue. In recent years the Government of India was willing to engage in dialogue and so were the armed groups. In 2004, the Union government engaged in a dialogue with the NSCN (IM);[22] The All Tripura Tiger Force (ATTF) in Tripura announced its willingness to negotiate with the Government of India in May 2004;[23] two factions of the National Liberation Front of Twipra (NLFT) decided to engage in talks in April, and one led by Mantu Koloi also agreed to lay down its arms in May 2004;[24] and the NDFB in October 2004 declared a ceasefire, announcing its willingness to initiate a dialogue.[25] In Jammu & Kashmir, in July 2000, the Government of India initiated negotiations with the Hizb-ul-Mujahideen.[26] Even the security forces, as part of building their public relations with the society, have initiated welfare programmes. For example, the Indian Army carries out welfare measures in both Jammu & Kashmir and the north-east, which have a positive impact.[27] In Jammu & Kashmir, the Indian Army has been carrying out a successful programme called *Operation Sadbhavana*.

In Nepal, since 2001, the government has engaged the Maoists in dialogue on many occasions, but has failed to convert the ceasefire into a permanent peace. In July 2001, the Maoists declared ceasefire, followed by three rounds of negotiations during August–November.[28] The next round of negotiations took place from February to August 2003, after the government and Maoists declared a ceasefire in January 2003.[29] In South Waziristan in Pakistan, the government initiated a series of negotiations with the tribal militants in 2004.

The success or failure of these negotiations has a crucial impact on the armed conflict. Whenever they have failed, as in the cases of Nepal, Sri Lanka, Jammu & Kashmir, and South Waziristan, the armed conflict has resumed with an added intensity. Where there has been relative success, adequate pressure is created by the civil society to maintain the ceasefire and take it to its logical conclusion. Besides, any success in one set of negotiations influences the other armed groups in the region to enter into negotiations. The recent success in select armed conflicts in India's north-east in terms of engaging the armed group in negotiations, to an extent, is the outcome of ongoing dialogue between the government and the NSCN (IM).

SUPPORT FROM THE DIASPORA

Support from the diaspora is another crucial element in sustaining the armed conflict in a region. Diaspora support is crucial, especially in terms of the economic and political sustenance of an armed conflict. The Sri Lankan diaspora in the case of Tamil Eelam movement and the present support to the LTTE, and the Punjabi diaspora during the Khalistan movement in India played a significant role in the armed conflict.

III. *Is there a Change in the Nature of Intra-State Conflicts in South Asia?*

Intra-state armed conflicts, in general, were primarily based on subnationalistic identities. Outside the leading subnational armed conflicts, South Asia also witnessed the naxalite movements, the intensity of the armed nature of which also waxed and waned over a period of time. Armed conflicts, to a large extent, have remained secular. However, there seems to be a slow but steady change in certain conflicts which are becoming sectarian and communal, or sectarian and communal conflicts becoming the dominant armed conflict in select regions. In Pakistan, the armed conflicts have assumed a sectarian nature, in the last couple of years. In Kashmir, there is a clear trend in which the struggle for an independent Kashmir is becoming a *jihad* and a fight for Islam. There have been numerous reports linking religion and militancy in the recent years in India's north-east.

Recent years have witnessed many reports on the growth of

Islamic militancy in India's north-east. The 2 October 2004 attack in Dimapur is worth mentioning, in which not only the state, but even the non-state actors have claimed a link between religion and militancy. Two bombs exploded simultaneously in Dimapur —in the railway station and a nearby market—killing more than twenty-five people.[30] An army officer was quoted as saying, 'We had positive information about a group of 20 fundamentalist organization-trained Bangladeshi *jihadis* sneaking into Nagaland through the Karimganj border. They had an agenda of carrying out large scale violence in the north-east, but nobody probably realised that it would be such a devastating attack in Dimapur.'[31] The Khaplang faction of the NSCN in Nagaland blamed the Al Qaida for the bomb blasts in October 2004.[32] Earlier an unknown outfit called 'Al Jehad-e-Islam' had claimed responsibility for this blast.[33] Select groups in India's north-east are also believed to have increased their contacts with the religious militant groups. For example, there are numerous reports linking the ULFA with fundamentalist organizations.[34]

The change is clearly visible in Jammu & Kashmir, where the armed conflict is slowly but steadily being taken over by the *jihadi* forces from militant groups. There were a series of attacks on the minority community in the last few years. Most of these attacks are not isolated, but well organized, with the objective to terrorize the minority community (see Table 12.1).

TABLE 12.1: ATTACK ON MINORITY COMMUNITY IN JAMMU & KASHMIR SINCE 1998

District	No. of Attacks	Persons Killed in each Attack	Total
Udhampur	6	9, 4, 5, 7, 8, 3	36
Doda	17	26, 15, 20, 29, 13, 4, 5, 6, 5, 5, 15	143
Rajauri	10	11, 9, 3, 12, 10, 5, 4	54
Poonch	4	9, 5, 2, 6	22
Anantnag	4	15, 7, 13, 2	37
Pahalgam	3	23, 5, 8	36
Jammu	4	13, 30, 28, 13	84
Pulawama	1	24	24

Source: Collected from various newspaper sources.

In Pakistan, the armed conflict in South Waziristan, besides the organized attacks in all parts of the country, has *jihadi* and sectarian undertones (see Table 12.2).

TABLE 12.2: SECTARIAN KILLINGS IN PAKISTAN

Month/Year	Persons Killed
June 2003	13
July 2003	54
March 2004	47
May 2004	15 & 18

IV. *Are the Intra-State Armed Conflicts Becoming More Violent?*

The intra-state armed conflicts have always been violent. However, a crucial question that needs to be asked is whether the intra-state conflicts are becoming more violent compared to the decade of the 1990s? An analysis of the armed conflicts in the recent years proves the case to be so, in select regions including Pakistan, Jammu & Kashmir, and India's north-east.

While there were always casualties on a regular scale, there is a trend in recent years in which there have been colossal attacks involving massive casualties. Also, some of these attacks are spectacular, minor in terms of human casualties but major in terms of the target chosen.

Why are the intra-state conflicts becoming more violent and spectacular? There could be several reasons. One, the state has been successful in its counter-militancy operations; hence the armed groups find it difficult to conduct their day-to-day operations. As a result, they plan meticulously to make their operations successful so as to make their presence felt. Two, due to continuous splits and also due to the mushrooming of new armed groups, there are several groups in the same region, at times fighting for the same cause. In order to make themselves popular or seen as the most active group, they each need to indulge in such spectacular activities. The fact that after every major attack a particular group owns responsibility for the attack could be taken as proof to substantiate this thesis. Three, perhaps the violence threshold of the local population has increased, thanks to the prolonged nature of an armed conflict in a region. People become indifferent to the killings and view them as a routine affair; hence these groups need spectacular attacks to capture popular attention.

Some of the recent attacks highlight the changing nature of armed conflict in terms of increased intensity and the target chosen (see Table 12.3).

TABLE 12.3: MAJOR ATTACKS SINCE 2001

April 2001	On 2 April, in Nepal, 300 Maoists attacked police post in Rukum district killing 31 policemen and abducting more than 20.[35]
July 2001	On 7 July 2001, Maoists killed 41 policemen in the remote districts of Nuwakot, Lamjung and Gulmi in Nepal[36]
November 2001	On 24 November 2001, in Nepal, 39 people were killed including soldiers and policemen.[37]
February 2002	On 17 February 2001, Maoists killed 138 people, mostly from the security forces in Nepal.[38]
September 2002	On 8 September 2002, in Nepal Maoists killed 65 people, mostly from the police forces.[39]
June 2003	On 8 June 2003, 13 Shiite police trainees were massacred in Quetta in Pakistan.[40]
July 2003	On 4 July 2003, 44 Shiites were killed in a sectarian attack in Quetta.[41]
December 2003	On 14 December 2003, a suicide attack was carried out against Pakistani President, General Musharraf.[42]
July 2004	On 30 July 2004, a suicide attack was carried out against Shaukat Aziz, who luckily survived. The attack killed 7 others in Fateh Jang.[43]

Suicide terrorism, though it has been witnessed in Sri Lanka since the late 1980s,[44] it has attained alarming proportions over the last few years in other parts of South Asia, especially in Pakistan and Jammu & Kashmir. The *Fidayeen* attacks in Jammu & Kashmir, though it cannot be strictly defined as suicide attacks, the fact is such attacks have increased the intensity of the armed conflict, affecting the morale of the security forces and creating a sense of helplessness in the society.[45]

NOTES

1. Uppsala University's Conflict Database has been following this definition; Peter Wallensteen and Margareta Sollenberg, 'Armed Conflict 1989–2000', *Journal of Peace Research*, vol. 38, no. 5, pp. 629–44; see http://www.pcr.uu.se/research/UCDP/
2. Mikael Eriksson, Margareta Sollenberg, and Peter Wallensteen, 'Definitions, sources and methods of conflict data', Appendix 2B in *SIPRI Yearbook 2003*, Oxford University Press, 2003, p. 122.
3. Margareta Sollenberg, Peter Walensteen and Andres Jato, 'Major Armed Conflicts', *SIPRI Yearbook 1999*, Oxford University Press, 1999, p. 15.
4. Mikeal Eriksson, Margareta Sollenberg and Peter Wallensteen, 'Patterns of major armed conflicts, 1990–2002', Appendix 2A in *SIPRI Yearbook 2003*, Oxford University Press, 2003, p. 109.
5. Mikael Eriksson and Peter Wallensteen, 'Armed Conflict, 1989-2003', *Journal of Peace Research*, vol. 41, no. 5, September 2004, p. 626. The study considers those intrastate conflicts with foreign interventions as 'internationalized intra-state conflicts'.
6. William I. Zartman (ed.), *Elusive Peace: Negotiating an end to Civil Wars*, Washington DC: Brookings Institution, 1995, p. 5.
7. 'From the State Autonomy Committee Report', *Frontline*, 8–21 July 2000.
8. 'Autonomy resolution within Constitution: PM', *The Hindu*, 1 July 2000.
9. *The Hindu*, 5 July 2000.
10. Anirudh Suri, 'Recent Developments in the Hurriyat—I', Article no. 1134, http://www.ipcs.org/Kashmir_articles2.jsp?action=showView&kValue =1143&issue=1012&status=article&mod=a, 13 September 2003; Anirudh Suri, 'Recent Developments in the Hurriyat—II', Article no. 1135, http://www.ipcs.org/Kashmir_articles2. jsp?action=showView&kValue=1144&issue=1012&status=article&mod=a, 13 September 2003; Anirudh Suri, 'Recent Developments in the Hurriyat—III', Article no. 1136, http://www.ipcs.org/Kashmir_articles2. jsp?action=showView&kValue=1145&issue=1012&status=article&mod=a, 13 September 2003; and Amin Masoodi, 'Is Hurriyat a Political Force', Article no. 1088, http://www.ipcs.org/Kashmir_articles2.jsp?action=showView&kValue=1097&issue=1012&status=article&mod=a; 11 August 2003.
11. Suba Chandran, 'Kashmir: Issues and Actors', in P.R. Chari and Suba Chandran (eds.), *Kashmir: The Road Ahead*, New Delhi: IPCS, 2001, p. 9.
12. S.D. Muni, *Pangs of Proximity: India and Sri Lanka's Ethnic Crisis*, New Delhi: Sage Publications, 1993, p. 132.

13. 'Special package for SULFA men soon: Gogoi', *The Assam Tribune*, 7 June 2004.
14. Bibhu Prasad Routrau, 'Surrendered Militants in India's Northeast: Outlived Utilities?', http://www.ipcs.org/North_east_articles2.jsp?action=showView&kValue=273&status=article&mod=a; Ajai Sahni and Bibhu Prasad Routray, 'SULFA: Terror by Another Name', *Faultlines*, vol. 9, pp. 1–38.
15. Nitin Gogoi, 'Assam police divided over disarming SULFA', 8 January 2001, http://in.rediff.com/news/2001/jan/08assam.htm
16. Kanwar Sandhu, 'Former militants and their law of diminishing returns', *Indian Express*, 9 December 1999.
17. '6 SPOs held for searching new infiltration routes', *Daily Excelsior*, 1 January 2001.
18. Sandhu, op. cit., 9 December 1999.
19. Saikat Datta, 'Army to explore new territory: Surrendered militants', *Indian Express*, 13 December 2003.
20. 'Many militants ready to discard gun: Mufti', *Daily Excelsior*, 11 February 2004.
21. 'ULFA, NDFB extortion unabated in State', *The Assam Tribune*, 1 May 2004
22. 'NSCN (IM) leaders to come India for talks', *The North-East Tribune*, 12 February 2004; Wasbir Hussain, *Naga Peace Talks: Can Delhi Convert The Truce Into A Deal?*, IPCS Issue, Brief no. 25, August 2004; 'NSCN (IM) leaders likely to visit India in Feb', *The North-East Tribune*, 17 January 2004.
23. 'Tripura militants to hold talks with New Delhi', *Hindustan Times*, 1 May 2004.
24. 'NLFT factions declare ceasefire for talks', *The Assam Tribune*, 17 April 2004; 'NLFT faction to lay down arms on May 6?', *The North-East Tribune*, 5 May 2004; 'Over 60 NLFT ultras to lay down arms today', *The Assam Tribune*, 6 May 2004; '72 NLFT bids farewell to arms', *The North-East Tribune*, 7 May 2004.
25. 'NDFB declares unilateral ceasefire', *The Assam Tribune*, 9 October 2004; 'NESO, AASU hail NDFB truce offer; urge ULFA to follow suit', *The Sentinel*, 12 October 2004; 'Centre asks NDFB to make formal offer', *The Assam Tribune*, 14 October 2004; and 'NDFB formally appeals for ceasefire', *The Assam Tribune*, 15 October 2004.
26. 'Centre invites J&K militants for talks', *The Hindu*, 29 July 2000; 'PM hails ceasefire offer', *The Hindu*, 26 July 2000; 'Security forces told not to jeopardize ceasefire', *The Hindu*, 27 July 2000; 'Positive development: Hizbul', *The Hindu*, 30 July 2000.
27. Nishit Dholabhai, 'Army project heals old scars', *The Telegraph*, 7 June 2004.

28. 'Government, rebels declare cease-fire', *The Kathmandu Post*, 24 July 2001; 'Priority to Dialogue: Maoists respond to Deuba's offer, halt offensive acts', *The Rising Nepal*, 24 July 2001; 'Maoists Call Off Violent Tactics: Hopes Rise For Resolving Problem', *The Rising Nepal*, 27 July 2001; Prem N. Kakkar, 'Government-Maoists' Talks: A Good Beginning', *The Rising Nepal*, 31 August 2001; 'Maoists to present agenda in next round of talks', *The Rising Nepal*, 1 November 2001; 'Govt-Maoist Talks Rekindle Peace Hope', *The Rising Nepal*, 1 November 2001; J. Pande and Kamal Panthi, 'Govt-Maoists talks get underway in Bardia', *The Kathmandu Post*, 14 September 2001.
29. 'Govt, Maoists announce ceasefire', *The Kathmandu Post*, 30 January 2003; 'Pun holds informal talks with Maoist team', *The Kathmandu Post*, 5 February 2003; 'Govt officially invites Maoists for talks', *The Kathmandu Post*, 7 February 2003; Yuvraj Acharya, 'Maoists commit to nationalism and peace: Sign 22-point code of conduct for peace talks', *The Kathmandu Post*, 14 March 2003.
30. 'Terror bursts, blood gushes', *The Telegraph*, 3 October 2004.
31. 'Army harps on jihadi hand', *The Telegraph*, 5 October 2004.
32. 'NSCN-K sees Al Qaeda footprints in Dimapur blasts', *The Assam Tribune*, 21 October 2004
33. 'Muslim outfit behind Dimapur blasts', E-Pao.net, 16 October 2004.
34. 'Police sees link between ULFA and Islamic fundamentalist groups', *The North-East Tribune*, 20 September 2004.
35. 'Rebel hits kill 35 policemen, Two dozen more abducted', *The Kathmandu Post*, 3 April 2004.
36. 'Maoists kill 41 policemen in Lamjung, Nuwakot and Gulmi: Rebels loose [*sic*] five in fierce gun battles', *The Kathamndu Post*, 7 July 2001.
37. 'A bloody end to the ceasefire: At least 39 killed in Maoists hit in Dang, Syangja', *The Kathmandu Post*, 25 November 2001.
38. 'Govt forces suffer heavy losses in Achham: At least 138 dead, Mangalsen torched, Bank looted', *The Kathmandu Post*, 18 February 2002.
39. 'Maoists kill 65 in Arghakhanchi: Toll could soar, as dozens reported missing', *The Kathmandu Post*, 9 September 2002.
40. '11 police recruits gunned down in Quetta', *Dawn*, 9 June 2003.
41. 'Attack on Quetta imambargah leaves 44 dead: Suicide bombing suspected; curfew clamped after rioting', *Dawn*, 5 July 2003.
42. 'Musharraf's convoy escapes bomb blast', *Dawn*, 15 December 2003.
43. 'Seven killed in suicide bomb attack: Shaukat survives assassination bid', *The News*, 31 July 2004.
44. R. Ramasubramanian and Beryl Anand, 'Suicide bombings in Sri Lanka: A Chronology (1987–2003)', *IPOST*, September 2004, vol. 1, no. 2, pp. 7–14, available at http://www.ipcs.org/02-IPOST-Sep04.pdf;

idem, *Suicide Terrorism in Sri Lanka*, IPCS Research Paper 5, New Delhi: Institute of Peace and Conflict Studies, August 2004, available at http://www.ipcs.org/IRP05.pdf.

45. B. Rajeshwari and R. Radhakrishnan, 'Suicide and Suicidal Attacks in Jammu and Kashmir: A Chronology', *IPOST*, October 2004, vol.1, no. 3, pp. 4–9, available at http://www.ipcs.org/03-IPOST-Oct04.pdf

CHAPTER 13

Indo–Bhutan Relations: Recent Trends

TASHI CHODEN

INTRODUCTION

The Kingdom of Bhutan is often described as being physically small with limited economic scope and military might. In spite of these limitations, Bhutan has earned the reputation of being a peaceful country where the development of threats from militancy, terrorism, and economic disparity within itself has virtually been absent. In this sense, Bhutan has thus far been more fortunate than many of its neighbours in the South Asian region.

This has been in part to its self-isolationist policy up until the second half of the twentieth century, and the preservation and promotion of a strong sense of identity which has ensured social cohesion and unity. Having never been colonized, nor feeling any direct impact of two world wars and the Cold War, Bhutan has been spared the conflicts and turmoil such as the legacy of hatred and mistrust generated by the partition of British India into present-day India and Pakistan.

Nevertheless, the Bhutanese have historically been sensitive to issues of security, with frequent disturbances occurring from internal warring factions prior to the unification and establishment of the monarchy in 1907. External threat was present during the seventeenth and eighteenth centuries with several failed attempts at invasion from the Tibetans; nineteenth century Bhutan saw the loss of the Assam and Bengal Duars to British India.[1] As such, preserving its sovereign independence and territorial integrity has always been a matter of great importance for Bhutan.

By the first half of the twentieth century, developments in the Himalayan region prompted Bhutan to re-evaluate the usefulness of its isolationist policy. Within this context, Bhutan began to develop political orientation towards its southern neighbour—nurturing a close relationship with India was one way of enhancing its own territorial security while at the same time enhancing the prospects for socio-economic development. As for India, with its contentious state of relations with China, Bhutan's strategic location between the two ensured its service as a buffer state which could enhance its own security.

The initiation of Indo–Bhutan friendship as it stands today is credited to the efforts of Indian Prime Minister Jawaharlal Nehru and His Majesty Jigme Dorji Wangchuck, the third king of Bhutan. Their meeting in the 1950s sparked the dialogue for development cooperation. Looking back over the decades since then, and under the continued guidance of the present king, His Majesty Jigme Singye Wangchuck, Indian assistance has greatly expanded in every field of Bhutan's development and socio-economic growth. To this day, India continues to provide the largest and most diverse assistance to Bhutan among all other donors. Often cited as a 'shining' example of friendship and cooperation between a large country and a small neighbour, relations between the two continue to grow at all levels.

A BACKGROUND ON INDO–BHUTAN RELATIONS

Recorded historic relations between Bhutan and India date back to AD 747, when the great Indian saint, Padmasambhava, introduced Buddhism in Bhutan, which has since then permeated all aspects of Bhutanese life. Aside from such shared cultural and religious heritage, other areas of interaction developed during the British rule in India, and include several Anglo–Bhutanese skirmishes and battles that were consequently followed by treaties and agreements. It was within this period of interaction with the British that trade between Bhutanese and Indians was also recorded to have taken place for the first time (1873).

China's invasion of Tibet (1910–12) and the subsequent claims made on Bhutan resulted in the signing of the Treaty of Punakha in 1910 with British India. Although this treaty served to expel any claims that China might have tried to make, it did not define Bhutan's status technically or legally; for the Bhutanese, this was a source of uncertainty over its relations with India at the time that the British rule was nearing an end. After India's independence in 1947, 'standstill agreements' with Sikkim, Nepal, and Tibet were signed to continue existing relations until new agreements were made; for Bhutan, its status became clearer following Nehru's invitation for a Bhutanese delegation to participate in the Asian Relations Conference in 1947. Following this, the negotiation for a fresh Indo-Bhutan Treaty began in the summer of 1949.

The basis for bilateral relations between India and Bhutan is formed by the Indo-Bhutan Treaty of 1949, which provides for, among others, 'perpetual peace and friendship, free trade and commerce and equal justice to each other's citizens'.[2] The much-speculated Article 2 in the treaty, in principle, calls for Bhutan to seek India's advice in external matters, while India pledges non-interference in Bhutan's internal affairs.

The geopolitical scene in the entire Himalayan region and Indian subcontinent underwent great change following the proclamation of the People's Republic of China in 1949, and the takeover of Tibet by the People's Liberation Army in 1950. These events, plus the presence of Chinese troops near Bhutan's border, China's annexation of Bhutanese enclaves in Tibet, and the perceived threat from China, all led Bhutan to re-evaluate its traditional policy of isolation; the need to develop its lines of communications with India became an urgent necessity. Consequently, Bhutan was more inclined to develop relations with India, and the process of socio-economic development began thereafter with Indian assistance. For India's own security, too, the stability of Himalayan states falling within its strategic interest was a crucial factor to consider. With border tensions between India and China escalating into military conflict in 1962, India could not afford for Bhutan to be a weak buffer state.

Against this backdrop, Indo-Bhutan relations began to take concrete shape following state visits made by the third king, His Majesty Jigme Dorji Wangchuck to India, and by Prime Minister

Jawaharlal Nehru to Bhutan between 1954 and 1961. Besides emphasizing India's recognition of Bhutan's independence and sovereignty in his public statement in Paro, Nehru's visit in 1958 was also significant in that discussions were initiated for development cooperation between the two countries.

Formal bilateral relations between Bhutan and India were established in January 1968 with the appointment of a special officer of the Government of India to Bhutan. The India House (Embassy of India in Bhutan) was inaugurated on 14 May 1968, and Resident Representatives were exchanged in 1971. Ambassadorial-level relations began with the upgrading of residents to embassies in 1978.

Beginning with India, Bhutan began to diversify its relations in the international community, thereby projecting its status as an independent and sovereign nation. With India sponsoring Bhutan's application for UN membership in 1971, the leaders of the two countries demonstrated that Article 2 of the Indo–Bhutan Treaty was not a restricting factor in the exercise of Bhutan's foreign policy.

AREAS OF COOPERATION

Development Assistance and Economic Relations

Planned development in Bhutan began in 1961, with the first two Five Year Plans (FYP) wholly financed by the Government of India (GOI). Over the years, Indian assistance has increased steadily from Rs. 107 million in the first FYP to Rs. 9,000 million in the eighth FYP. Road construction by the Indian Border Roads Organization started in the first FYP (1962–6); the second FYP (1966–71) focused on public works, education, agriculture and health. While Bhutan's source of foreign aid has diversified significantly since it became a member of the United Nations, India continues to be the major donor of external aid to Bhutan–Indian assistance accounted for about 41 per cent of total external outlay during the eighth FYP (1997–2002). Over the last four decades, India has provided assistance mainly in the social sectors such as education and human resource development, health, hydropower development, agriculture, and roads. In addition, India also provides partial or full grant assistance and gradually, economic relations have evolved with cooperation extending towards mutually beneficial projects such as hydropower development and industrial projects.

These projects are taken up outside of the FYP programmes with many major works awarded to Indian companies. Important projects invested in under Government of India–Royal Government of Bhutan (GOI–RGOB) cooperation include the Chhukha (336 MW), Kurichhu (60 MW), and Tala (1020 MW) Hydropower Projects; the Penden and Dungsam Cement Projects; and the Paro Airport Project. A Memorandum of Understanding for preparing a detailed project report for the proposed 870 MW Puna Tsangchhu Hydropower Project was also signed between the two governments in September 2003. With the huge Indian market for electricity currently facing domestic supply difficulties, Bhutan has high potential to offer supply relief to India—presently, approximately 90 per cent of the electricity generated in Bhutan is exported to India, and this translates only to 0.5 of the total demand. Other mutual benefits generated by the Indian-assisted and Bhutanese government-owned projects include assured business opportunities in the manufacturing and other industries in both India and Bhutan.

Trade and Investment

A new era in Bhutan's foreign trade commenced following the closure of trade routes between Bhutan and Tibet in 1960, and the construction of roads linking the Bengal–Assam plains to Phuentsholing, and Phuentsholing to Thimphu and Paro in 1962.

Over the period 1981–2001, Bhutan's exports to India accounted for an average of 86.5 per cent of its exports, and imports from India accounted for an average 79 per cent of the total imports. Bhutan's main items for export to India are electricity, mineral products, products of chemical industries, base metals and products, and wood and wood products, with hydropower generation being the most important area of comparative advantage. Imports from India include a wide range of items such as machinery, mechanical appliances, base metals, electronic items, foodstuff, and other basic necessities and consumer items.

Besides trade, Indian involvement extends into many other areas of Bhutan's private and public sector activities. In the area of Foreign Direct Investment, Bhutan has so far pursued a conservative policy, and the first and only foreign investor in Bhutan for almost two decades since 1971 was the State Bank of India (SBI). The SBI has worked in collaboration with the Bank of Bhutan (BOB) since its identification as partner in management and shareholding in the capital of BOB, in addition to imparting banking expertise. BOB's collaboration with SBI was last renewed on 1 January 2002 for a period of upto 31 December 2006.

In addition, Indian nationals operate a range of small-scale trading and service activities on licenses issued by the Ministry of Trade and Industry in Bhutan. Such ventures include small shops trading in a variety of products like groceries, auto parts, and furniture, as well as scrap dealers, distribution and dealership agencies. Indians in Bhutan also run hotels/restaurants, saloons, tailoring and cobbler services. On a larger scale, Indian investment in Bhutan exists in the manufacturing and processing industries, construction, service, engineering, steel and electronic industries, and consultancy. Indian companies such as the Jaiprakash Industries and NHPC carry out major works for the Tala and Kurichhu Power Projects respectively. Similarly, many other Indian and Bhutanese companies (or joint ventures) benefit from the current requirements of massive power projects and manufacturing industries.

Although there is no in-depth study available on the level of informal trade between the two, it has been noted that such activities are tolerated in practice partly because of the open and porous border between Bhutan and India.[3] Another informal but common practice is the operation of a wide range of businesses by Indian persons using the licenses of Bhutanese nationals as indigenous fronts. These include anything from small shops trading in petty consumer items to large-scale investment businesses such as construction. To quote a CBS study:

The prevalence of small-scale Indian investment as well as business fronting is understandably concentrated in southern Bhutan owing to proximity of bordering Indian towns. The border town of Phuentsholing is the centre of commercial hub in the country from where the exit and entry of goods as well as travelers largely takes place; the Indian town Jaigoan under Jaipalguri district is 'just across the fence' where tailor-made foods suited to Bhutanese needs are especially stocked. Although statistics are not available, it is apparent that the business community in Jaigoan has prospered in large part owing to the level of trading activities with Bhutanese businessmen and other customers.

Labour Relations

Beginning with the inception of development plans in the 1960s, Bhutan's requirement of semi-skilled and unskilled labour has been filled by expatriates, particularly Indians, first in road construction and then in other sectors such as mining, agro-based industries and hydropower projects with the shift in development priorities. This dependence has sprung from the lack of in-country experience and skills in road construction as well as technical skills and equipment. Indian personnel and labourers were recruited in large numbers, mainly from neighbouring Indian states. While Indian labourers found employment on Bhutanese roads, Bhutanese labourers (who were mostly farmers) were spared the burden of solely undertaking the construction works. Currently, public road maintenance is entrusted mainly to Project Dantak,[4] and at any given time it has an average of 2,000 Indian labourers working on roads in various parts of Bhutan.

Considering that the modern system of formal education in Bhutan was initiated only after 1955, and that it was a few decades before the first generation of qualified Bhutanese entered the civil service, many Indian personnel were recruited by the Bhutanese government to fill administrative posts and posts related to development programmes in the 1960s. While Bhutanese nationals have gradually replaced Indians in these posts, many of the latter continue to serve in both public corporations and the civil service to this day.[5] However, a turning point has come where the successes of modern education have helped Bhutanese nationals to gradually replace Indian expatriates in various professions such as teaching, health and medics, engineering, accounting, and administration.

Additional Areas of Cooperation

India's assistance to Bhutan's security and defence arrangements, specifically in training and equipping the Royal Bhutan Army, was prompted by several factors which include Bhutan's location in India's strategic defence system, the Chinese occupation of Tibet, the 1962 border war between India and China and the perception of increasing Chinese threat. Besides training and courses for army personnel conducted by the Indian Military Training Team (IMTRAT) in the past, Bhutanese army cadets continue to be sent to the National Defence Academy (NDA) in Pune, and the Indian Military Academy (IMA) in Dehra Dun, India. The presence of IMTRAT can be seen when one travels between the districts of Paro, Haa and Thimphu in western Bhutan. The headquarters of the IMTRAT in Bhutan is located in Haa district, which is adjacent to Tibet's Chumbi valley. Its establishment in Thimphu includes the Friendship Hospital, locally called the IMTRAT Hospital, which offers invaluable services to Bhutanese patients as well. In addition to building schools and hospitals in the country, an important defence consideration has been the construction of extensive roads by India's Border Roads Organization, called Project DANTAK, in Bhutan.

The benefits of Indo–Bhutan relations are also prominent in other areas such as education and culture where there is a high level of interaction. The Indian government provides about fifty scholarships annually to Bhutanese students for higher studies in India. A significant number of Indian teachers contribute to education in Bhutan, with many of them posted in the remote areas of Bhutan. In addition, Sherubtse College in eastern Bhutan has developed into a premier institution for tertiary education, with affiliation to the University of Delhi in India. The exchange of cultural troupes and artists between Bhutan and India has also become a regular activity under the bilateral cultural exchange programme. In 2001, a cultural exhibition titled, 'The Living Religious and Cultural Traditions of Bhutan' was hosted by the

Indian government at New Delhi and Kolkata; consequently, a six-month Festival of India was held in Bhutan from June to November 2003. The main purpose of these initiatives has been to strengthen the ties of friendship, and to create awareness among the people of the many areas of the commonalities between the two countries.

Other areas of cooperation include bilateral civil aviation dating back to 1983, when Bhutan's national airline Druk Air began commercial operations to India with flights from Paro to Kolkata and later from Paro to Delhi in 1988. An Air Services Agreement signed with India in September 1991 granted Druk Air Fifth Freedom Rights; following a new commercial agreement in May 1998, these Rights were provided on concessional terms. A Government of India notification that same year qualified Druk Air to avail itself of fuel at bonded rates, and its fuel continues to be supplied by the Indian Oil Company. By 2000, Druk Air was also granted permission to use Bagdogra as a diversionary airport for refuelling, technical halts, and during bad weather conditions. With permission from the Department of Civil Aviation in India, Druk Air inaugurated flights on the Paro–Bodhgaya Sector on 11 November 2003, thus offering services to Bhutanese making their annual pilgrimage.

In the international forums too, India and Bhutan can be seen to be supportive of each other. While Bhutan has not always voted identically with India on every issue thereby expressing its own choices, it has maintained a consistent pattern of support to India on many occasions and significant issues. To name a few, the vote on the Comprehensive Test Ban Treaty (CTBT), the establishment a of Nuclear Weapons Free Zone in South Asia, India's aspirations to be a permanent member of the UN Security Council, India's candidature to various international bodies, negotiations in the WTO, and the importance of India in the success of SAARC.[6]

A strong tradition of official visits at various levels has further enabled views to be exchanged and areas of cooperation to be enhanced between the two countries. Besides everyday people-to-people contact at the informal level, ministers, parliamentarians, civil servants, as well as representatives of the business community all make regular official visits. His Majesty King Jigme Singye Wangchuck himself has made at least fifteen visits to India since 1971.

SOME ISSUES OF CONCERN

While India and Bhutan share an extraordinarily warm friendship, issues such as the state of relations with China continue be a cause of some concern to both countries. Considering the importance of Bhutan's economic relations with India, the liberalization policies and their implications for Bhutan is an additional development to take into account. More recently, in 2003, the illegal presence of militants using Bhutan as a base and hideout while rebelling against the Indian government resulted in the Bhutanese army taking military action to flush out the insurgents.

Relations with China

In the light of the contentious state of Indo–China relations, it is no secret that Bhutan with its strategic location factors into India's security interests. Therefore, whatever course Indo–China relations may follow in the future, it is likely that they will bear implications for Indo–Bhutan relations as well. While it may not be realistic to expect that Indo–China relations will normalize in the immediate future, it is not something that should be considered impossible over the course of time. Some confidence-building measures are being taken by both sides, for example, discussing the boundary issue, the regular exchange of high-level visits, and agreements to enhance cooperation in areas such as culture, trade, science and technology. In the long term, normalization in Indo–China relations, and consequently the degree to which strategic considerations influence India's policy towards Bhutan, is a possibility that should be considered. And even as current geopolitical and geoeconomic realities ensure that India will continue to be one of the most critical elements in Bhutan's foreign relations, Bhutan has to consider the reality of China to its north. As such, for Bhutan to maintain friendly relations with

China without undermining its own relations with India is a challenge that deserves careful consideration.

India's Liberalization Policies

Up until the 1990s, Bhutan had enjoyed a more or less protected status in its trade relations with India. With economic liberalization on the rise in India, however, Bhutan is facing a gradual loss of this status, and unless Bhutanese industries are able to remain competitive they could lose their market share in the increasingly open market in India. Bhutan has already felt the impact of the reforms in India's subsidy policies which has resulted in a gradual phasing out of subsidies and a decrease in its budget for assistance to Bhutan. Bhutan will also have to face the effects that would be brought on by India gradually moving towards privatizing its power, petroleum, and other traditional public sectors.

Military Operations Against Indian Militants

Over the 1990s or so, the illicit establishment of camps by the United Liberation Front of Assam (ULFA), National Democratic Front of Bodos (NDFB) and the Kamtapuri Liberation Organization (KLO) militant outfits[7] in the dense jungles of south-east Bhutan has been a matter of great concern and security threat for Bhutan. In addition to hampering businesses and the implementation of development activities in many parts of the country, the presence of these militants had the potential to adversely affect the friendly relations enjoyed by Bhutan and India.

In consideration of the close ties between Bhutan and India, and recognizing that the militants (despite their actions) are nonetheless Indian citizens from the neighbouring states of Assam and West Bengal, the Bhutanese government repeatedly urged them to leave the country peacefully. But in spite of the Bhutanese government having spent almost six to seven years in trying find a peaceful solution to the problem,[8] it was apparent by the final months of 2003 that the militants had no real intention of leaving Bhutan until their own objectives had been fulfilled.[9] Again to quote the CBC study:

In December 2003, with the talks with the ULFA and NDFB having failed, and the KLO not even responding, the Bhutanese government's repeated attempts at a peaceful solution came to an end. On the morning of 15th December 2003, the Bhutanese army finally launched military operations to flush out the militants. Even as security forces took over all thirty of the militants' camps into the second day of offensive, the combing process and the implications of the operations have brought forth the reality, that the long spell of peace and tranquility that has been the proud inheritance of the present Bhutanese generation can no longer be taken for granted.

Although the operation was considered successful, Bhutan has come to realize the need to be wary of possible repercussions following such an action. Having long kept the military option at bay in consideration of possible retaliation against Bhutanese from the militants as well as their relatives and supporters from Assam, the Bhutanese now have to be more cautious than usual while travelling through Indian territory.[10]

CONCLUSION

Aware of its small size, lack of advanced technology and military defence capabilities, Bhutan has had to rely on alternative security measures such as 'national identity for cultural cohesion, and neutrality to renew its long-term security'.[11] An added bonus to this strength has been its natural location in the Himalayas along the lines of India's strategic security interests, and consequent prospects for internal growth.

However, such a location has been a factor not only of strength but also its vulnerability. Being a landlocked, mountainous country, Bhutan's trade routes and access to the sea pass through India, and it is thus largely dependent on the latter for its economic security. While Bhutan has diversified its political and economic relations and has attained a good level of socio-economic development, the reality of its position and shared borders with India means that destabilizing elements from external sources continue to pose threats to its stability. These have been evident from the spillover effects of militancy from Assam, and of cross-border economic migration driven by regional poverty.

As the world globalizes and traditional barriers are broken down, Bhutan too is being swept into the process. Along the way, its traditional strongholds of national identity and cultural cohesion will continue to face increasing challenges, just as its long spell of internal peace and tranquility was challenged by issues emanating from regional situations like poverty, economic migration, and militancy.

Bhutanese, however, can take pride in the fact that the leadership, in particular of the present king, has guided the country along a unique development path of its own without submitting incorrigibly to external influences. And while the illicit presence of the ULFA–NDFB–KLO militants on Bhutanese soil was a shared concern of both India and Bhutan, Bhutanese leaders were clear in their stand that such an immediate security threat to its sovereignty would be taken in its stride. Thus, the military operations launched by the Bhutanese army to flush out the militants in December 2003 not only provided an assurance of Bhutan's capability to safeguard its own security, it was also another commitment made towards the maintenance of strong Indo–Bhutan ties.

Ever since Bhutan and India embarked upon the road of friendship and cooperation, the two countries have demonstrated that a journey of peace and mutual benefit between two neighbours can be pursued, even in a region where the level of economic disparity, terrorism, and conflict is high. We can perhaps look at such a relationship as a model of friendship and cooperation between close neighbours.

NOTES

1. Karma Ura, 'Perceptions of Security', in Dipankar Banerji (ed.), *South Asian Security: Futures*, Colombo: Regional Centre for Strategic Studies, 2002, pp. 59–79.
2. As quoted on the website of the Indian Embassy in Bhutan at <http: www.eoithimphu.org/indo.html>
3. The study on *Economic and Political Relations between Bhutan and the Neighbouring Countries* (CBS et al., 2004) notes that much of the informal trade is not considered illegal economic activities, but more as 'extra-legal' trading; informal trade is described here as those that are unregistered, unlicensed, and not recorded by the government.
4. An organization of the Indian Border Roads Organization.

5. In 2002, there were a total of 11,499 Indians working in 30 Indian companies undertaking joint ventures in Bhutan. There were also 734 Indians working in 24 different public corporations. In the civil service, Indians number 871 of which 128 are regular employees and 743 contract employees. Nearly 84 per cent of them are teachers in Bhutanese schools. As of August 2003, the total number of regular Indian employees was 32,776 (CBS et al., pp. 79–189).
6. CBS et al., pp. 79–189.
7. The ULFA, fighting for the independence of Assam, NDFB, fighting for an independent state of Bodoland, and KLO, fighting for an independent state of Kamtapur, had an estimated 1,560 militants in 13 camps, 740 militants in 12 camps, and 430 militants in 5 camps respectively, as reported by Bhutan's Home Minister to the 81st session of the National Assembly prior to the launch of military operations in December 2003.
8. The issue was deliberated extensively in successive sessions of the National Assembly—the 77th session in 1999 passed a three-point resolution to make the militants leave peacefully: steps would be taken to stop rations and supplies from reaching militant camps; any Bhutanese or Indian national helping militants on Bhutanese territory would be prosecuted under the National Security Act; and the government would hold talks with the leaders of the militants to reach a peaceful solution.
9. Prior to the final round of talks with the militants in December 2003, the Bhutanese government had held four rounds of talks with the ULFA, reaching an agreement during the 3rd round that camps would be removed and their cardres reduced in phases; however, camps were soon relocated and cardre strength increased. In two rounds of meetings with the NDFB, they gave no commitment to leave Bhutan and thereafter refused to come for further talks; as for the KLO, correspondence from the Bhutanese government to remove their camps were flatly ignored, and talks scheduled to be held with a high-level delegation was instead attended by junior-level leaders of the outfit.
10. Trade routes to at least twelve of twenty districts of Bhutan have to pass through Indian territory in Assam.
11. Ura, 'Perceptions of Security', pp. 59–79.

REFERENCES

CBS et al., 'Economic and Political Relations Between Bhutan and the Neighbouring Countries', in *Sub-Regional Relations in the Eastern South Asia: With Special Focus on Bangladesh and Bhutan*. Joint Research Program Series No.132, Chiba, Japan: Institute of Developing

Economies-Japan External Trade Organization (IDE-JETRO), 2004, pp. 79–189.

Chari, P.R. (ed.), *Perspectives on National Security in South Asia: In Search of a New Paradigm,* New Delhi: Manohar, 1999.

Development Towards Gross National Happiness (Main Document, 7th RTM), Thimphu: Department of Debt and Aid Management, Royal Government of Bhutan, 2001.

Hasrat, B.J., *History of Bhutan: Land of Peaceful Dragon*, Thimphu: Education Department, Royal Government of Bhutan, 1980.

Kohli, Manorama, *From Dependency to Interdependence—A Study of Indo–Bhutan Relations*, New Delhi: Vikas Publishing House, 1993.

Kuensel, Thimphu, 9 June 2001.

Mathou, Thierry, 'Bhutan-China Relations: Towards a New Step in Himalayan Politics', paper submitted for the International Seminar on Bhutanese Studies, Thimphu: The Centre for Bhutan Studies, 20–23 August 2003, pp. 174–88.

Parmanand, *The Politics of Bhutan*, Delhi: Pragati Publications, 1998.

Planning Commission, *Bhutan 2020: A Vision for Peace, Prosperity and Happiness*, Thimphu: Royal Government of Bhutan, 1999.

———, *National Accounts Statistics 1980-1999*, Thimphu: Central Statistical Organisation, Royal Government of Bhutan, 2000.

———, Five Year Plan Documents (1st, 2nd, 3rd, 4th, 5th, 6th, 7th, 8th and 9th Plans), accessed at < http://www.pcs.gov.bt/ on 7 June 2003.

Sonam, Kinga, *Changes in Bhutanese Social Structure: Impacts of Fifty Years of Reforms (1952–2002)*, Chiba, Japan: Institute of Developing Economies, 2002.

Ura, Karma, 'Perceptions of Security', in Dipankar Banerji (ed.), *South Asian Security: Futures.* Colombo: Regional Centre for Strategic Studies, 2002, pp. 59–79.

Yadav, Lal B., *Indo-Bhutan Relations and China Intervention*, New Delhi: Anmol Publications, 1996.

CHAPTER 14

Security and Governance in South Asia

JAYA RAJ ACHARYA

INTRODUCTION

Security has been one of the most important concerns of individuals, communities, and states ever since they came into existence. During the Cold War period, the major ideological camps perceived threats to their security interests from each other. The post-Cold War world has witnessed a proliferation of internal security threats in many states. The Soviet Union collapsed because of internal reasons, and the security of Russia has been challenged by the separatist movements, for example Chechnya. The USA has felt shocks such as the bombing of the Federal Sate building in Oklahoma in April 1995, and the terrorist attacks of 11 September 2001.

South Asia as a whole is one of the poorest and most conflict-ridden regions in the world. There have been many books and papers on the South Asian countries, dealing with the 'security threats' perceived as 'coming from external sources', namely, the neighbours and the global powers. There have been books and papers on the South Asian countries also facing the problems of 'security threats' or 'terrorism' for a long time. However, they do not focus much on the problem of governance, or misgovernance as a major cause for 'internal conflicts, insurgencies and terrorism.'

CAUSES OF INTERNAL CONFLICT

This study is particularly focused on incidence of mis-governance, which has resulted in the failure to substantially reduce poverty, one of the main breeding grounds of 'terrorism' and 'security threats.' It is argued in here that the main causes of internal conflict are: (i) poverty; (ii) oppression or the lack of equal freedom (autonomy, decentralized power or right to self-determination); (iii) unemployment or the lack of opportunity; (iv) injustice; and (v) misgovernance, which builds up the environment of insecurity to the people as well as the governments themselves when a group of people or a community takes up arms or uses violent means against these negative conditions that it suffers.

Conversely, (i) prosperity; (ii) equal freedom; (iii) employment opportunities; (iv) fair justice; and (v) good governance result in internal security as the people enjoy life in those positive conditions, and see no reason to take to insurgency or violent 'terrorist' activities.

South Asia as a whole has been suffering from abject poverty and deprivation leading to violent conflicts. It contains about 22 per cent of the world's population, but makes a meager 6 per cent of the world's income. More than 46 per cent of the world's illiterate live in South Asia, and 50 per cent of the world's malnourished children also live in this region (Huq 1997). There is no room, nor any need, in this study for an elaborate discussion of poverty in each country of this region.

Oppression is another major cause of conflict and national insecurity. Ethnic minorities and smaller religious communities and regional groups in South Asian countries feel oppressed since they do not enjoy the same freedom and rights and equal treatment as the traditionally privileged groups. Even in India, where politics operates more or less within the framework of democracy, the ethnic groups in the north-eastern states seem to have felt as marginalized, and there are conflicts leading to insurgencies (Verghese 1996). In Sri Lanka, the Tamils felt the same and have taken up arms. In Bangladesh, the indigenous people of the Chittagong Hill tract seem to feel insecure as they are overpowered or gradually outnumbered by the majority Muslims. In Bhutan, the Nepali-speaking people feel oppressed by the royal government. The Maoist insurgency of Nepal does not seem to have originated from the oppression of ethnic groups alone as all the poor people, regardless of their ethnic or caste identity, feel oppressed. In Pakistan, the religious minorities seem to be at the centre of such conflicts. In Sri Lanka, the Tamil–Sinhalese conflict seems to have the same cause—oppression of the minorities by the majority.

There is also a high unemployment rate in South Asiam which fuels conflict and insecurity at the individual, social, and national levels. Almost all South Asians working abroad, particularly, the Nepalese, Bangladeshi, Pakistani, and Indian labourers in the Arab countries working under harsh conditions, indicate the lack of employment opportunities at home, which is often described under the Poverty of Opportunity Index (POPI)—an example of bad or weak governance. This situation decreases the people's faith in their respective governments, and alienates them from the functioning of the state machinery as a whole.

SOUTH ASIA'S VICIOUS CIRCLE OF POLITICAL INSTABILITY AND CONFLICT

As a result of misgovernance, there has been severe political instability in certain countries of South Asia such as Nepal and Pakistan. While Nepal has presented itself as a classic case of infighting in the political parties and witnessed fourteen governments in the last fourteen years, Pakistan is playing a game of see-saw between military rule and democracy. A civil-war like situation has embroiled Sri Lanka in a very debilitating conflict for over two decades, whereas Bangladesh suffers from the non-participation of the opposition party in the parliamentary procedures, raising questions about the very validity and usefulness of the periodic general elections.

Political instability engenders instability in civil administration or bureaucracy as every new political leadership makes changes in the bureaucracy by transferring the civil servants at critical positions, thus hampering the development programmes that are meant to improve the socio-economic conditions of the society in general. And as the poverty-stricken societies of South Asia feel the despair of economic stagnation and unemployment, they become ready for any action including violence. Such violence then destabilizes the position of the government at the very top level of political leadership.

Unlike other countries in the region, India has had a more or less stable democracy. Since its independence, it has not had such a detrimental political instability (defined as 'too frequent changes in the government sometimes by military coup or other political debacles') as the changes in the governments have taken place within the framework of democracy. However, there have been other factors at the policy and practical levels, which have hindered the pace of desired socio-economic development in the country, giving rise to insurgencies and terrorism. If the state ownership and management of several industries in India before the early 1990s hampered efficiency and productivity which could have otherwise contributed to a significant reduction of poverty in the country, privatization and liberalization (in the 1990s and more recently) without proper safety nets for the poor have resulted in thousands of suicide by farmers. That is a serious matter in a country which is still predominantly agricultural.

According to *Human Development in South Asia* (1999), 'around 1,000 people took their own lives, many committing public self-immolation as a final act of protest in Pakistan during 1998–9'. This is just a part of the story of the poverty and deprivation caused by political instability and misgovernance. In Sri Lanka, Bangladesh, Nepal, and Bhutan, political instability and the resulting disruption of socio-economic development have clearly given rise to insurgencies and various types of serious social unrest.

GOVERNANCE OR MISGOVERNANCE

Political scientists have discussed the issue of governance as the function of the government, mainly the executive branch of the state. Atul Kohli (1990), Lok Raj Baral (1993), K.M. De Silva, (1993), Mushahid Hussain (1993), Urmila Phadnis et al. (1986), Bahavani Sen Gupta (1993), all put particular emphasis on the political aspects and administrative capacity of the government to maintain peace and security in the country. Economists have discussed the question of governance in terms of its role in the economic growth and equity in society. The *Nepal Human Development Report* (2001), for example, is titled 'Poverty

Reduction Governance'. Undoubtedly poverty reduction, through economic growth, is one of the main functions of the government in any South Asian country.

However, for a citizen or a lay person, it is clear that governance is a broad concept, and much more than the function of the executive branch of the state described by the political scientists, or just the question of economic growth and equity described by the economists. It involves the legislative, executive, and judiciary and other bodies such as the bar associations, the election commission and human rights commission, political parties, and the role of the civil society. It involves the very process of the creation of the state power: the question of the legitimacy of the government, its authority to rule, or its monopoly in the use of violence at times when it may be necessary indeed.

The legislative part of the state does not seem to properly represent the people in the region. Almost half of the parliamentarians in India and Pakistan are landlords (Mahbub ul Huq Human Development Centre, 1999). Once elected, the parliamentarians do not remain in touch with the people. Some of them have not spent even the special budget given to them by the government for the socio-economic development of their constituencies. Although the practice of giving such a special budget to the incumbent MPs may be questionable since it gives them an additional edge against their rivals in the periodic elections that are expected to be fully free and fair, there is such a provision in many South Asian countries. But wherever the MPs have spent the budget, there have been allegations of misappropriation. In the highly stratified society of the region, a huge number of poor people, ethnic or tribal communities, and caste groups feel unrepresented or under-represented in the parliaments, wherever they exist. There are conflicts associated with ethnic or tribal identities in almost all countries of South Asia.

The executive branches of the sates in South Asia are allegedly acting in a manner that is not accountable to the people. Though the bureaucracies are highly bloated, there is inefficiency, corruption, and a rent-seeking tendency. Some countries in the region are ranked by Transparency International as some of the highest in the corruption scale. Even India witnessed cases like the Bofors scandal. There does not seem to be adequate decentralization of authority in smaller countries such as Nepal and Bhutan. Development planning and implementation of projects ignore the people from whom they are meant.

The people have little faith in the judiciary. The people of South Asia in general find it very difficult to get justice in the legal courts in their own countries. 'A basic deficiency of the judicial system throughout the region has been the lack of effective access to justice for large sections of the population, mainly due to poverty' (ibid.). Justice is also delayed in South Asia for several reasons. Many countries have a huge number of pending cases in the court: Bangladesh (6.5 million), India (22.0 million), Nepal (0.08 million), Pakistan (0.75 million), thus about 29.3 million cases in total. Also, there have been persistent allegations of corruption in the legal courts of these countries. In summary, bad governance characterizes South Asia in general.

The Election Commissions and Human Rights Commissions are weak. Elections in India have become much fairer since the power of the Election Commission were strengthened. Booth-capturing or vote-tampering were common even in India where democracy has been regarded as in relatively better condition than in other South Asian countries. Sociologists and political analysts had therefore developed the theory that such cases of booth-capturing took place only where political parties had their strongholds anyway, so the election results would be more or less the same even if there were no such incidents. In a way, such theories gave a certificate of validity to the elections, despite their being so flawed. In Nepal, the incumbent parties usually won the elections by the misuse of power.

The political parties in South Asia have not been able to organize themselves on the basis of ideology, policies, and programmes. There is a culture of personal loyalty and oppor-tunism, which can hardly be called 'a political culture'. The tendencies of dynastic rule are cited not only in smaller countries such as Bhutan, Nepal, Sri Lanka, Bangladesh and Pakistan, but also in India. This seems to be a South Asian political culture.

GOOD GOVERNANCE

The quality of governance is determined ultimately by popular perception. The questions are: How are the elections organized? How do the people feel about them? Are they fair—not just in terms of free and fair polling and the correct counting of votes but also in terms of who the candidates are, and whether they represent various sections and the moral expectations of the society or not? If the legislative body and the executive branch do not emerge as representatives of, and accountable to, all the sections of the society in a true sense, the elections hardly establish the legitimacy of the government.

In summary, people's participation, accountability to them and transparency (PAT) are the three main elements of good governance, that must be reflected in all the bodies and functioning of the state. They are inter-related in such a way as to form a three-sided prism. Free and fair elections become a legitimizing process only if the people's participation in them is truly voluntary, and if the elected leaders are truly representative. Accountability is related with the moral obligation of the elected leaders and the bureaucrats performing the duties of the state on the one hand, and the people's perception as such on the other. Legislators passing laws to increase their own perks and benefits such as pensions and duty-free cars can hardly be seen as working with a sense of public accountability. Similarly, transparency is like a glass through which people can see what the state machinery (legislative, executive, and judiciary) is doing and vice versa.

It is a universal fact that the people—educated or not—are the ultimate source of legitimacy, and keep the latent energy and power with them to pick-up the gun, and challenge the mono-poly of the state by the use of violence, if the governance is not fair to them. South Asia as a whole is replete with such examples. In fact, the insurgencies around the world have originated from the problems of governance or misgovernance.

India may not be facing a really serious crisis of security originating from governance problems—it has a relatively better-functioning democracy, more credible parliament, more decentralized and pluralistic power distribution, more credible judiciary (at least at the Supreme Court levels), more free press, and more educated elite in the power centres—however, the country's marginalized states and societies do pose the problems of insurgency. The north-eastern states of India seem to be hotbeds of insurgencies caused by the people's sense of oppression and alienation from the centre. Sections of people in the states of Bihar, Jharkhand, Andhra Pradesh, and other parts seem to carry a sense of economic deprivation and socio-political and cultural exclusion, leading to insurgencies and 'terrorism' which pose serious internal security challenges to the state and central governments. Recently, the question of equity and justice came into focus when thousands of Indian farmers were reported to have committed suicide despite the impressive economic growth rates presented in the economic growth reports.

SENSE OF MORAL OBLIGATION AND NATIONAL VISION

For good governance to happen, what is needed is a sense of moral obligation to the people, and a national vision with a capacity to build institutions to translate that vision into reality. Despite their questionable democratic credentials, leaders like Lee Kuan Yew of Singapore, Muhammad Mahathir of Malaysia, and Park Chung Hee of South Korea brought their countries from Third World status to almost First World status with their hard work, inspired by their own national visions and a sense of moral obligation to their people.

LEADERSHIP

A former foreign secretary of India in a private and informal chat with the present author said: 'India has to (1) maintain good relations with its neighbours, (2) reduce its defence budget, and (3) spend more on social and economic development in order to achieve its national security goals.' Obviously, that is true for all the SAARC member states. In fact, from the people's point of view, that is what constitutes good governance and security indeed.

But for that to happen we need true leadership. Lee Kuan Yew, writing a brief Preface to his autobiography, *The Singapore Story*, says, 'I hope that they will know that the honest and effective government, public order and personal security, economic and social progress, did not come about as the natural course of events.' To quote the *Human Development in South Asia* (1999) again:

> Five decades ago, 'governance' had not been established as the buzz word among policy makers; yet for the vast majority of South Asians who had won their freedom from the British colonial rule and the right to determine their own lives as South Asians, the concept of effective governance was firmly embedded in the popular imagination and associated with the heroes of the era: Gandhi and Nehru, Jinnah, and Bandaranaike. But that dream withered over time, with governments retreating into military dictatorships, one party rule, and the same feudal relation which had persisted under the British Raj. Pakistan's democratic era barely lasted a decade before an era of military regimes began, followed by the turbulent break up of the country in 1971, and the tumultuous early years of Bangladesh. India witnessed a decay of the Congress party, and the shattering Emergency years. Nepal's monarchy gave way partially, but to a still weak democracy, while Bhutan's monarchy remained in place. Sri Lanka saw years of peace and prosperity give way to Tamil-Sinhalese divisions and finally the ongoing, horrific war with the LTTE.

Now, the question is: Do we have a leadership that can rescue and revive the region with a moral authority and vision?

REFERENCES

Acharya, Jaya Raj, 'USA and South Asia: Before and After 9/11, 2001', in *Institute of Foreign Affairs Policy Studies Series 4*, Kathmandu: Institute of Foreign Affairs, 2003.

———, 'Nepal's Rough Road to Democracy: The Fall of Nepali Congress Government, 1994', paper presented to the Centre for International Affairs, Cambridge, MA: Harvard University, 1996.

Alexander, P.C., *The Perils of Democracy,* New Delhi: Somaiya Publications, 1993.

Baral, Lok Raj, *The Regional Paradox: Essays in Nepali and South Asian Affairs,* Delhi: Adroit Publishers, 2000.

———, *Nepal: Problems of Governance,* New Delhi: Konark Publishers, 1993.

Belbase, Narayan, Prakash Mani Sharma and Kedar Khadka, *Asal Shasan: Srot Sangalo* (*Good Governance: A Resource Book*), Kathmandu: Pro Public Janahit Samrakshan Manch, 2001.

Bhattachan, Krishna B. et al. (eds.), *NGO, Civil Society and Government in Nepal: Critical Examination of their Roles and Responsibilities*, Kathmandu: Central Department of Sociology and Anthropology, Tribhuvan University, 2001.

Bhattarai, Baburam, *The Nature of Underdevelopment and Regional Structure of Nepal*, Delhi: Adroit Publishers, 2003.

Bose, Sugata and Ayesha Jalal, *Nationalism, Democracy and Development*, New Delhi: Oxford University Press, 1998.

Brown, Louise T., *Challenges to Democracy in Nepal: A Political History*, London: Routlege, 1996.

Chadda, Maya, *Building Democracy in South Asia; India, Nepal, Pakistan*, New Delhi: Vistar Publications, 2000.

De Silva, K.M. (ed.), *Sri Lanka: Problems of Governance*, New Delhi: Konark Publishers, 1993.

Fukuda-Parr, Sakiko, Carlos Lopes and Khalid Malik, *Capacity for Development: New Solutions to Old Problems*, Virginia: Earthscan and UNDP, 2002.

Gajurel, Deepak, *Security and Cooperation South Asia*, Kathmandu: Spotlight Newsmagazine, 2003.

Gellner, David N. (ed.), *Resistance and the State: Nepalese Perspectives*, New Delhi: Social Science Press, 2002.

Gersony, Robert, *Sowing the Wind: History and Dynamics of the Maoist Revolt in Nepal's Rapti Hills*, Mercy Corps International, 2003.

Gunaratna, Rohan, 'Indian Intervention in Sri Lanka: The Role of India's Intelligence Agencies', Colombo: South Asian Network on Conflict Research, 1994.

Huntington, Samuel P., *The Third Wave: Democratization in the Late Twentieth Century*, Oklahoma: University of Oklahoma Press, 1991.

Huq, Mahbub ul, *Human Development in South Asia, 1997*, Karachi: Oxford University Press, 1997.

Huq, Mahbub ul and Khadija Huq, *Human Development in South Asia, 1998: The Education Challenge*, Karachi: Oxford University Press, 1998.

Hussain, Mushahid, *Pakistan: Problems of Governance*, New Delhi: Konark Publishers, 1993.

Institute of Foreign Affairs, *Policy Study Series 2: Security in South Asia*, Kathmandu: Institute of Foreign Affairs, 2001.

———, *Future of South Asia, A New Generational Perspective*, Kathmandu: Institute of Foreign Affairs in Co-operation with Friedrich Ebert Stifstung, 2004.

International Crisis Group, *Nepal Backgrounder: Ceasefire—Soft Landing or Strategic Pause?* Brussels: International Headquarters, ICG, 2003.

Kaiwar, Basanta and Sucheta Mazumdar, *South Asia Bulletin: Comparative*

Studies of South Asia, Africa and the Middle East, Durham, NC: Duke University Press, 1993.

Karki, Arjun and David Seddon (eds.), *The People's War in Nepal: Left Perspectives,* Delhi: Adroit Publishers.

Kashyap, Subhash C. (ed.), *South Asia Politics*, vol. 3, no. 3, New Delhi: Rastriya Jagriti Sansthan, 2004.

K.C. Khadga, *The Institutionalization of Democratic Polity in Nepal,* Pokhara, Nepal: Department of Political Science/Sociology, Tribhuvan University, 2000.

Khnal, Y.N., *Nepal's Non-Isolationist Foreign Policy,* Kathmandu: Satyal Publications, 2000.

Khatri, Sridhar, K. (ed.), *Regional Security in South Asia,* Kathmandu: Centre for Nepal and Asian Studies, 1987.

Khoj Patrakarita Kendra (Investigative Journalism Centre), 2056, *Bigreko Bato* (*Bhrastacharama Khoj Patrakarita*), Kathmandu: Himal Association, 1998.

Kohli, Atul, *Democracy and Discontent: India's Growing Crisis of Governability,* New York: Cambridge University Press, 1990.

Kumar Dhruba (ed.), *Domestic Conflict and Crisis of Governability in Nepal,* Kathmandu: Centre for Nepal and Asian Studies, 2000.

Mahbub ul Huq Human Development Centre, *Human Development in South Asia 1999: Crisis of Governance,* Karachi: Oxford University Press, 1999.

———, *Human Development in South Asia 2001,* Karachi: Oxford University Press, 2001.

Muni, S.D., *Maoist Insurgency in Nepal: The Challenge and the Response,* New Delhi: Rupa and Company, 2003.

Nepal Rastriya Buddhijibi Sangathan (Nepal National Intellectual Organization), *Nepalma janayuddha (People's war in Nepal),* Kathmandu: Nepal Rashtriya Buddhijibi Sangathan, 1997.

National Human Rights Commission, *Human Rights in Nepal: A Status Report, 2003,* Kathmandu: National Human Rights Commission, 2003.

Panandiker, V.A. Pai (ed.), *Problems of Governance in South Asia,* New Delhi: Konark Publishers, 2000.

Pandey, Nishchal Nath, 'Security in South Asia: A Future Perspective', in *Future of South Asia: A New Generational Perspective*, Kathmandu: Institute of Foreign Affairs in Cooperation with Friedrich Ebert Stifstung, 2004.

Phadnis, Urmila, S.D. Muni and Kalim Bahadur (eds.), *Domestic Conflicts in South Asia* (2 vols.), New Delhi: South Asia Publishers, 1986.

Rajbhandari, Achyut Bahadur et al. (eds.), *Nepalama Prajatantrako Ek Dashak* (*A Decade of Democracy in Nepal*), Kathmandu: Prajatantra ra Sushashanko lagi Adhyayan Kendra, 2000.

Rose, Leo E. and John T. Scholtz, *Nepal: Profile of a Himalayan Kingdom*, New Delhi: Selectbook Syndicate, 1980.

Sen Gupta, Bhavani, *India: Problems of Governance,* New Delhi: Konark Publishers, 1993.

Sobhan, Rehman, *Bangladesh: Problems of Governance,* New Delhi: Konark Publishers, 1993.

Shrestha, Nanda R., *In the Name of Development*, Kathmandu: Educational Enterprise, 1997.

Shrestha, Shanta B. et al., *Sushasan* (*Good Governance*), Kathmandu: Sushasan Adhyayan Tatha Anusandhan Kendra, 2001.

Shrestha, Surya P., Shailendra Sigdel and K.C. Tarak, *Governance Assessment* (*Nepal*), Kathmandu: Nepal Administrative Staff College, 1998.

Srestha, Anand P. and Hari Uprety, *Conflict Resolution and Governance in Nepal,* Kathmandu: Nepal Foundation for Advanced Studies (NEFAS) in cooperation with Friedrich Ebert Stiftung (FES), Nepal, 2003.

Srestha, Anand P. and Shiv Raj Dahal, *Issues of Governance in Nepal,* Kathmandu: NEFAS, CASAC and FES, 2001.

Subedi, Kedar, *Charchit Prasanga* (*Current Issues*), Kathmandu: Niani Prakashan, 1999.

Thapa, Deepak and Bandita Sijapati, *A Kingdom under Siege: Nepal's Maoist Insurgency, 1996-2003,* Kathmandu: The Printhouse, 2003.

Thapa, Deepak (ed.), *Understanding the Maoist Movement of Nepal,* Kathmandu: Martin Chautari, 2003.

Thapa, Hari Bahadur, *Anatomy of Corruption,* Kathmandu: Sangita Thapa, 2002.

UNDP, *Poverty Reduction Governance: Nepal Human Development Report,* Kathmandu: United Nations Development Program, 2001.

———, *Governance for Sustainable Growth and Equity: Report of International Conference,* United Nations, New York, 28–30 July 1997.

Verghese, B.G., *India's Northeast Resurgent: Ethnicity, Insurgency, Governance, Development,* New Delhi: Konark Publishers, 1996.

World Bank Country Study, *World Development Report, 2000/2001: Attacking Poverty,* Washington, DC: World Bank, 2001.

———, *Nepal: Policies for Improving Growth and Alleviating Poverty,* Washington, DC: South Asia Regional Office, World Bank, 1989.

———, *Nepal: Development Performance and Prospects*, Washington, DC: South Asia Regional Office, World Bank, 1983.

World Bank, *World Development Report, 1997,* Washington, DC: World Bank, 1997.

Yew, Lee Kuan, *The Singapore Story: Memoirs of Lee Kuan Yew,* Singapore: Singapore Press Holdings, 1998.

CHAPTER 15

Comprehensive Security in South Asia: Problems and Prospects

MOHAN LOHANI

The right of a country to preserve its national security which has become increasingly vulnerable to the menace of international terrorism cannot be questioned. Security, however, in a comprehensive sense, transcends the ability of a country to protect its territory from external aggression, extra-regional threats, global wars and violence as V.R. Raghavan rightly observers: 'The existing state-centred approach to national security, confined to the defense of a country against territorial aggression, has been widened to the idea of security inclusive of a larger set of threats to the people of the state.'[1] A similar view is maintained by P.R. Chari: 'An understanding of South Asian national security requires the military and non-military threats in the region to be considered.'[2] Such non-military threats, as Baral points out, include ethnic crisis, national and transnational terrorism, religious fundamentalism, atmospheric pollution, population, poverty, transborder migration and redefinition of state sovereignty in accordance with the burgeoning trend of supranationalism.[3]

Our approach to South Asian security has been lopsided as it has hitherto focused mainly on the military component, including the nuclear potential, of some South Asian Countries, namely, India and Pakistan.[4] With the end of the Cold War, the ambit of security studies has expanded to include human, environmental, social, and economic security, as Abdur Rob Khan opines: 'Military security is still perhaps the dominant paradigm, but it is being increasingly realized that military security cannot respond to some of mankind's fundamental needs like freedom from poverty, threats to individuals and groups from multiple sources.[5]

The purpose of this study is to bring home the point that security in South Asia is threatened today as much by massive poverty—the ever-widening gap between the rich and the poor, including economic disparity within states,[6] population growth disproportionate to economic growth, social tensions caused by ethnic strife and communal clashes, large-scale migrations within and between states in search for a better life, urbanization at an accelerated pace and deterioration in the environment—as by the arms race between two major countries of the region, acts of violence and terror perpetrated by terrorists to coerce individuals, groups, communities or governments into conceding their political demands, and religious fundamentalists threatening to radicalize the society of the region.

South Asia comprising seven nations accounts for over one-fifth of the world's population. With a civilization regarded as one of the most ancient, the region derives its identity and uniqueness from a common geography, a common ecosystem and shared bonds of culture, history, and the economics of neighbourhood.[7] It is recognized that poverty alleviation is the greatest challenge facing the peoples of South Asia.[8] Endemic poverty is responsible for creating political and social tensions in South Asia. Despite more than four decades of development effort, the overall rate of growth in the region has remained too low to have a substantial impact on living standards and the quality of life of nearly 40 per cent of the people. Growth has failed to 'trickle down' in any significant manner, and the magnitude of poverty remains staggering.[9] The Report of the Independent South Asian Commission on Poverty Alleviation (ISACPA), 1992, draws our attention to how large-scale unemployment of educated youth all over the region has given rise to much disenchantment and alienation with the development process and, for that matter, with the democratic process itself. We further learn from the study that conflicts and militancy, in many cases, are partly the result of the inability of the economies of the region to grow fast enough to satisfy the awakened aspirations of the people.[10] ISACPA, now reconstituted, has already submitted its Report 'our Future our Responsibility', and the 12th SAARC Summit held in Islamabad in January 2004 declared poverty alleviation as 'the overarching goal of all SAARC activities'.[11]

Nepal's Tenth Five-Year Plan has accorded priority to poverty alleviation. Despite the implementation of pro-poor programmes, the percentage of people living below the poverty line is somewhere between 35 and 40 per cent. The Human Development Report 2004 ranks Nepal 69th among 95 developing countries in the Human Poverty Index (HPI).[12] Nepal has a long way to go before the target of reducing the poverty of the people to 15 per cent below the poverty line is achieved within the next twelve years. Poverty reduction is still a mirage, as Jan Sharma writes: 'Most poverty-fighting programmes designed to benefit the poorest of the poor and other disadvantaged groups have left out these very groups for one reason or the other.'[13]

With the gradual erosion of the credibility of the state and anomie in other political institutions,[14] it is hardly surprising that social groups mired in abject poverty and alienated from the mainstream have, in some countries of the region, already resorted to violent means or methods to express their resentment and frustration. South Asia seems to have embraced a culture of violence in recent years, as insurgency and counter-insurgency operations and movements have become the order of the day in most countries in the region.[15] While ethnic strife in Sri Lanka, where secessionist Tamil Tigers (LTTE) have waged an armed struggle for more than two decades, remains unresolved despite peace talks between the government and the rebels through international mediation, Maoist insurgents in Nepal, where 'violence exploded in 1996 as "People's War" for the seizure of state power and has continued as a protracted conflict',[16] have, in recent years, unleashed a reign of terror in different parts of the country, in particular far the western districts that are woefully backward, neglected, and deprived of the minimum infrastructure for development. A large number of people who include security personnel, Maoists and other innocent civilians have lost their lives in the crossfire between insurgency and counter-insurgency operations. The insurgents twice walked out of the negotiations, despite several rounds of peace talks and have intensified their indiscriminate acts of violence, terror, and insurgency through intimidation, extortion, abduction, and senseless killings. Recently, the rebels intensified the campaign of forcible recruitment of youths in their militia.[17]

Maoist insurgents have been dubbed terrorists by the state. The close connection between the Nepali Maoists and their counterparts in India is no longer an open secret. They have received arms supplies from across the border, albeit clandestinely. The former Indian Ambassador, Shyam Saran, in an interaction with the media described the Maoist insurgency as a common threat to Nepal and India. While admitting that arms smuggling happens, he stressed the need for vigilance and extended India's cooperation to resolve the problem politically. He categorically stated: 'The problem of Maoist insurgency Nepal is facing does not respect our national boundaries.'[18] In this context, it is encouraging to note that India has recently taken steps to deploy the Special Security Bureau (SSB) on the border to control cross-border arms and explosives smuggling. Some Maoist leaders have been apprehended and handed over by India to Nepal, while some are in Indian custody. Nepal has appreciated India's gesture of cooperation.

A unique feature of the Nepal–India relationship is the open border which has been misused for large-scale migration,[19] as well as for undesirable activities such as terrorism, subversion, drug smuggling, and trafficking in women.[20] Such activities are bound to give rise to occasional irritants, tensions, and misunderstanding in bilateral relations. The cross-border movement of terrorist and criminal elements who sneak into each other's territory to carry out their sinister designs is a matter of serious concern to both Nepal and India. Experts and policy makers on both sides have realized and highlighted the need for regulating the open border through joint endeavours, vigilance, patrolling and strict record keeping of the movement of goods and people. Nepali fears that the continued presence of terrorist and criminal elements across the border might jeopardize its security and make the country vulnerable to external intervention are not completely unfounded.

A glaring instance of the misuse of the open border was the influx into Nepal of over 1,00,000 refugees from Bhutan in the

1990s. Victims of ethnic cleansing these refugees have been languishing in seven UNHCR-sponsored camps in eastern Nepal for more than a decade. The plight of these refugees, who have been waiting impatiently for repatriation to their own country with dignity and honour and who are mostly uneducated, unemployed, and demoralized, is bound to further embitter the otherwise friendly relations between Nepal and Bhutan. The two countries have worked together in international forums for the cause of landlocked and least developed countries (LDC). The lingering refugee crisis, it is feared, might turn the refugee camps into a breeding ground for terrorists and other anti-social elements, posing a threat to the security of both Nepal and India. There is already rising incidence of crime, and forests in the surrounding areas are being felled causing damage to the ecosystem of the region. Experience has shown that a landslide in Nepal would wreak havoc in the Ganga and sweep away an entire village in Bangladesh. The longer the process of repatriation is delayed, the more difficult will it be for governments of the region to devise concrete programmes of cooperation in order to curb further deterioration in the environment.

Despite fifteen rounds of talks between Nepal and Bhutan, the refugee imbroglio remains unresolved. There is a strong feeling that the problem cannot be solved without the cooperation of India, which was the first entry point of asylum for refugees from Bhutan. India is reluctant to mediate, insisting that it is a bilateral problem. A noted human rights' activist and senior Bhutanese leader, Tek Nath Rizal, who spent ten years in Bhutan's prisons does not accept the argument that the refugee problem is a bilateral one where the two countries, Nepal and Bhutan, sit and find a lasting solution.[21] While Nepal has not abandoned efforts to arrive at a solution through the bilateral process, the issue has already become internationalized.[22] There is mounting pressure on Bhutan from the international community, including the European Union and donor agencies, to expedite the repatriation of already verified refugees in the Khudunabari camp and launch the process of verification in other camps without further delay. The crux of the problem is the lack of political will in Thimpu. The Bhutanese government buying time to postpone indefinitely the return of the refugees to their country with dignity and honour.

The dominant presence of India in the region is a reality which cannot be left out of a discussion on comprehensive security in South Asia. India is the largest of all countries in the region in terms of size, population, and resource endowment, and shares common borders with all its neighbours, except for the island states of the Maldives and Sri Lanka. Ever since the Partition of India in 1947, which brought Pakistan into existence as an independent country, India and Pakistan with nuclear capabilities have already fought two wars over Kashmir and avoided, fortunately, another military confrontation verging on war in the Kargil Sector of Jammu & Kashmir in 1999. The deep distrust and hostility between the two countries has been compounded by the lingering dispute over Kashmir.[23]

Kashmir remains, without doubt, a festering sore in Indo–Pak relations. The international community, including countries in the region, welcomed the peace overtures made by the Congress (I)-led coalition government of India. Both countries have reaffirmed their commitment to the peace process and the resumption of composite dialogue. At the SAARC ministerial meeting in Islamabad, July 2004, the foreign ministers of India and Pakistan discussed bilateral matters, including the issue of Kashmir, in a cordial atmosphere, for improving relations through peaceful dialogue. There was, however, no reference to the increase in India's defence expenditure by 17 per cent and the same increase in Pakistan's military budget by 6 per cent. Observers, reacting to the increase in military expenditures in the region, have expressed their apprehensions that the arms race between the two nuclear rivals might be a setback for regional peace and stability.[24]

While Indo–Pak relations have remained strained due to cross-border terrorism, a major irritant in India–Bangladesh relations is the alleged illegal presence of immigrants from Bangladesh, particularly in the north-eastern states of India. The militant separatist rebels from Assam, called ULFA, crossed into Bhutan and used it as a base for hostile operations against their own country of origin. The majority of the Sinhala community in Sri

Lanka continues to believe that the Tamil rebels, known as the LTTE, were trained, aided and abetted in the Tamil Nadu state of India in the early 1980s. The death toll in the civil war in Sri Lanka has already risen to over 60,000 during the last two decades. As stated earlier, the Nepal–India open border continues to be misused by criminal, anti-social elements and terrorists, including Maoist insurgents. These few instances confirm the state of insecurity in the region, which has not only contributed to the internal displacement of people and intra-state conflicts but also cross-border migration and inter-state conflicts.[25]

Democracy, good governance, economic growth, and social justice are interrelated and call for an integrated and holistic approach in the context of comprehensive security in South Asia. Commenting on the process of governance in South Asia dominated by special interest groups, P.R. Chari observes that good political governance requires the decentralization of powers to the people; accountability and transparency in public affairs; access to prompt and affordable justice; elimination of discrimination against women and minorities; and, finally, maintenance of peace and social cohesion within states.[26] Since South Asian society is multiracial, multi-ethnic, multi-religious and multilingual, the legitimacy of the democratic process and the rationale of democratic institutions are bound to be questioned if the policy makers and administrators in the region fail to accommodate the interests of the various ethnic groups and minorities that are seeking to assert themselves in the pursuit of their separate identities. In the Nepalese context, Harka Gurung refers to the change triggered by the 'awareness among the nationalities to establish their cultural identities'.[27]

Owing to the fragility of the democratic regimes in South Asia, politicians in the region, with a few exceptions, have little or no time to think in the larger interest. They are so infatuated with power that they have failed to rise above petty self-interest and short-term political gains. There is an erosion of the value system in South Asian politics, and the credibility of political institutions is at stake. Dipankar Banerji is more forthright in his observation: 'Rule of law, pluralism, tolerance, openness, transparency and respect for each other's beliefs, values and religions appear to be fast eroding.'[28] No less incisive is Devendra Raj Pandey's observation: 'The fundamental issue today is that the constitutional systems and political institutions that we thought were near perfect no longer appear to be so. People are losing faith in them, not only in South Asia but almost all over the world. The reason is not any structural problem as such, but the behaviour of those who manage the system and the others including citizens, who are expected to oversee the process'.[29] Pandey also deplores the exclusion of the majority poor from political participation, which is dominated by traditional elites or neo-elites through corruption.[30]

The restoration of parliamentary democracy in Nepal in 1990 was a positive development. It raised the people's expectations for a better life and a prosperous future. Euphoria was, however, shortlived as it soon gave place to disillusionment. Although Nepal has had three general elections and two elections to local bodies since 1990, factional infighting in the ruling party (Nepali Congress), which had a comfortable majority in Parliament, led to the premature dissolution of Parliament twice, in 1994 and 2002. King Gyanendra dismissed the Deuba government in October 2002 as it had failed to conduct elections in time, and he invoked Article 127 of the Constitution to appoint three prime ministers in less than two years. Sher Bahadur Deuba, who headed a coalition in 2004 of four political parties and two independent persons close to the palace, had a royal mandate to restore peace by resolving the Maoist problem through fruitful and result-oriented dialogue and conduct general elections peacefully not later than April 2005. Prime Minister Deuba could not hold talks with the Maoist rebels and conduct elections in the stipulated time hence was sacked in February 2005. During the last thirteen years, Nepal has witnessed thirteen governments with constitutional legitimacy, while raising fears of instability, chaos, confusion and a state of near anarchy.

While the common people continue to grumble against rising prices, income disparities, mass unemployment, and overall economic stagnation, political corruption at the top and bureaucratic lethargy and inefficiency have combined to whip up public discontent resulting in rebellion followed by acts of violence and terror. Experts opine that there is a nexus between parties, leaders, ministers, bureaucrats, police, and army personnel working in tandem with commission agents and underground gangs.[31] Baral's analysis ends on a note of caution: 'If the political institutions continue to rot and if the political leaders fail to identify with the common people, the legitimacy issue would surface again placing the country and the polity in serious jeopardy.'[32]

In the changing regional security environment, the state is at once the power and non-power to deal with challenges confronting human society. The best strategy for comprehensive security for South Asia lies in the capacity of each country to face challenges and overcome social, economic, political, and environmental constraints with renewed vigour, vitality and commitment. Imtiaz Ahmed pleads for the notion of national security to be replaced by a more sober and practical notion of societal security. He concludes by saying that only a combination of creative thinking and bold action could make a lasting difference to the issue of security in South Asia.[33]

While recognizing the important role of non-state actors in promoting comprehensive security in South Asia, no state in the region can shirk its responsibility to provide remote and backward regions opportunities in terms of basic education, primary health care and gainful employment. Each state must keep its own house in order by improving social, economic, political and environmental conditions within its territory. Governments of the region must incorporate the regional agenda in their national development strategy. While sharing experiences at the regional level is useful, poverty alleviation is primarily a national responsibility.

The SAARC process needs to be reactivated as it has suffered setbacks in the past owing to bilateral tensions. The promotion of mutual trust and understanding is a prerequisite for achieving the aims of promoting peace, stability, and amity in the region. SAARC's future and the prospects of comprehensive security in the region hinge on the willingness of India and Pakistan to accommodate each other on a 'give and take' basis.[34] The emphasis of all SAARC Summits has been on fostering good neighbourly relations, relieving tensions, and building confidence. Notwithstanding existing contentious issues of a bilateral and regional nature, the countries of South Asia should make an effort to channel their energies towards socio-economic issues, since non-military issues ranging from politics to economics and environment do not act in isolation but have a spillover effect on the other countries.[35]

NOTES

1. V.R. Raghavan, 'Introduction', in V.R. Raghavan (ed.), *Comprehensive Security in South Asia: Seminar Proceedings*, Delhi Policy Group, January 2001, p. 1.
2. P.R. Chari, 'Security and Governance in South Asia: Their Linkages', in P.R. Chari (ed.), *Security and Governance in South Asia*, Colombo: RCSS, 2001, p. 12.
3. Lok Raj Baral, 'Non-military Threats and Governance', in Muchkund Dubey and Nancy Jetly (eds.), *South Asia and Its Eastern Neighbours*, New Delhi, 1999, pp. 243–67.
4. M.P. Lohani, 'South Asia Comprehensive Security Perspectives: Nepal', in V.R. Raghavan (ed.), *Comprehensive Security in South Asia: Seminar Proceedings*, Delhi Policy Group, January 2001, pp. 23–35.
5. Abdur Rob Khan, 'Introduction', in Abdur Rob Khan (ed.), *Globalization and Non-traditional Security in South Asia*, Colombo: RCSS, 2001, p. 12.
6. Indian Finance Minister, P. Chidambaram made a statement, as reported in *The Kathmandu Post*, 7 August 2004, that India's wealthier states are getting richer while poorer states are lagging behind, creating an economic gulf that has dangerous implications for the country's stability.
7. *Meeting the Challenge*: Report of the Independent South Asian Commission on Poverty Alleviation, SAARC Secretariat, November 1992, xii.
8. 'Twelfth SAARC Declaration', in *Report on Nepal's Foreign Affairs (2002–2003)*, Kathmandu: IFA, March 2004, p. 170
9. *Meeting the Challenge*, p. 15.
10. Ibid., p. 14.
11. 'Twelfth SAARC Declaration', p. 170.
12. *The Himalayan Times*, Kathmandu, 20 July 2004.
13. Jan Sharma, 'Tackling Exclusion', *The Kathmandu Post*, 19 July 2004.
14. 'South Asia', states Jayadeva Uyangoda, 'is fast reaching a phase of political anomie. One of its key features is the weakening, from within as well as without, of the old forms of the state along with the erosion of their structures of legitimation', in 'Security's Insecurity: South Asia's States, Societies and Citizens in the Age of Globalization', Rajesh M. Basrur (ed.), *Security in the New Millennium*, New Delhi: India Research Press, 2001, p. 116.

15. Lohani, 'South Asia Security Perspectives', 2001, p. 30.
16. Dhruba Kumar, 'Proximate Causes of Conflict in Nepal', unpublished paper presented at an International Workshop on 'Causes of Internal Conflict and Means to Resolve Them: Case Study of Nepal', Kathmandu, 22–24 February 2004, p. 1.
17. *The Kathmandu Post*, 19 July 2004.
18. *The Himalayan Times*, Kathmandu, 10 July 2004.
19. John Woodall, a senior International Labour Organization (ILO) officer, made a statement, as reported in *The Kathmandu Post*, 7 August 2004, that Nepal and India sharing a porous open border has also fuelled cross-border migration and that the increasing trend of migration from Nepal could be linked to flaring insurgency.
20. Lohani, 'Nepal's Security at the Turn of the Century', in Kousar J. Azam (ed.), *Discourse in Trust; US- South Asia Relations*, New Delhi: South Asian Publishers, 1999, pp. 275–86.
21. 'Interview with Tek Nath Rizal', *The Kathmandu Post*, 19 July 2004.
22. 'Bhutan', *Report on Nepal's Foreign Affairs (2002–2003)*, Kathmandu: IFA, March 2004, p. 17.
23. Lt. Gen. (Retd.) Talat Masood, 'Security in South Asia: A Pakistani Perspective', *Security in South Asia* (*Policy Studies Series 2*), Kathmandu: IFA, 2001, p. 96.
24. *The International Herald Tribune*, 13 July 2004.
25. Imtiaz Ahmed, 'Security in South Asia: A Bangladesh Perspective' *Security in South Asia* (*Policy Studies Series 2*), Kathmandu: IFA, 2001, pp. 1–29.
26. P.R. Chari, 'Security and Governane', p. 14.
27. 'Hindus' growth rate falls in Nepal', *The Himalayan Times*, Kathmandu 3 August 2004, p. 1.
28. Dipankar Banarji, 'Foreword', in Rajesh M. Basrur (ed.), *Security in the New Millennium*, New Delhi: India Research Press, 2001, p. viii.
29. Devendra Raj Pandey, 'Governance and Political Corruption: A Perspective on Prospects of Regional Cooperation in South Asia', in K.K. Bhargava and Shridhar K. Khatri (eds.), *South Asia 2010: Challenges and Opportunities*, Delhi: FES, 2001, p. 275
30. Devendra Raj Pandey, *Nepal's Failed Development*, Kathmandu: Nepal South Asia Centre, April 1999, pp. 280–1.
31. Lok Raj Baral, 'Governance and Security in Plural Societies', in P.R. Chari (ed.), *Security and Governance in South Asia*, Colombo: RCSS, 2001, p. 100.
32. Ibid., pp. 104–5.
33. Ahmed, 'Security in South Asia', p. 24.
34. Y.N. Khanal, unpublished address to the young officers of the Ministry of Foreign Affairs (MOFA), Kathmandu, 2 August 1998.
35. V.R. Raghavan, 'Comprehensive Security', p. 3.

CHAPTER 16

China in South Asia: An Emerging Dynamic

M.R. JOSSE

INTRODUCTION

Of late China's perceived interest and/or presence in South Asia is increasingly being heard or talked about—in academic seminars, diplomatic circles and, indeed, the media. In 2002, a seminar was held on the subject of 'SAARC and China' in which several participants from South Asia, and a Chinese scholar, participated.[1]

Among those who presented papers on that occasion were Ma Jiali, Research Professor at the China Institute of Contemporary Relations, Beijing,[2] and the first Secretary-General of SAARC, Ambassador Abu Ahsan of Bangladesh.[3] Professor Ma, in his paper, explained that 'China only wants to establish good relations with surrounding countries and regional organizations' and recalled that 'China has already set up a good tie with ASEAN and built the Shanghai Cooperation Organization together with Russia and Central Asian countries'.

Ahsan, for his part, not only pointed out that 'during 2001 and 2002 ASEAN Summits, ASEAN and China reached major understanding which is significant for South Asia in several ways' but also expressed the conviction that 'ASEAN–China provides a good guide in as much as our socio-economic background is similar'. He, however, added the caveat that 'any viable arrangement with China will have to involve a number of ASEAN countries as full partners'.

The China and South Asia relationship was also underlined by former Pakistan Foreign Secretary Niaz A. Niak in a paper presented at the 'SAARC and China' seminar in Kathmandu in

2002. Therein, Naik recommended that Nepal and Pakistan should pursue 'a sub-regional economic and development cooperation agreement between China, Pakistan, Nepal and Bangladesh'.[4]

CHINA AND SAARC

In recent times, at the official or diplomatic level too, Beijing has signaled its interest in forging some form of association with South Asia, principally through SAARC.

For instance, the Chinese Ambassador to Nepal, Sun Heping, in March 2004, in response to a specific query from a journal on China's possible interest in SAARC, had the following to say:

> We appreciate that SAARC has made positive efforts to (further) economic development, social progress and cultural exchange in South Asia. Being (a) close neighbour of South Asian countries, China has always attached great importance to the cooperative relations with SAARC. The Chinese government is ready to work together with the governments of all South Asian countries to promote the cause of peace and development in the region. The time is now basically ripe to establish relations between China and SAARC.[5]

Equally significant, if less direct, were the observations contained in Chinese Premier Wen Jiabao's congratulatory message to the 12th SAARC Summit in Islamabad several months earlier. In it, Premier Wen declared:

> Since its founding SAARC has played an active role in enhancing the economic development, social progress and cultural exchange in South Asia thanks to the common efforts of its member states. Today, leaders of SAARC member states meet to discuss major issues of further stepping up South Asia regional cooperation and moving towards common prosperity. I am sure that this Summit will exert a positive influence upon the regional development and cooperation in this part of the world.
>
> China and South Asian countries enjoy long-standing friendly relations and cooperation. The Chinese government is ready to work together with the governments of all South Asian countries to promote the cause of peace and development in the region.[6]

Ambassador Sun once again took the opportunity to stress publicly that, as Premier Wen's message had subtly implied, 'the time is now basically ripe to establish relations between China and SAARC'.[7]

The South Asian media, too, has become increasingly alive to the China/South Asia connection. Thus, according to *The Nation* in Pakistan, quoting unidentified diplomatic sources on the eve of a SAARC Council of Ministers meeting in Islamabad, 20–21 July 2004, said:

> Sources said the foreign ministers of all member countries can deliberate upon some new issues such as the expansion of SAARC with more states joining its fold. They said that one such country is China, which is an important regional player, while another can be Afghanistan.
>
> Sources said having close friendly ties with China, Pakistan is of the desire that it joins SAARC and it can also lobby for its membership. However, they added that India will feel uneasy about China's possible inclusion in SAARC.[8]

In an exclusive PTV interview in Islamabad covered live by India's NDTV channel on 21 July 2004, Pakistan foreign minister Khursheed Mehmood Kasuri, sitting alongside SAARC Secretary-General, Q.A.M.A. Rahim, when queried about China's possible membership in SAARC, in the context of a report that it figured in Pakistan's Prime Minister Sujaat Hussain's speech, responded that it was something that some newspapers had referred to, but it had not been on the agenda of the Council of Ministers which had been finalized months in advance: hence it was not discussed by the Council of Ministers.[9]

Interestingly, however, a news anchor of the NDTV channel, which broadcast the PTV item reported that Pakistan had brought it up recently, at an informal level.[10]

One can thus safely assume that while the subject of China's possible association with, if not membership of, SAARC had not been *formally* discussed at the SAARC Council of Ministers in Islamabad on 20–21 July 2004, it had nevertheless been raised *informally* by Pakistan, the current Chair of the regional organization.

CHINA AND SOUTH ASIA

China's interest in, or nexus with, South Asia—quite apart from SAARC—has lately also attracted the notice of public commentators, at least in Nepal. One commentator, for example, noted that 'history, geography and culture closely link China and South Asia to each other', pointing out, among other things, that China has common borders with India, Pakistan, Afghanistan, Nepal, and Bhutan.[11]

Another referred to China's association with the Kathmandu-based International Centre for Integrated Mountain Development (ICIMOD) where 'since 1983, it has been a member along with Afghanistan, Bangladesh, Bhutan, India, Myanmar, Nepal and Pakistan as equal partners in integrated mountain development of the Hindu Kush–Himalayan region'.[12] He continued, 'it can, if it likes, be engaged in two trans-border, sub-regional co-operation programmes to integrate the highland mountain economies and societies of the Hindu Kush–Himalaya to involve Afghanistan–China–Pakistan, on the one hand, and Bangladesh–Bhutan–China–India–Myanmar–Nepal to encompass the Himalayan sub-region, on the other hand'.[13]

Going even further, he was of the view that 'Together China and South Asia can establish spiritual and adventure tourism resorts and wilderness parks capitalizing on the mountains, their pristine beauty and aura. The high altitudes can be the laboratory for all manner of organic farming for fruit, vegetable, and seed production.'[14]

Finally, he proposed that 'through the modality of sub-regional cooperation, using ICIMOD as the platform or 'entry point' it is felt that China should take the 'short route to SAARC' and thereby contribute to the peace and prosperity of the peoples living in high altitudes that have, so far, been by-passed by national development efforts because of their remoteness and isolation, as well as because of their political fragmentation into several nation states at the cost of the integrity of their natural endow-ments and social capital.[15]

Meaningfully, China's interest in South Asia, aside from the SAARC dimension, has been articulated at the official level. Thus, speaking at a public forum in Kathmandu, the former Chinese envoy to Nepal, Ambassador Wu Congyong, specifically linked China's 'Develop West Strategy' with South Asia. In Wu's words, 'The "Develop West Strategy" which is now pursued by China opens up new wider vista for the economic cooperation between China and the South Asia(n) countries including Nepal.'[16]

At this juncture, it may be noted that 'China's western region consists of twelve provinces/autonomous regions and a national level municipality. Four of them are Yunnan and Sichuan provinces, Tibet and Xinjiang autonomous regions. Yunnan borders Myanmar, Tibet borders India, Bhutan, Sikkim (the official Chinese map does not show Sikkim as a part of India), Nepal, and Pakistan, and Xinjiang borders Pakistan.

'Sichuan province (with an area of 480,000 sq. km and population of 83.29 million) and Chongqing Municipality (with an area of 82,000 sq. km and population of 30.9 million) perform as the industrial, natural resources (gas, minerals, water, etc.) and security backbone for several constituent provinces and autonomous regions of west China.'[17]

DEFINITIONAL ISSUES/MYTHS

Quite aside from the growing Chinese interest in SAARC in particular, and more generally in South Asia, as noted earlier, there is, I believe, the important definitional aspect of recognizing exactly what 'South Asia' means. Thus far, there is no uniform or universal definition of that essentially arbitrary geographic terminology. This definitional issue must be tackled satisfactorily before any in-depth consideration can be attempted on the subject of comprehensive security in South Asia.

At one level, there is a common or knee-jerk tendency to equate South Asia with SAARC. Yet many foreign offices and scholars tend to include Afghanistan and Myanmar, non-SAARC member states, as falling within the ambit of South Asia. That is not satisfactory if for no other reason than it fails to recognize a pre-SAARC 'South Asia'.

Furthermore, despite the general perception that Nepal lies wholly south of the Himalayas, it needs to be pointed out that its territory, in fact, encompasses both sides of that mountain range. If 'South Asia' is thus narrowly defined as including territory south of the Himalayas, clearly Nepal cannot be considered entirely as a South Asian state. Phrased otherwise, Nepal also shares many geographic or topographical characteristics with China's Tibet Autonomous Region. If Nepal is an integral part of part of 'South Asia' is Tibet, then, too?

In any case, the frailty of any terminology that locates states arbitrarily within one single convenient geographical box or the other has by now been thoroughly exposed. Thus, if one were to take the case of Pakistan, clearly it possesses Central Asian/West Asian geographic characteristics or moorings, in addition to its South Asian linkages. Despite Pakistan's membership of SAARC, can those geographical realities, then, simply be wished away in the framing of its foreign and security policy, among others?

Besides, there is the pat, if erroneous, theory that tends to project the Himalayas as a watertight security barrier or cordon between South Asia and the territories beyond, and in so doing, advances the notion or corollary that South Asia lies entirely south of that magnificent and towering mountain range.

Before proceeding any further, let us attempt to deal with the fragility of the commonly held perception that the Himalayas form a natural or impregnable divide that separates or isolates South Asia from China's Tibet. As Pakistani scholar, Noor A. Husain, has perceptively argued:

> It is wrong, it is a broad sweeping generalization, to say there has been no invasion across the Himalayas. I do not want to go into the lessons of history, but till as late as the 7th century, Tibetans came right through the Himalayas. The Chinese and Tibetans moved into Gilgit to support the Rajah against an external invasion and stayed there for five years.[18]

As the present author noted in a seminar in Kathmandu in 2003, Nepal, after unification under the House of Gorkha, launched two military expeditions into Tibet, across the Himalayas; in 1788 and 1791. In 1792, 10,000 Chinese troops crossed over the Himalayas from the other side to assist the Tibetans and advanced as far as Nuwakot, the northern gateway to Kathmandu, forcing Nepal to sue for peace.

Indeed, in the case of Sikkim too, conflicts with Tibet across the Himalayas were not unknown, including those in 1888 when a British expeditionary force was mounted resulting in the settlement of Sikkim–Tibet hostilities.[19] Similarly, 'five or six times, the Tibetans attempted to conquer Bhutan' in the sixteenth century alone.[20]

In fact, that the Himalayas constituted an impenetrable obstacle for the security of India (or British India, before that) in the colonial era was disproved when the British themselves launched a successful military expedition against Tibet in 1904 through Sikkim and the Chumbi Valley. This carefully propagated myth was even more dramatically exploded when China's People's Liberation Army almost reached Tejpur in the plains of northern Assam through passes in the eastern Himalayas, after a short and one-sided armed conflict between India and China in 1962.

Moreover, China's maiden nuclear explosion in 1964, followed thereafter by rapid advances in the development of intercontinental ballistic missile capability, has surely rendered the theology that the Himalayas constitute an insurmountable barrier between South Asia and Tibet entirely untenable or outmoded. Clearly too, the overt nuclearization of India and Pakistan in May 1998, and their development of ballistic missiles capable of traversing the Himalayas, if necessary, may be considered to have given that carefully fostered creed or belief system a final burial.

To return, however, to the central focus of this discussion, it is difficult to summarily reject the 'China (Tibet/Xinjiang) in South Asia' reality on the grounds of either geographical or historical logic.

LINKED BY MOUNTAINS AND RIVERS

The Chinese often refer to the fact that China (Tibet/Xinjiang) is linked to South Asian states by 'mountains and rivers'. That expression, is not merely a diplomatic platitude; it is a hard geopolitical fact of life that must be taken into account in any academic exercise that seeks to probe the emerging 'China in South Asia' dynamic.

Reference has already been made to the fact that China is a member of the Kathmandu-based ICIMOD, along with Afghanistan, Bangladesh, Bhutan, India, Myanmar, Nepal and Pakistan—countries to which it is linked by the Himalayas–Hindu Kush mountain ranges.

As Chinese publications indicate, however, China's Tibet is connected by the Himalayas to India, to Nepal, and to Bhutan. At the Karakorom (Kala Kulun in China) Mountains, China's Xinjiang Uygur Autonomous Region adjoins Kashmir, a disputed territory between India and Pakistan.[21] Thus, as Husain reminds us, 'we must not close our eyes to the fact that China, historically, geographically, geo-politically by virtue of being in Tibet and Sinkiang (Xinjiang) is a South Asian power'.[22]

Moreover, Chinese maps, even today, show China's eastern boundary with India as lying along the foothills, east of Bhutan, and just north of the plains of Assam. As the Sino–Indian border remains disputed in this sector till today, can one justifiably assert outright that China possesses no South Asian credentials?

As far as Bhutan—whose very etymology 'Bhot Ant' suggests the 'end' of 'Tibet' (Bhot)—is concerned, not only do the Himalayas connect it with Tibet but also 'four passes, three in the west and one in the east were once the most important gateways to Tibet'.[23]

That aside, considering that China has, in India's eyes, taken possession of a significant chunk of the territory of Kashmir it claims as China's, as per the March 1963 Sino–Pak Treaty, to dispute China's South Asian linkage would be to assert that Kashmir falls outside the ambit of South Asia!

Let us now examine the significance of the geopolitical reality that major South Asian rivers and/or their tributaries originate in the high Tibetan plateau. Perhaps the most important of them is the Yarlung Zangbo River, better known in Nepal, as well as in India and Bangladesh, as the Brahmaputra. Travelling for considerable distances along the northern and southern banks of the mighty Yarlung Zangbo, in spate due to prolonged rains, it is easy to imagine the severe impact that it would have downstream in India and in Bangladesh. This was underscored, among other things, by the UN's appeal for US $210 million for flood victims facing 'grave' food shortages after two-thirds of Bangladesh was submerged, destroying crops and killing over 700 people.[24]

'Great rivers of Asia that find their origin in Tibet include the Ganges, Hindus (Indus), Brahmaputra, Mekong, Salween and Irrawaddy' Chinese publications point out.[25] Several tributaries of the Ganga flow into Nepal directly from Tibet before merging with the river that Hindus regard as sacred. Among them are the Karnali, the Narayani (Gandak) and the Kosi rivers. The Raibok River rises in Tibet, flows through Bhutan, enters India and ultimately merges with the Brahmaputra in Bangladesh. Moreover, the Sutlej also originates in Tibet and flows into India before it joins the Indus in Pakistan.

It will perhaps be instructive to recall that the claim that the origin of the Ganga is in Tibet is not well advertised in India; certainly, the claim and a large-scale Chinese physical map the present author scrutinized in Lhasa at the Tibet Environment Administration office seemed to indicate that the claim was valid.

One must thus wonder why there has not been a greater acknowledgment of this fact in India. In schools and colleges in India one was taught that its origin, unlike the Brahmaputra's, was entirely in India! Incidentally, other authoritative documents also indicate as much.[26]

Before proceeding further into this discourse it may be germane to note a recent turn of events that forcefully underlines the 'China in South Asia' angle. China informed India that 'a lake formed by landslides in the Tibet Autonomous Region of China is threatening to burst its banks and inundate hundreds of villages in neighbouring India'.[27] A later news story went on to report that Himachal Pradesh authorities 'reviewed the preparedness to meet any eventuality in case of flood in the Sutlej'.[28] Yet, despite such intimate physical integration between China, 'an important, though virtually unacknowledged, upper riparian state'[29] and South Asia, there has been a studied reluctance in the past to bring China into the South Asian fold, even for exploiting or harnessing the abundant water resources of the Himalayan region for shared benefit.

That has been particularly true for India, and the reasons are no doubt political—despite the proclaimed improvement in relations with China. One explanation for India's reluctance in doing so would seem to lie in her colonial past. Indeed, 'Delhi's insistence on a bilateral over a river basin or multilateral approach is largely viewed as a legacy from the British Raj.'[30]

As the present author argued at a seminar in Kathmandu in 1994:

> If a breakthrough in achieving a truly meaningful cooperative development in Himalayan water resources is desired, a completely fresh strategy has to be fashioned. . . . The key obstacle is the old fashioned

balance-of-power, spheres-of-influence mind-set that dictates that bilateralism, not international river basin or regional methodology, be considered the cornerstone of the edifice of such cooperation. The sooner that reality is grasped the better. If it means China must come into the picture, so be it.[31]

Here it may be salutary to note that India ignored the late King Birendra's regional water resources exploitation vision thus articulated at the 26th Colombo Plan Consultative Committee meeting in Kathmandu on 5 December 1977, attended, among others, by senior Indian officials.

If water constitutes one of the potent sources for Nepali economic growth, we do not intend to look upon them from the standpoint of national interest alone. It is our conviction that if cooperation can be called for, especially, cooperation of Asian countries such as Nepal, India, China, Bhutan, Bangladesh, Pakistan and Sri Lanka, and all other regional countries, a vast resource of bountiful nature can be tapped for the benefit of man in this region.[32]

Especially noteworthy is that Nepal's 1977 proposal, a direct precursor to SAARC, envisaged regional cooperation *only* in the sphere of water resources exploitation and that China, still does not figure in the SAARC arrangement. However, as indicated earlier, in the not too distant future some sort of linkage may be established between China and SAARC, perhaps as a 'dialogue partner'.

A well-known Bangladesh scholar and water-resources expert has observed: 'Water impinges on the security of the states and their peoples: political, economical, social and ecological. . . . So far, the Brahmaputra has remained practically untouched.'[33] Then, referring to the late King Birendra's proposal, he recalled that American President Jimmy Carter and British Prime Minister James Challagan 'in separate statements made in New Delhi in January 1978, offered their countries' technical and financial support to any regional water development project that India, Nepal and Bangladesh may put up. But India did not react favourably to the offer. This was in line with India's insistence on bilateralism in dealing with the problem of the Ganges inspite of the fact that the river is international.'[34]

If India has had problems of associating multilaterally with Nepal and Bangladesh in such efforts, it is easy to understand why it has shied away from any common river exploitation project that would include China, which, as we have noted, is the source of many of South Asia's major rivers. Yet experts are increasingly of the view that 'only river basin development can solve the problems of floods and droughts' as in tragically witnessed virtually every year in South Asia.[35]

To return to the central theme of this study, acceptance of the emerging new dynamic of 'China in South Asia' would greatly help in bringing economic prosperity and hope into the lives of a huge chunk of the world's population that inhabits this region.

At this juncture, an explanation for China's non-inclusion in the Mekong Committee may be in order. According to the Secretariat of the Interim Committee for Coordination of Investigations of the Lower Mekong Basin:

> Although part of the territories of Burma (Myanmar) and China were located within the Mekong upper basin, political reasons prevented both nations from being included in the new cooperative venture in 1957. China at that time was not a member of the United Nations community and provided the main reason for not creating a Mekong Committee made up of six riparian countries of the Mekong. Burma, for its part, did not exhibit any particular interest in membership for political or geographic reasons.[36]

FICTION OF SEPARATION

It should also be mentioned that China's interest in the Mekong basin issues have increased as is underscored by its participation in a ten-day workshop on 'Water Law and Management of the Mekong River Basin' in Bangkok, 2–11 June 1992.[37]

Much more recently, or after the change in government in India in May 2004, another important dimension to the emerging 'China in South Asia' dynamic may be considered to have been added, specifically, Indian external affairs minister K. Natwar Singh's proposal for a common nuclear doctrine between India, Pakistan and China, first unveiled at his maiden press conference in the Indian capital after the change of regime.[38]

As reported in the mainstream India media, the proposal represents a further refinement to former Indian Prime Minister Rajiv Gandhi's disarmament proposals.[39] Despite the initial excitement over the proposal in New Delhi, and some puzzlement or cautious optimism in Islamabad, China soon shot it down. Indeed, Chinese Assistant Foreign Minister Shen Guofeng stated in Beijing that China was not in favour of welcoming India and Pakistan into the international nuclear club. 'The international community should stick to the spirit and principles enshrined in the Nuclear Non-Proliferation Treaty (NPT) as well as the consensus reached in the UN Security Council resolution 1172.'[40] Subsequently, Singh told Parliament that no talks had been held with Pakistan and China on his proposal.[41]

Although Singh's common nuclear doctrine clubbing India, Pakistan and China together has admittedly not taken off, the point to be emphasized here is that there is inherent in that concept an admission by India of China's vital role in matters directly impinging on a key strategic issue. Phrased differently, that proposal correctly acknowledges that China cannot be viewed in isolation or separately from South Asia, particularly in matters relating to comprehensive security, environment security, trade liberalization in South Asia, and so forth.

In an altogether different way, the process of globalization now underway in much of the world would also tend to militate against the fiction of treating China and South Asia as if they existed on two very different planets. As it is, post-Deng Xiaoping, China has not only morphed from an ideological state into a strictly geopolitical power, it has also become one of the most important players on both the global as well as the broad Asian stage.

The latter, incidentally, is well underlined by the Qingdao Initiative, emerging from the June 2004 conference in Qingdao in China's Shàndong Province, on South-South cooperation in Asia. Similarly, it is also reflected in China's hosting, since 2001, of the Boao Annual Forum for Asia, in the Hainan Province of China. As will be recalled, the latest Boao conference was held on 24–25 April 2004, bringing together 'on a common platform government leaders of Asia, other politicians, academics, experts and representatives of the business community, civil society and the media who . . . meet in the spirit of cordiality, camaraderie, constructive exchange and shared interests'.[42]

Finally, let us recall two concrete recent developments that would reinforce the 'China in South Asia' dynamic or emerging reality: one relates to anti-terrorism cooperation and the other to environment security affecting South Asia.

Not long ago, China and Pakistan, it was reported, were to hold anti-terrorism exercises (they have since been held). They were intended to 'improve the capacity of jointly combating terrorism'.[43] They were also designed 'to contain and crackdown on the forces of separatism, extremism and terrorism'[44] and were to take place in the mountainous terrain of Taxkorgan Tajik Autonomous County in the Xinjiang region, bordering Tajikistan, Afghanistan, and Pakistan.[45]

Since trans-border terrorism is a scourge that afflicts South Asia today, clearly active Sino–Pakistan cooperation in that area enhances the view that China's role in South Asian security is indeed an emerging reality or dynamic.

Reference has already been made to the news report about the nexus between the expected imminent burst of a landslide-created lake in Tibet and fears of flooding on the Sutlej downstream in Himachal Pradesh and India's request for a flood warning mechanism on the Chinese side that has reportedly gone unheeded.[46] As per the same news report, there are three flood-monitoring stations on the Brahmaputra (the Yarlung Zangbo in Tibet).[47] China's role in promoting environmental security in South Asia is, in any case, obvious enough.

The conclusion from this is clearly that China cannot be artificially separated from a region with which it is so inextricably connected: by history, geography, ecology, and vital common interests, whether they have to do with military security, terrorism, or environmental security. Enlightened self-interest would clearly suggest that the emerging 'China in South Asia' dynamic be freely acknowledged and acted upon appropriately by all concerned.

NOTES

1. 'SAARC and China', seminar organized by China Study Centre, Kathmandu, 23 December 2002.
2. Ma Jiali, 'Relations between China and SAARC', paper presented at the 'SAARC and China' seminar, Kathmandu, 23 December 2002.
3. Abu Ahsan, 'SAARC-China Relations', paper presented at the 'SAARC and China' seminar, Kathmandu, 23 December 2002.
4. Niaz A. Naik, paper presented at the 'SAARC and China' seminar, Kathmandu, 23 December 2002.
5. Suntheping, interview to *People's Review* weekly, Kathmandu, 25–31 March 2004.
6. Sun Heping, 'China's Foreign Policy in South Asia', address delivered on 28 May 2004 in Kathmandu, at a lecture jointly sponsored by the Nepal Council of World Affairs and the China Study Centre, Kathmandu.
7. Ibid.
8. *The Nation*, Islamabad, 16 July 2004.
9. Paraphrase of statement heard/seen by the present author, 21 July 2004.
10. Ibid.
11. Upendra Gautam, *People's Review*, Kathmandu, 29 May–4 June 2003.
12. Madhukar S.J.B. Rana, 'China in South Asia?, *Kathmandu Post*, 1 June 2004.
13. Ibid.
14. Ibid.
15. Ibid.
16. Wu Congyong, address to a gathering organized jointly in Lalitpur on 8 May 2003 by the Nepal Council of World Affairs and the China Study Centre, Kathmandu.
17. Gautam, *People's Review*, 29 May–4 June 2003.
18. Sridhar K. Khatri (ed.), *Regional Security and South Asia*, Kathmandu: Centre for Nepal and Asian Studies, Tribhuban University, 1987, p. 242.
19. V.H. Ceolho, *Sikkim and Bhutan*, Delhi: Vikas Publication, 1970, p. 20.
20. Ibid., p. 122.
21. *Tibet*, China Intercontinental Press, West China series, June 2001, p. 8.
22. Khatri (ed.), *Regional Security in South Asia*, p. 242.
23. *Bhutan: Himalayan Kingdom*, Published by The Royal Government of Bhutan, 1979, p. 8.
24. AFP news item, *Himalayan Times*, Kathmandu, 13 August 2004.
25. *Tibet*, p. 13.

26. *Map of The People's Republic of China*, Beijing: China Cartographic Publishing House, January 2001.
27. AP news item, *Himalayan Times*, Kathmandu, 8 August 2004.
28. PTI news item, *Himalayan Times*, Kathmandu, 9 August 2004.
29. M.R. Josse, 'The Case for "New Thinking"', in Ajaya Dixit (ed.), *Water Nepal*, vol. 4, no. 1, Kathmandu, September 1994, p. 258.
30. Ibid., p. 260.
31. Ibid., pp. 265–6.
32. Proclamations, Speeches and Messages, HMG, Ministry of Communications, Kathmandu.
33. B.M. Abbas A.T., 'Water Resources and South Asian Regional Cooperation: Development Prospects or Security Problems', in Sridhar K. Khatri (ed.), *Regional Security in South Asia*, p 187.
34. Ibid., p. 187.
35. Ibid., p. 188.
36. Josse, 'The Case for "New Thinking"', quoting *The Mekong Committee: A Historical Account 1957–89*, Bangkok: Mekong Secretariat, p. 264.
37. Ibid., p. 264.
38. *Indian Express*, New Delhi, 2 June 2004.
39. *The Telegraph*, Kolkata, 6 June 2004.
40. PTI news item, *The Times of India*, New Delhi, 30 June 2004.
41. *The Hindu*, Chennai, 8 July 2004.
42. Mohan Lohani, *Kathmandu Post*, 30 April 2004.
43. *Xinhua* report quoted by AFP, *Himalayan Times*, 30 July 2004.
44. Ibid.
45. Ibid.
46. *Indian Express*, New Delhi, 11 August 2004.
47. Ibid.

CHAPTER 17

Refugees in South Asia and Impact on Regional Security

NISHCHAL NATH PANDEY

When nowhere seems safe,
And it's the only place you can go.
When nothing makes sense,
And it's the only thing you know.
When the fear is so much it hurts,
And the pain just can't be healed.
When your life is no longer yours,
And your home no longer anywhere.
When all you can do is run and not look back,
And hope that someone cares!

LOUISE ALLCOCK

BACKGROUND

The history of mankind is repeatedly interspersed with mass expulsions of people forced to flee from famine, wars, revolutions and natural disasters. Early examples of the movement of refugees around the world in considerable number include the expulsion of the Jews and the Moors from Spain in the late fifteenth century, the flights from religious persecutions to the New World in the sixteenth and seventeenth centuries, and the exodus of the émigrés during the French Revolution. The twentieth century witnessed the greatest of refugee flows than at any point of history. The partition of India, the break-up of the Ottoman Empire, the creation of Israel and Bangladesh, civil wars in Sudan and Nigeria, the independence of Algeria, the westward surge of the Polish refugees after World War II, Paraguayans settling in Argentina,

Ugandans settling in Kenya, Jews from Arab nations moving to Israel . . . the list can go on and on and is likely to extend into the future.[1]

However, until the twentieth century, there was little or no methodical attempt to help refugees either to repatriate them to their place of origin or to resettle them. Clearly, it seems that the refugee problem is older than the concept and definition of refugees. After the First World War, international organizations were created to give assistance and, finally in 1921, the League of Nations appointed Fridtj of Nansen its high commissioner for refugee work. Later, the International Labor Organization and the Nansen International Office for Refugees took charge. Nansen effected repatriation wherever possible by even arranging 'Nansen Passports', which gave the holder the right to move around freely. But the Second World War further displaced civilian populations in huge numbers. At the War's end, the United Nations Relief and Rehabilitation Administration (UNRRA) had the responsibility of caring for some 8 million 'displaced persons'. With the end of UNRRA, the UN created the International Refugee Organization to carry on its work. Since 1951, the office of the UNHCR has coordinated international activities and worked for independent solutions. Despite its best efforts, there are approximately 22 million refugees in the world today.

In the last fifty years, there has been an increase in awareness in both scholarship as well as pedagogy to the complexities of the movements of people, caused by varied reasons ranging from 'forced booting out' by oppressive regimes to ethnic or political violence and colossal natural calamity, as well as economic chaos. Furthermore the economic globalization and the end of the Cold War meant to be 'a liberal humane place, with liquid nationalism' have led to a steady rise in cross-border flows since 1990. With a host of intra-state conflicts centering around ethnicity, separatism and religion, the mass exodus of people living in make-shift huts has become a stark reality of the New World Order. According to the World Refugee Survey, 2003, published by the US Committee for Refugees, 'Afghanistan, Palestine, Myanmar, Sudan, Angola, Democratic Republic of the Congo, Burundi, Vietnam, Somalia, and Iraq are the top ten principal sources of refugees'.

In November 2004, the magnitude of the humanitarian crisis in the Greater Darfur region of Sudan, where a violent conflict has been raging since early 2003 has resulted in the deaths of thousands of people as a direct or indirect consequence of the ongoing conflict. About 2 million people—a third of the entire population of the Darfur region—are badly affected. One million people have been displaced within Sudan and approximately 200,000 people have fled across the border into Chad. Serious violations of human rights have been reported by the UN and human rights organizations and observers warn that the humanitarian situation may only get worse.[2]

There are various routes through which security can be threatened by refugees or by migratory movements—when refugees or migrants work against the regime of their home country, when they pose a social, economic or cultural threat to the host country, or even when the host country uses them as instruments to threaten the home country.[3] Nowadays, grave humanitarian consequences of the failure of the state capacity to protect and assist its own citizens can also lead to outside intervention. There is a growing tendency to link 'sovereignty' with 'responsibility'.[4]

SOUTH ASIA

The case of South Asia is poignant, pertinent, and problematic. The largest migration of South Asians occurred in 1947, accompanying the partition of India into two nations—India and Pakistan—on the basis of religion. In the nine months between August 1947 and the spring of the following year, by unofficial counts, at least 18 million people were forced to flee their homes and become refugees; at least a million were killed in communal violence.[5] In the later years, the plight of the growing millions of refugees in South Asia is swamping the resources of their host countries as well as those of the UNHCR. All South Asian countries involved suffer from overpopulation and extreme poverty. Refugees who have been dispossessed but are returning to their homeland—as in Afghanistan—are inevitably in need of assistance, but their own countries and the UN do not have sufficient resources.

With the multifarious causes of refugee origination not mitigated, South Asia hosts one of the world's largest population of refugees even today. This phenomenon has created problems (*either to the refugee generating* or *to the refugee hosting country*) which pose as one of the greatest sources of non-traditional threat to security in the region:

- Economic burden
- Political complexities
- Diplomatic pressures and embarrassment
- Legal challenges
- Environmental degradation
- Sociological and psychological impact
- Rise in drug abuse/prostitution/unemployment/petty crimes
- Rise in tension among various ethnic and religious groups
- Adverse affect on law and order

'[Therefore] with the expansion of the concept of security, refugees today are regarded as a source of non-military threat to national security. While scholars and policy makers have devoted time and resources to the study of refugees *per se*, not much work has been done on the implications of the presence of the refugees on the security of the state that hosts them'.[6] This is further accentuated by the wicked fact that the 'state' in South Asia, and its 'authority' has not yet solidified itself and both the 'state' and 'nation-building processes' continue to generate turmoil and displacement. Therefore, while a proper analysis of the links of insecurity and refugee inflows inside South Asian states needs to be carried out, it has also to be understood that the refugees themselves are products of conflict and insecurity situations and their presence further exacerbates conflict, tension, and insecurity.

The actual security implication of the refugee movements needs to be assessed apropos of the refugee generating (home state), the refugee receiving (the host state), and external aspects of the home and the host states' security. 'The home state, by driving its citizens out, exposes itself to international criticism and embarrassment, pressures and even intervention for atrocities on its own people. Whereas, the security implications of the refugees in the host country are far-reaching and multi-dimensional evident both in relations to internal and external security.'[7] This trend is witnessed in a four-way traffic of the refugees, i.e. movement within the region; movement from the region; movement into the region; and movement within the country of domicile.

On the other hand, a major problem is that a maximum number of refugees in South Asia have been absorbed inside the region itself. The refugee management process in the region is not uniform and there have been shifts in terms of policy framework and strategy to mitigate its adverse impacts on the society, its polity, economy, and the environment. Three factors—humanitarian, economic responsibility and national security—largely shape states' attitudes in either accepting or declining the refugees, but interestingly, all South Asian countries adopt haphazard and ad hoc policies on this intricate issue. The realization that refugees are people, they need family support and reunion, and that they too need freedom, seldom figures in the outlook of the refugee-generating countries, and the end result is delay and separation, and a useless life in pitiable conditions behind barbed wire.

Generally, a comparable illustration can be cited of the impact of refugees in individual South Asian states, i.e. the effect on the economy (which even otherwise faces difficulty in sustaining its own populace), a bearing on the law and order situation of these countries (which even without these refugees is prone to violence and perpetual disturbance), impact on the overall political situation of these countries (which remains murky and unstable), and the general pressure on the environment that sends offshoots to the region as a whole. Whereas identical consequences of the general impact of the refugees inside South Asian countries has been a hallmark, it also occasionally leads to strained bilateral relations affecting overall regional accord and harmony.[8] With the easy availability of small arms, landmines and explosives to fuel armed movements by refugees, the presence of large-scale 'idle minds' in one's territory always produces unease rather than sympathy in the governments of the host countries.

REFUGEE CONDITIONS IN SOUTH ASIAN STATES

The UNHCR definition of refugees states that '[they] are people who flee their country because of a well-founded fear of persecution for reasons of race, religion, nationality, political opinion or membership of a particular social group. A refugee either cannot return home or is afraid to do so'.[9] Additionally, Internally Displaced Persons (IDPs) have developed into a major trouble for at least some South Asian countries, like Nepal.

India

According to one estimate, some 345,000 refugees were living in India alone at the beginning of 2002. They included: 144,000 from Sri Lanka; 110,000 from TAR, China; 52,000 from Myanmar; 15,000 from Bhutan; 12,000 from Afghanistan; 5,000 to 20,000 from Bangladesh;[10] and nearly 300 from other countries. Additionally, refugees from the Chin state in Myanmar have been fleeing to Mizoram in India since 1988. In early 2003, their number in Mizoram rose to 50,000. These Chin refugees face the danger of being either expelled or arrested unlike those from Sri Lanka or the Tibet Autonomous Region (TAR), whom India protects as refugees.[11]

Being the largest country in the region, the second most populous nation in the world, with a porous border, and also being a democracy, India has had to receive the inflow of refugees from any given conflict situation in the region. Its democratic credentials, a free and an open polity and media inspire political activists fighting for democracy to live inside India while struggling for their cause. Others from poverty-stricken countries take up low-wage jobs in Indian cities. However, there is always a sizeable section in India opposed to the influx of refugees from outside, as it feels the refugess will further complicate the problems of unemployment, scarce resources, and the poor law-and-order situation in the Indian states.

Tamil refugees from Sri Lanka began fleeing to India in 1983 when violence broke out between the majority Sinhalese and the minority Tamils. Although many of the refugees have been repatriated over the years, at present 61,000 are living in 103 government-run camps in Tamil Nadu. An additional 20,000 refugees live outside the camp. Since the outbreak of the hostilities in Sri Lanka, several lakh Muslim Tamils have fled the island. As of mid-1999, approximately 66,000 were housed in 133 refugee camps in south India, another 40,000 lived outside the Indian camps, and more than 200,000 Tamils have sought refuge in America, Canada, and other Western countries. Following the assassination of Rajiv Gandhi, restrictions have been placed on their freedom of movement and they are treated with some degree of suspicion by the local police. The refugee camps have been moved away from the coastal areas to isolated interior regions so as to prevent contact between refugees of different camps.

With the ceasefire and the initiation of peace talks between the Sri Lankan government and the Liberation Tigers of Tamil Eelam (LTTE), the security situation in Sri Lanka has improved considerably. Tourism is up and the economy too is growing. Several thousands of refugees have returned, perhaps nearly 10 per cent. But the refugees are not convinced that the ceasefire will hold. Plus there is fear of the LTTE which still recruits child soldiers, and since most of their homes lie in high security zones occupied by the Sri Lankan army, returning home does cause a certain degree of nervousness among these refugees.[12]

Seasonal economic migrants from both sides criss-cross the Indo–Nepal open border regularly. Today there are a large number of Nepalese settlers from the Maoist affected areas of rural Nepal in India, the official numbers, however, are not known. Human trafficking, mainly the trafficking of Nepalese girls for prostitution in major Indian towns such as Mumbai and Delhi, is yet another persistent problem for both India and Nepal.

Pakistan

Pakistan has certainly been a generous host to Afghan refugees for much of the decades of the 1980s and the 1990s. During its war with the former Soviet Union (1979–89), one-third of Afghanistan's people fled the country, with Pakistan and Iran sheltering a combined peak of more than 6 million refugees. By early 2000, 2 million Afghan refugees still remained in Pakistan and about 1.4 million in Iran. It was cited in a survey that in Peshawar—a city of 1 million people 35 miles from the border in the north-west of Pakistan, there were four times more Afghans than Pakistanis; another 40,000 Afghans lived in refugee camps south of the city. Nevertheless, since the defeat of the Taliban, the UN plans to help at least 1 million Afghans return. More than 2 million Afghans who fled from Taliban oppression to neighbouring Iran and Pakistan have already been repatriated.[13] In the mid-1990s, Pakistan became increasingly hostile to those fleeing from Afghanistan because of sociological, environmental, political, and more importantly, financial reasons. After 9/11, Pakistan also had to keep a closer vigil on extremist elements, especially in the bordering towns and villages with a substantial Afghan refugee population.[14] About 200,000 fled to Pakistan during the US-led bombing campaign in 2001.

However, the real problem is that even after they return home the lack of education, dearth of financial resources, lack of safety, and the slow pace of the reconstruction of their country make it difficult for Afghans to earn their daily living. Afghanistan has been particularly unfortunate in that it harbours one of the largest illiterate populations owing to the long-standing conflict and *warlordism*; hence it generates refugees unintentionally.

Nepal

At the beginning of the 1990s, Bhutan adopted a discriminatory policy and started expelling thousands of its citizens of Nepalese origin from its territory, which lead to one of the worst humanitarian cataclysms in this part of the subcontinent. These *Lhotsampas* had been living in Bhutan for generations and also owned houses, land and other property in southern Bhutan. They had contributed significantly to the economic development of Bhutan but were victimized by the authorities for their alleged role in the pro-democracy movement of 1990.[15] India too, which has compassionately harboured thousands of refugees from other countries was unkind, particularly to the *Lhotsampas*. '[Today] The Bhutanese refugee problem is no longer a bilateral issue between Nepal and Bhutan. Nepal provided them shelter on humanitarian ground as they entered Nepal's territory through Indian territory more than 12 years ago. India was, thus, the first entry point of asylum for refugees from Bhutan. This crisis can be resolved with Indian cooperation [which] as an emerging great power and also a regional power, is a common friend of both Nepal and Bhutan. It should help its small neighbours in tackling this long lingering issue through its good offices'.[16]

However, in the last twelve years, the issue of the Bhutanese refugees has remained a very ticklish, complex and a challenging problem in Nepal–Bhutan relations. Nepal has tried its best to utilize all available avenues to solve this humanitarian problem in a peaceful manner so that the refugees can go back to their motherland with honour and dignity. 'The random exodus of Bhutanese refugees into the kingdom of Nepal has been a box of contention and has created [constant] uneasiness between the two countries.'[17] Nepalese leaders and officials have been trying to impress upon Bhutan the need for a durable and lasting solution of the problem through bilateral negotiations. Despite efforts to arrive at a solution through the bilateral process, the issue has become internationalized.[18]

The US Ambassador to Nepal, James F. Moriarty, has recently said in an interview that the question of the repatriation of the Bhutanese refugees is very important as people are not meant to live their entire lives inside refugee camps. 'The United States which gives 25 per cent of the total assistance provided to the refugee camps obviously has [an] economic stake to settle the problem and close down the camps', he has stressed.[19] The United States has additionally put pressure on the Druk government of Bhutan for the resolution of the Bhutanese refugee problem.[20]

Nepal and Bhutan—both kingdoms, both landlocked and both situated in almost the same politico/geographic reality, between India and China—have many things in common on the basis of which bilateral relations can be strengthened in the areas of tourism, trade, culture, sports, intellectual exchanges, etc. People-to-people contact between the two kingdoms has been going on since time immemorial, and it is this bond of cultural and religious affinity that needs to be nurtured in the days ahead. One such interesting illustration of the intimate relations between the two kingdoms is evident from a paragraph of the famous memoirs of Yab Ugyen Dorji, father of the four queens of Bhutan. In his memoirs, *Of Rainbows and Clouds* (written by HM Queen Ashi Dorji Wangmo Wangchuk), Mr Dorji recollects that during the restoration of *Sangchhoekar dzong* in Bhutan, the central idol of Guru Rimpoche on the first floor of the *Utse* was under the patronage of the queens themselves. The head and hands of the idols were refined by silversmiths in Bhutan and the brass work was done in Kathmandu, closely supervised by his wife's uncle.

'As a predominantly Buddhist country, Bhutan sees many of its people going to Nepal and India on pilgrimage as many holy sites for Buddhists including Bodhgaya and Lumbini are in [these countries]. Bhutanese pilgrims maybe [*sic*] encouraged to visit these places so that appreciation for [the] culture and history of another country is increased.'[21] However, this complicated issue of the refugees needs to be resolved without further delay. Dilly-dallying, indecision, and a deliberate game of buying time on the part of Thimpu with the hope of forever shelving this core issue might actually fan the flames of frustration among the refugees who are one hundred thousand in number, are idle and situated near the strategically important chicken-neck area of India.[22] If these idle minds, out of utter impatience or exasperation, join hands with the Maoists or with the numerous outfits fighting for varied causes in north-eastern India, the whole subregion will go up in flames. In such an unwanted scenario, Bhutan will find itself to blame for its sheer indifference to the complexity of the problem and the need to swiftly arriving at a lasting solution. 'While, there does not appear to be a danger of a full-blown conflict breaking out, between them [Bhutan and Nepal], the tensions that arise from the ethnic divide are a source of perennial concern.'[23]

Even so, until the issue is amicably resolved, Nepal will continue to face tremendous economic, political, sociological, environmental, and cultural pressures arising due to the presence of the Bhutanese refugees, at a time when the Maoist insurgency has crippled its national economy and diverted the attention of its security apparatus. Hence not only for India and Nepal, but for Bhutan too—which has recently embarked on a course of sustainable economic development by harnessing its natural resources whereupon its per capita income has risen manifold in the last decade—a lasting solution of this refugee entangle would mean a relief from international pressures, an end to serial negative newscasts in the foreign media, and a cessation of strained bilateral relations with Nepal.

An estimated 20,000 Tibetan refugees in Nepal arrived between 1959 and 1989. At the end of 1989, Nepal stopped registering Tibetan refugees. Of the remaining registered refugees, some 12,000 live in Kathmandu's Bouddha district or in Pokhara, Baglung, and other places. China considers these refugees as illegal immigrants. It has been a consistent policy of Nepal that Tibet is an integral part of China. Sino–Nepal relations in political, economic, and cultural spheres have grown from height to height since diplomatic relations was established in 1955. Occasionally, Nepal faces criticism from the US and some European countries with regard to its Tibetan refugee policy. For instance, expressing her dismay that the government of Nepal deported eighteen Tibetan refugees who fled in April 2003, Senator Feinstein from California announced her intention to withdraw her sponsorship of the legislation she had introduced to grant duty-free status to Nepalese garments in the United States. To counter this, Nepal's foreign secretary, at the time, Madhuraman Acharya during his visit to Washington on July 2003, discussed the bill granting duty-free and quota-free access for Nepalese garments in the American market with Under Secretary of State Marc Grossman and Assistant Secretary of State Christina B. Rocca. He also met a number of Senators and Congressmen to lobby for the bill. The negative publicity about Nepal which had grown considerably in America following the refugee controversy was much subdued after Acharya's visit.

Bangladesh

Bangladesh has had the lion's share of the refugee problem in South Asia. A country which once every other year faces the wrath of Mother Nature in the form of floods, torrents and drought has also to take care of the diverse implications emanating from the refugee problem. About 250,000 Rohingyas fled to Bangladesh from Myanmar in late 1991 and early 1992. Many of these refugees who came first have been repatriated back to Myanmar. By the end of 2003, fewer than 20,000 remained. But there are strained relations between the local inhabitants and the Rohingyas.[24] These Rohingyas have not received recognition as refugees from the Bangladeshi government and are considered to be illegal economic immigrants in search of work. In spite of the appalling conditions, the refugees prefer living in the slums to going back to Myanmar.

In the mid-1980s, the appropriation of land belonging to ethnic minorities in Bangladesh's Chittagong Hill Tracts (CHT) region by Muslim settlers had caused some 64,000 Chakma to flee to India and more than 60,000 others to become internally displaced. In December 1997, the government signed a peace accord which ended a 25-year conflict, which paved the way for the repatriation of all the refugees. Despite provisions in the accord for the 'rehabilitation' of both the refugees and the internally displaced, the situation of the more than 60,000 Chakmas who had become internally displaced during the previous three decades remained unresolved at the end of 2001.

INTERNALLY DISPLACED PERSONS (IDP)

IDPs are the single largest group at risk in the world. An estimated 20 to 25 million persons have been forcibly displaced within the territories of over 50 countries due to violent conflicts and resulting human rights' violations (conflict-induced), or by natural disasters or development projects (development-induced). With around 13 million, Africa has more IDPs than the rest of the world put together.

Unlike refugees, IDPs are not covered by any kind of international conventions or protocols. What is available is only the '*Guiding Principles on Internal Displacement*' that identifies specific needs of internally displaced persons and their rights and guarantees relevant to the protection of persons from forced displacement and their protection and assistance during displacement as well as during return or resettlement and reintegration. As the title suggests, these Principles are only for 'guidance' and therefore not obligatory. Definitely, IDPs fall within the ambit of international humanitarian law and the national law of the state concerned. However, these legal provisions cannot be properly enforced due to the lack of any legal instrument for IDPs.[25]

An estimated 157,000 persons of various ethnicities were displaced in several states in north-east India, a geographically and politically isolated area that is home to many tribal groups. Once sparsely populated, north-east India's population has swelled with the arrival of millions of ethnic Bengali Hindus and Muslims from Bangladesh and from India's West Bengal state in recent decades. The resulting population growth has led to competition for land and jobs, and also given rise to tensions among various minority ethnic groups. Those tensions gave rise to ethnic and politically based insurgencies which in turn cause widespread displacement. More than 500,000 people are today internally displaced in India, from Kashmir to the north-east.[26]

Displacement has also occurred within Sri Lanka during various periods of its history. Since 1983, the number of the internally displaced has increased manifold. The IDPs unlike the refugees, belong to all three ethnic groups—Tamil, Sinhalese and Muslim. The displacement of the majority Sinhala population has been in the Tamil majority areas.

In Bangladesh, it is estimated that in the direct aftermath of the general elections of 2002, an estimated 5,000 to 20,000 Bangladeshi Hindus and other minorities fled to India to escape Bangladesh's post-election violence against the minorities. An unknown number of Hindus, perhaps as many as 200,000, became internally displaced.

In Nepal, due to the ongoing Maoist insurgency, a growing number of Nepalese from rural areas have taken shelter either in cities like Kathmandu, Nepalgunj, Biratnagar and Pokhara, or in India in order to save themselves and their families from violence. The people from mid-west Nepal, especially, owing to food shortages, economic bedlam and unpredictable security situation, have sold/abandoned their property in their villages and begun to resettle in other areas. As a direct consequence, property prices in major cities have soared. People fleeing the conflict and insecurity have tended to move as urban and economic migrants, amid continued urbanization and traditional migration patterns from rural areas to urban centres, or emigration to India.[27] The Nepalese government has formed a nine-member task force led by the vice-chairman of the National Planning Commission, Shankar Sharma, to carry out a detailed study for providing relief to IDPs.[28] Although no one knows the exact figures, it has been roughly estimated that more than 100,000 people have been internally displaced in Nepal owing to the Maoist insurgency that started in 1996. But these IDPs remain largely unrecognized; receiving little assistance to cope with their displacement. Young people in particular have been uprooted from the countryside by the effects of war. Whether moving to cities, with their families in rural areas or migrating to India, conditions for IDPs vary greatly. Displaced children in cities appear to be among the worst affected. [29]

CONCLUSION

The strategy adopted so far by refugee-hosting states in South Asia has been to try and engage the home state in negotiations to resolve the refugee impassé. However, most of the time bilateral negotiations are tedious, laborious, and complex processes that take years, even decades, to arrive at an amicable and an honourable arrangement. The refugees themselves are seldom represented in these negotiations. South Asia needs to focus on ways to prevent refugee flows by either political or economic means rather than pondering on what to do once the refugees are already settled in their respective territories. Nevertheless, preventive measures are not likely to succeed without regional mechanisms. It would hence be useful if SAARC was formally involved in this process and not bilateralism but a regional structure in order to deal with this humanitarian cataclysm in a comprehensive manner would prove useful. Although SAARC does not permit 'bilateral and contentious issues' to be brought into its agenda, what has to be understood is that almost all South Asian countries are affected in one way or another by the presence of refugees/illegal immigrants and would collectively benefit by the regional organization getting involved in this issue. People have historically moved to places where there is safety and economic opportunity. Managing the refugee crisis therefore has much to do with effectively managing the overall state and regional security.

NOTES

1. Martin Ira Glassner, *Political Geography*, 2nd edn., John Wiley and Sons, Inc., 1996, pp. 635-6; Ineke Haen Marshall (ed.), *Minorities, Migrants and Crime*, London: Sage Publications, 1997.
2. 'EU Humanitarian Aid for Greater Darfur-Sudan' >http://europa-eu-un.org<
3. Warren Zimmermann, 'Migrants and Refugees: A Threat to Security?', in Michael S. Teitelbaum and Myron Weiner (eds.), *Threatened Peoples —Threatened Borders*, Universal Book Traders, 1995, p. 90.
4. 'Report of The International Commission on Intervention and State Sovereignty', *The Responsibility to Protect*, International Development Research Centre, December 2001.
5. Patrik French, *Liberty or Death: India's Journey to Independence and Division*, London: Harper and Collins, 1997; Sumit Sarkar, *Modern India 1885-1947*, New Delhi: Macmillan India, 1983.
6. Suba Chandran, 'Refugees in South Asia: Security Threat or a Security Tool', in P.R. Chari, Mallika Joseph, Suba Chandran (eds.), *Missing Boundaries*, New Delhi: Manohar, 2003, p. 151.
7. S.D. Muni and Lok Raj Baral (eds.), *Refugees and Regional Security in South Asia*, Colombo: RCSS, 1996, p. 24.
8. Nishchal Nath Pandey 'Security in South Asia: A Future Perspective', in *Future of South Asia: A New Generational Perspective*, Kathmandu, IFA/FES, 2004.
9. UNHCR website >www.unhcr.org<
10. Bangladeshi economic migrants in India are estimated to be about 12 million according to Minister of State for Home Affairs of India Sriprakash Jaiswal. 'The Bangla Bogey', *The Times of India*, 29 July 2004, p. 12.
11. Chin refugees come under the 'Government of India's Foreigners Act-1946' which makes no distinction between illegal immigrants and refugees.
12. 'Sri Lankan Refugees in India: Hesitant to Return', >www.refintl.org<
13. Source >www.irinnews.org<
14. 'President Musharraf says Terror will be Crushed', *Dawn*, 14 August 2004.
15. Pandey, 'Bhutanese Refugees in Nepal: Trouble to the Host', in A. Vandana and Ashok C. Shukla (eds.), *Security in South Asia: Trends and Directions*, Delhi: APH Publishing, 2004, p. 155; D.N.S. Dhakal and Chistopher Strawn, *Bhutan: A Movement in Exile*, New Delhi: Nirala Publishers, 1994; and Mathew Joseph C., *Ethnic Conflict in Bhutan*, New Delhi: Nirala Publishers, 1999.
16. Mohan P. Lohani, 'Five Questions', *The Telegraph Weekly*, 4 August 2004.

17. Biswo Pradhan, 'Diplomatic Strategy for Nepal', Kathmandu: Mrs. Durga Devi Pradhan Publisher, 2003, p. 135.
18. *Report on Nepal's Foreign Affairs 2002-2003*, Kathmandu: Institute of Foreign Affairs, March 2004.
19. 'Perspective', *The Spotlight news magazine*, vol. 24, no. 33, 23–24 July 2004.
20. Dev Raj Dahal, 'Effects of War on Nepal' >www.fesportal.fes.de<
21. Tashi Choden, 'Security Problems of Bhutan: Confidence Building Measures', in Mohammad Humayun Kabir (ed.), *Confidence Building Measures and Security Cooperation in South Asia: Challenges in the New Century*, Dhaka: BIISS, 2002, p. 179.
22. 'SOS from Kathmandu', *The Times of India*, 6 July 2004, p. 16.
23. Satish Nambiar, 'Promoting Transparency and Cooperation in the Region: Role of Regional Research Institutions', in Dipankar Banerji (ed.), *South Asian Security: Futures*, Colombo: RCSS, 2002, p. 153.
24. >www.refugeesinternational.org<
25. N. Manoharan, 'Internally Displaced Persons (IDPs): An Overview' >www.ipcs.org<
26. >www.refugees.org<
27. The population of twelve municipalities of Nepal grew by 5.2 per cent in 2002–3, compared to 3.6 per cent between 1991 and 2001, according to a survey by an UNDP–Rural–Urban Partnership Programme conducted in the twelve municipalities in 2002. This represents an increase of 80,000 rural–urban migrants in 2002–3.
28. *The Kathmandu Post*, 9 August 2004, p. 1.
29. >www.reliefweb.int<

CHAPTER 18

Indo–Nepal Relations: Future Prospects

PRAKASH A. RAJ

The purpose of this study is to assess the likely prospects of Indo–Nepal relations in the twenty-first century in view of the changes in strategic equations and globalization not only in the region but also worldwide.

BRIEF REVIEW OF INDO–NEPAL RELATIONS IN THE LATTER HALF OF THE TWENTIETH CENTURY (1950–1999)

Nepal was ruled by the Rana oligarchy until 1950, when there was a revolution and the Nepalese people and King Tribhuwan succeeded in overthrowing the Ranas and establishing democracy in the country. King Tribhuwan fled to India and the Indian government supported the democratic forces in Nepal. Had it nor been for India's support it would have been difficult for the democratic forces in Nepal to succeed in ending the despotic regime. Most of the leaders of the Nepali Congress were living in India and had close rapport with leaders of the freedom movement in India. There was a time in the 1950's when India had paramount influence not only in international relations but also in the domestic affairs of Nepal. Prime Minister Nehru stated in the Indian Parliament in 1950 that '. . . we have had from immemorial times, a magnificent frontier that is so say, the Himalayas. . . . The principal barrier to India lies on the other side of Nepal and we are not going to tolerate any person coming over that barrier'.[1] Nehru had reiterated in 1954 that the 'foreign policy of the Nepalese Government should be co-ordinated with the foreign policy of India'.[2]

B.P. Koirala became the first prime minister of Nepal after Parlimentary elections were held in 1958. However, King Mahendra dismissed Koirala in a coup in December 1960 and assumed powers himself. Prime Minister Nehru was unhappy and said the step represented a 'setback for democracy'. Anti-monarchial forces protesting against this step launched a movement inside the borders of Nepal and in India. The Indian government did not do anything to stop such activities from the Indian soil initially. As the movement was gathering momentum, the Sino–Indian border conflict began in 1962, which was to have a profound impact on relations between Nepal and India as well. The Chinese defence minister Chen Yi, said that the Chinese people would help Nepal if it were to be attacked.[3] The Chinese signed an agreement to construct a road linking Kathmandu with the Chinese border and assisted Nepal in constructing a ring road around the capital city and in setting up some industries. The Indians who had always regarded Nepal as their own backyard were unhappy but were unable to prevent the construction of the road to the border. King Mahendra was very successful in the realm of foreign affairs as Nepal was able to assert its independent identity and reduce its dependence on India. On the other hand, when the Chinese agreed to construct parts of the East-West Highway along the Terai in the southern part of Nepal, there were protests from the Indian side as they didn't want the Chinese working too close to their borders. They offered to build those parts themselves. The King respected Indian sensitivities in this regard and parts of the highway in the far eastern and far western sectors were built with Indian assistance. Nepal had established diplomatic relations with many countries and exchanged residential diplomatic missions with them. On the other hand, India continued to regard its relations with Nepal as being 'special'. This was mainly due to the open border between the two countries and the Treaty of Friendship signed in 1950.

King Birendra succeeded his father in 1972 and he attempted to gather international support to declare Nepal as a 'Zone of Peace'. More than 100 countries supported Nepal's proposal but India did not. K.V. Rajan, the former Indian ambassador to Nepal state that the Zone of Peace proposal was a 'thinly disguised attempt to bury Nepal's security obligations to India under the 1950 Treaty'.[4] Nepal had purchased anti-aircraft guns, medium-range SSMs, and assault rifles from China in 1988 which was regarded by India as 'provocative' and a contravention of the 1950 treaty. India declared a blockade of goods to Nepal after delays in the renewing Trade and Transit Treaty between the two countries causing hardship to the people. The popular movement against the Panchayat system—which King Mahendra had instituted in 1962, under which powers were concentrated in the monarchy amd political parties were banned—gathered momentum and King Birendra had to dismantle the party-less system and transfer sovereignty to Parliament in 1990.

There was an elected government of the Nepali Congress throughout most of the 1990s headed by Girija Koirala. India separated the Trade Treaty with Nepal from the Transit Treaty and guaranteed Nepal's access to the sea for all time—not something that had to be renewed every seven years as in the past.

The hijacking of an Indian Airlines aircraft from Kathmandu Airport on Christmas eve in 1999 and its landing at Kandahar Airport in Taliban-ruled Afghanistan was to make profound changes in the Indo-Nepal relationship. India expressed concern about the threat to its security by foreign forces operating from Nepalese soil.

The beginning of the new millennium also marked two events, that were to affect Nepal profoundly. The first was the royal massacre in June 2001, when Crown Prince Dipendra massacred his entire family including his parents, King Birendra and the Queen, and then allegedly committed suicide. The late king's brother Prince Gyanendra succeeded him. The second event was the rise in the Maoist insurgency in the country.

FUTURE PROSPECTS OF INDO-NEPAL RELATIONS

It is essential to examine the future prospects of Indo-Nepal relations from strategic and economic perspectives. Such recent developments in the world arena as the end of the Cold War, the emergence of the United States as the sole superpower, the strategic partnership between India and the United States as common allies against international terrorism, and the increasing economic clout of two of Nepal's immediate neighbours, India and China, are bound to affect Indo–Nepal relations as well. The non-aligned movement is less relevant today than it was during the days of the Cold War. Steps taken in the past few years to normalize Indo–Pak and Sino–Indian relations and, above all, the extension of the Chinese railway network to Lhasa in Tibet are especially important in this context.

STRATEGIC PERSPECTIVE

India on the eve of the new millennium faced problems with some of its neighbours. Afghanistan, a country with which it had friendly relations till the end of 1980s was ruled by a hostile Taliban regime. It had a long-standing dispute on the Jammu & Kashmir with Pakistan and was facing cross-border raids by Islamic militants based in Pakistan. Some of the militants were Taliban. The Taliban were on friendly terms with Pakistan, which felt its 'strategic depth' had increased in relation to India. Sino–Indian relations had not been normalized, as there were still boundary problems in the north-east and the Aksai Chin area of Ladakh in Kashmir. The hijacking of an Indian Airlines aircraft from Nepal represented a serious setback to its security interests. This incident must have come as a shock to India. The territory of the only Hindu kingdom in the world, which India had assumed would remain in friendly hands, was used to conduct a terrorist attack against the airline of the country with the largest Hindu population. S.D. Muni of Jawaharlal Nehru University (JNU) has said that monarchy as an institution in Nepal had done precious little in accommodating legitimate security and economic interests and concerns in Nepal.[5] However, an elected government was in power in Nepal at the time of the hijacking. This indicates a biased attitude of some Indian intellectuals towards Nepal as many of the security concerns of the Indians were generated during the rule of the Nepali Congress government than during the Panchayat era when the monarch was the paramount power in the country.

The attacks by the Al Qaida in New York and Washington on 11 September 2001 and retaliation by the US in Afghanistan against the Taliban led to a commonality of interests between India and the US in fighting international terrorism. India, the US, and Israel were branded as the common enemy by the Taliban. Pakistan also sided with the US and provided valuable support in destroying the Taliban. India and the US had become strategic allies. When the Maoist insurgency in Nepal escalated, the US provided arms assistance to Nepal. India did not protest as it had when arms were purchased by Nepal in 1988. As both of Nepal's immediate neighbours, India and China, as well as Pakistan, a fellow SAARC member sharing the same subcontinent, are now nuclear powers. Nepal's strategic importance in the region has increased. This is especially so as South Asia is likely to continue as a high conflict potential area in the near future due to India and Pakistan being nuclear powers and the existence of missiles capable of delivering nuclear weapons.[6] Nepal has not remained unaffected due to the fallout from nuclear tests conducted in the region, in Pokhran in Rajasthan or Baluchistan or Sinkiang.

The Annual Report on Patterns of Global Terrorism 2003, published by the US Department of State had this to say about Nepal:

> Limited government finances, weak border controls and poor security infrastructure have made Nepal a convenient logistic and transit point for some outside militants and international terrorists. The country also possesses a number of relatively soft targets that make it a potentially attractive site for terrorist operation.

There are indications that India is now concerned about the impact of the Maoist insurgency in Nepal, which has spilled over into Uttaranchal state in India. There also appears to be a nexus between the Maoists in Nepal and similar outfits in India such as the People's War Group in Andhra Pradesh, Jharkhand, Bihar and Orissa. The annual report of the Indian Defence Ministry for 2002–3 states 'the growing influence and grip of the Maoists throughout the country, particularly the terai areas bordering India and their links with Indian left extremist outfits are a cause of serious concern'.[7] India is linked to its north-eastern part by the 'Chicken's Neck', a narrow strip of territory between Nepal and Bangladesh. If the insurgency in the Jhapa district of Nepal were to spread to the Chicken's Neck, India's control of the entire north-east might be endangered. It may be remembered that India is fighting many separatist insurgencies in such states as Nagaland and Manipur in the north-east.[8]

A meeting of the chief ministers of the states affected by movements similar to the Maoists in Nepal was organized in September 2004 in Delhi. It was attended by the chief ministers and senior officials of Uttar Pradesh (UP), Bihar, Jharkhand, Madhya Pradesh, Chhattisgarh, Andhra Pradesh, West Bengal, and Maharastra. The meeting expressed concern about linkages between the Maoists in Nepal and similar outfits in India, and emphasized better coordination between security and intelligence agencies, and noted with concern Maoist threats to assassinate Indian leaders with human bombs.[9]

A peaceful resolution of the Maoist insurgency in Nepal is also in India's strategic interests. It was precisely because of the open Indo–Nepal border that the Maoist insurgency could spread so fast as the insurgents would often take shelter across the border. Many of the security concerns of the Indians could have been addressed had the border been better regulated by such means as keeping a record of movements and providing residents in areas close to the border with identity cards which could be used while crossing the border. India has so far been reluctant to regulate the open Indo–Nepal border, but there are indications that it is now changing.

ECONOMIC PERSPECTIVE

An article in the *International Herald Tribune* by Robert Radtke, Vice-President of Asia Society in the US, raises interesting questions about economic development in two of Nepal's neighbours, India and China.[10] Radtke believes that the economies of India and China, which are competing with each other, might become more complementary in the future. He concludes China may believe it has more to gain by establishing an amicable relationship with India. Steps taken in recent years to normalize Sino–Indian relations should also interest Nepal. Both India and China have enjoyed impressive growth rates in the 1990s. Both are on their way to becoming economic giants. Nepal is situated just north of the heavily populated states of Uttar Pradesh and Bihar in India, which have remained relatively backward. The Tibet Autonomous Region (TAR) is sparsely populated but will be linked with the eastern part of China by railway. Nepal is already linked with Tibet by the Kodari Highway built in the 1960s. A second highway is being constructed which will link Kathmandu by Rasuwa to Keyrong. Nepal should be able to take advantage of its proximity to both Indian and Chinese markets. China was able to get foreign investments of US $54 billion in 2003, which was ten times more than that received by India. While the strength of the Chinese economy is in manufacturing, that of India is in services.[11]

India has made tremendous progress in the IT sector in recent years and has developed as an outsourcing market for the US and some countries of western Europe. Nepal could also benefit from such development.

Nepal could also be an attractive destination for FDI from India. It is already the largest investor in Nepal. Indian investors have identified advantages offered by Nepal such as attractive incentives, the government's positive attitude towards investors, low-cost locations, cheap labour costs, and an easily trainable workforce.[12] Indian investment in Nepal is 36 per cent of the FDI and includes such sectors as tourism, consumer durables, garments and carpets. Such Indian companies as Dabur, Colgate, and Hindustan Lever have set up factories in Nepal with the objective of exporting their finished products to India.

Tourism and hydropower development are two sectors in which Nepal enjoys a comparative advantage and could be attractive for Indian investors. Nepal is an attractive destination for Indian tourists who visit the country for pilgrimage and sightseeing. It is increasingly becoming a popular destination for young Indian honeymooners and for adventure tourism. It could also attract more tourists in summer to get away from the heat of the Indian plains. The difficulty in obtaining airline seats had been a major impediment. However, since 2004, such private airlines from India as Air Sahara and Jet Air have started flying to Nepal, and some private Nepalese airlines such as Cosmic Air are flying to some Indian cities. There are also prospects of developing health tourism.

There is scope for cooperation in hotel management between India and Nepal.

There are already Chinese tourists visiting Nepal. There are prospects that pilgrimage tourism to such places as Lumbini, Bodhgaya, Sarnath and Kushinagar in Nepal and India will attract a large number of Chinese tourists who have more disposable income due to economic development. Many Indian pilgrims already visit Manasarovar via Nepal.

Nepal has one of the highest potentials for the development of hydroelectric power because of the variation in altitude and adequate amounts of water. It is estimated that Nepal enjoys a power-generating capacity of 83,000 MW. The demand for electric power in north India has increased dramatically in recent years. There are prospects for cooperation between the two countries in this sector.[13] Bilateral and multilateral donor agencies are interested in funding hydroelectric power development projects in Nepal when they are assured that a market in India exists. There has been some apprehension in Nepal that India is unwilling to depend for such a vital source of energy on areas outside its own borders. Nepal's experience in utilizing water resources in cooperation with India has not always been encouraging. The Kosi Project was the first major river project. It was primarily a flood-control project that benefited Bihar and only a very small amount of power was produced which could benefit Nepal in view of the size of project. Similarly, the Gandak Project utilizing another major river of Nepal was primarily for the irrigation of UP and Bihar in India, and gave some benefits to Nepal as well.

An Indian columnist has written about Nepal's potential to become an economic bridge between India and China in view of the opening of the new rail line to Lhasa from eastern China by 2006, which could be extended to Shigatse on the one hand and the possibility of linking the railhead south of the border with India on the other.[14]

The leadership in India in the two decades after Indian independence consisted of people associated with the Indian National Congress or the Socialists. Many of these leaders came from the north Indian states of UP and Bihar. On the other hand, many of the Nepalese leaders had close links with India as they were educated in such north Indian cities as Varanasi, Allahabad, and Kolkata. Some were even born there. However, the leadership in both India and Nepal in the beginning of the new millennium is from a different background. Parties that are more regional than national now rule the two Indian states in the Gangetic Plains. The coalition governments in New Delhi in the recent past have also included representatives of many regional parties. Similarly, the new leadership in Nepal is younger and does not have the same linkage with UP and Bihar as in the past as there are more educational institutions within Nepal itself and educational opportunities in foreign countries other than India. The leftist leadership in Nepal now may have a close rapport with West Bengal. This could generate a new perspective in the Indo–Nepal relationship.[15]

In a nutshell, it could be said that one of the major issues concerning Indo–Nepal relations is what has been alleged as insensitivity to India's security concerns as a former Indian ambassador has written.[16] Actually, Nepal should not allow its territory to be used against either of its two neighbours. On the other hand, there is ample scope for cooperation in harnessing the water resources of Nepal which will benefit both countries provided it is transparent and the benefits are distributed equitably.

NOTES

1. A.S. Bhasin (ed.), *Documents on Nepal's Relations with India and China, 1949-66*, Bombay: Academic Books, 1970.
2. Rishikesh Shaha, *Nepali Politics Retrospect and Prospect*, New Delhi: Oxford University Press, 1975, p. 143.
3. New China News Agency Report, 6 October 1962.
4. J.N. Dixit (ed.), *External Affairs, Cross-Border Relations*, New Delhi: Roli Books, 2003.
5. S.D. Muni, *Maoist Insurgency in Nepal,* New Delhi: Rupa, 2003.
6. Rifaat Hussain, 'Challenges and Prospects for Peace in South Asia', paper presented at the 'Conference on Security and Co-operation in South Asia', Kathmandu, 6 August 2003.
7. *The Hindu*, 6 November 2004.
8. Prakash A. Raj, 'Nepal, India Offensive against the Maoists', *The Himalayan*, 5 November 2004.
9. *The Kathmandu Post*, 23 September 2004.

10. Robert Radtke, 'India, China and the US', *International Herald Tribune*, 23 June 2003.
11. Ibid., 11 June 2004.
12. Vijaya Katti, 'Emerging Trade and Investment Opportunities for Nepal and India', paper presented at the Workshop on Indo–Nepal Economic Co-operation, organized by the Nepal Council of World Affairs and B.P. Koirala Foundation, Kathmandu, 21 December 2003.
13. S. Sen, 'Indo-Nepal Trade and Industrial Co-operation', paper presented at the Workshop on Indo–Nepal Economic Co-operation, 21 December 2003.
14. C. Rajamohan, 'India, Nepal and the Politics of Regional Economic Integration', paper presented at the Workshop on Indo–Nepal Economic Co-operation, 21 December 2003.
15. Nishchal Nath Pandey, 'Indo-Nepal Relations . . .', *Spotlight*, 3 August 2004.
16. Dixit, *External Affairs.*

Contributors

JAYA RAJ ACHARYA received his Masters degrees in Sanskrit and English from Tribhuvan University and Ph.D. in Linguistics from Georgetown University, Washington, D.C. Nepal's Permanent Representative at the United Nations (1991–4), he was a Fellow at Harvard University Centre for International Affairs (1995–6), where he wrote a paper on 'Nepal's Rough Road to Democracy'. He has retired after 25 years of teaching.

SUBA CHANDRAN is Assistant Director at the Institute of Peace and Conflict Studies, New Delhi. Some of his recent publications include *Missing Boundaries: Refugees, Migrants, Stateless and Internally Displaced Persons in South Asia* (New Delhi: Manohar, 2003) (co-edited); *Terrorism Post 9/11: An Indian Perspective* (New Delhi: Manohar, 2003) (co-edited). He was a Ford Fellow at the ACDIS, University of Illinois (June-December 2003) where he completed a study titled '*Limited War with Pakistan: Will it Secure India's Interests*?'

PERVEZ IQBAL CHEEMA is the Director of the Islamabad Policy Research Institute. He was earlier Professor of International Relations at the Quaid-i-Azam University where he served as the Chairman of both the departments of International Relations and Defence and Strategic Studies. He has also held the post of Educational Planning and Management, Islamabad. He was a visiting fellow at Australian National University, John Hopkins University and University of Illinois at Urbana-Champaign.

TASHI CHODEN is Research Officer at the Centre for Bhutan Studies (CBS), an autonomous research institute carrying out policy and inter-disciplinary studies related to Bhutan. With a background in Politics, Philosophy and Economics (BA in PPE), she has worked on a variety of studies including local grassroots-level elections; traditional and emerging practices in understanding civil society from a Bhutanese perspective; economic and political relations between Bhutan and neighbouring countries; security problems of Bhutan; and studies related to gender.

DEV RAJ DAHAL is Head of the Nepal office of Friedrich Ebert Stiftung. Until recently, he was Associate Professor at the Central Department of Political Science at Tribhuvan University. He is also the former visiting research scholar at the Institute of East Asian Studies, University of California, Berkeley during 1987–8. Dahal is the author of *Challenges to Good Governance: Decentralization in Nepal* (Kathmandu: GDS, 1996); *State, Society and Development in Nepal* (Kathmandu: IIDS, 1998) and *Civil Society in Nepal: Opening the Ground for Questions* (Kathmandu: CDG, 2001)

NARAYANI GANESH is Assistant Editor of *The Times of India*. She has a Masters degree in Economics from the University of Madras and has been with *The Times* since 1987. She is a lead writer on the editorial page and has written on issues that impact the environment, science, space biotechnology, security, travel, tourism and heritage. She also writes on Indo–Nepal issues besides contributing regularly to *The Economic Times* Travel section. Narayani edits two columns on spirituality and philosophy that appear in the *TOI*, Monday to Saturday in all editions.

GHANI JAFAR is associated with the Institute of Regional Studies, Islamabad. He has earlier been Senior Research Fellow, Institute of Strategic Studies, Islamabad, Editor, *Pulse Weekly*, Executive Editor, *The Muslim*, Diplomatic Correspondent, *The Pakistan Times*, and Deputy Editor, *Pakistan Observer*. He has travelled widely; most recently to attend the Executive Course at the Asia-Pacific Centre for Security Studies, Honolulu, Hawaii, US.

M.R. JOSSE, a former Chief Editor of *The Rising Nepal*, was Nepal's Deputy Permanent Representative to the United Nations, 1985–90. During 1988–9, he also served as Nepal's Alternative

Representative to the UN Security Council. Presently associated with a number of Nepalese newspapers and magazines, including as a weekly columnist for two broadsheet English dailies, he has served as foreign correspondent or contributing editor for a number of South Asian newspapers and journals.

MOHAMMAD HUMAYUN KABIR is Research Director at the Bangladesh Institute of International and Strategic Studies (BIISS), Dhaka. A recipient of several prestigious academic awards including Commonwealth Scholarship in the United Kingdom and Senior Fulbright Fellowship in the United States, he studied International Law at the Kiev State University, Ukraine, and International Relations at the University of Oxford, UK. He has to his credit more than forty research works including books, monographs and articles published in South Asia, Europe and North America.

MOHAN PRASAD LOHANI is Executive Director of Institute for Sustainable Development, Kathmandu. He was Royal Nepalese Ambassador to Bangladesh and Deputy Permanent Representative to the United Nations. A well known academic of Nepal, he served in the Tribhuvan University for forty years. He was also Executive Director of the Institute of Foreign Affairs from 1998 to 2001.

INDRA NATH MUKHERJI is currently Professor, South Asian Studies in the Centre for South, Central and South-East Asian Studies of the School of International Studies, Jawaharlal Nehru University, New Delhi. Earlier he served as Chairperson of the Centre and Dean of the School. He has authored two books and co-authored and edited several others. He is currently Member, Editorial Board, *South Asian Economic Journal* and *Journal of Himalayan Studies.*

LT GEN (RETD) SATISH NAMBIAR served as the first Force Commander and Head of Mission of United Nations forces in the former Yugoslavia from March 1992 to March 1993. He was earlier Military Advisor at the High Commission of India in London. He retired as the Deputy Chief of the Indian Army Staff in 1994. He has been awarded the Vir Chakra for gallantry in battle in the 1971 Indo-Pak conflict. He is also the recipient of the Ati Vishist Seva Medal and Param Vishist Seva Medal in 1991 and 1994 respectively.

NISHCHAL NATH PANEDY is Officiating Executive Director at the Institute of Foreign Affairs (IFA), Kathmandu. He has been with the IFA for the past 6 years in various capacities. Previously, he was advisor in the National Planning Commission of Nepal and Task Force member to draft the Ninth Five Year Plan of His Majesty's Government of Nepal for the tourism and civil aviation sectors. He was also sub-editor of *The Rising Nepal* daily. MABL from Tribhuvan University, Kathmandu, he writes frequently in various national and foreign newsmagazines; and has edited the book, *Trade Facilitation: Nepal's Priorities* and presented research papers in seminars and workshops abroad.

JEHAN PERERA is Media Director at the National Peace Council of Sri Lanka where he is responsible for analysis and policy recommendations relating to peace process, liaison with media and other agencies, advocacy, fund raising, providing conflict resolution training for media and grassroots politicians and developing project proposals. He is also political columnist for the *Daily Mirror* newspaper and *Lanka Monthly Digest Magazine*.

NAJAM RAFIQUE is Senior Research Fellow at the Institute of Strategic Studies, Islamabad. In addition to his research assignments, Najam is also Associate Editor of the quarterly journal *Strategic Studies* and periodical *Islamabad Papers*. He holds a Masters degree in Political Science from the University of Illinois, Urbana-Champaign, USA, and a Masters in Defence and Strategic Studies from Quaid-i-Azam University, Islamabad.

C.V. RANGANATHAN was in the Indian Foreign Service from 1959 to 1991. He was Ambassador of India to China and France. He served in different capacities in the United Nations, Germany, Hong Kong, Ethiopia and Moscow. He has been a Nehru Fellow on India–China relations and is an honorary fellow at the Institute of Chinese Studies, New Delhi. He is a former Convener of the National Security Advisory Board.

FAROOQ SOBHAN is the President and Chief Executive of Bangladesh Enterprise Institute. He was Executive Chairman, Board of Investment and Special Envoy to the Prime Minister, Foreign Secretary, Ambassador to India, China, Malaysia and Deputy Permanent Representative to the UN. He served as Chairman of the Group of 77 at the UN and was Chairman, UN Commission on TNCs. Mr Sobhan is a Member of the International Research Committee of the Centre for Security Studies, Colombo and member of the Board of Governors of the South Asia Centre for Policy Studies (SACEPS), based in Dhaka.

B.C. UPRETI is an Associate Professor at the South Asia Studies Centre, University of Rajasthan, Jaipur. He was Director of the Centre between 1999–2002. He has been associated with South Asian studies in general and the studies on Nepal in particular for the last 28 years. He has published 17 books and more then 80 papers in reputed journals and books. He has also been Editor of *South Asian Studies.* Dr Upreti's latest work is *Contemporary South Asia* (Delhi, 2004).